MW00683144

PRAISE FOR THE BOOK

'*Patriots and Partisans* makes for compelling reading . . . It asserts the voice of a liberal who would not stay supine, but would fight his corner vigorously'—*The Hindu*

'If there is one theme that connects the essays, which are otherwise independent, it is about how arguments driven by the decencies of reason, not the intolerance of ideologies, redeem democracy. The arguments of Ramachandra Guha are delightfully powered by those virtues'—*India Today*

'Beautifully crafted pieces that balance research and storytelling expertly and are an education to all aspiring non-fiction writers . . . It's heartening to read an analysis of contemporary India that isn't stifled by everything that's awry and holds out some hope . . . Among the things that *Patriots and Partisans* manages to do is make you hungry for the stories from India's history that no one but Guha seems to be interested in recording and telling'—*DNA*

'These socio-political essays by the pre-eminent chronicler of Indian history, laced with catchy anecdotes and fascinating character sketches, make a delightful read. Guha's prose can match the best creative writer's. *Patriots and Partisans* is an invaluable volume for a student of history, and an inspiring companion to the dispassionate reader'—*Deccan Herald*

'Engaging, incisive and eminently readable'—*Business Standard*

'Ramachandra Guha is much more than a pure historian. He writes with his heart, too. And this new book, *Patriots and Partisans*, reflects this very fact'—*Business World*

'One would do well to read this book and not only for the pleasure of the prose. It is the range of ideas and personalities, institutions and processes that Ramachandra Guha writes so elegantly about that should force us to think about what we are becoming and what we are gaining and losing in the process. His repertoire is wide as is the range of the sources he draws upon or the individuals he admires'—*Biblio*

'He writes with a joy that contrasts the dour objectivism seen in much academic work . . . His remains an interesting, provocative, distinctively brilliant and uniquely Indian voice'—*Sunday Guardian*

ALSO BY RAMACHANDRA GUHA

The Unquiet Woods:
Ecological Change and Peasant Resistance in the Himalaya

Savaging the Civilized:
Verrier Elwin, His Tribals, and India

Environmentalism:
A Global History

The Use and Abuse of Nature (with Madhav Gadgil)

An Anthropologist among the Marxists and Other Essays

A Corner of a Foreign Field:
The Indian History of a British Sport

The Last Liberal and Other Essays

How Much Should a Person Consume?
Thinking Through the Environment

India After Gandhi:
The History of the World's Largest Democracy

EDITED WORKS

Social Ecology

The Picador Book of Cricket

Nature's Spokesman: M. Krishnan and Indian Wildlife

Makers of Modern India

PENGUIN BOOKS

PATRIOTS AND PARTISANS

Ramachandra Guha's many books include a pioneering work of environmental history (*The Unquiet Woods*, 1989), an award-winning social history of sport (*A Corner of a Foreign Field*, 2002), and a widely acclaimed and bestselling work of contemporary history (*India after Gandhi*, 2007). The first volume of his landmark biography of Gandhi, *Gandhi before India*, was published in 2013; the second and concluding volume will be published in early 2018.

Guha's awards include the R.K. Narayan Prize, the Sahitya Akademi Award, the Ramnath Goenka Award and the Padma Bhushan. In 2014, he was awarded an honorary doctorate in the humanities by Yale University, and in 2015, he won the Fukuoka Prize for contributions to Asian culture and scholarship.

RAMACHANDRA GUHA

PATRIOTS AND PARTISANS

PENGUIN BOOKS

PENGUIN BOOKS

USA | Canada | UK | Ireland | Australia
New Zealand | India | South Africa | China

Penguin Books is part of the Penguin Random House group of companies
whose addresses can be found at global.penguinrandomhouse.com

Published by Penguin Random House India Pvt. Ltd
7th Floor, Infinity Tower C, DLF Cyber City,
Gurgaon 122 002, Haryana, India

Penguin
Random House
India

First published in Allen Lane by Penguin Books India 2012
Published in Penguin Books 2013

Copyright © Ramachandra Guha 2012

All rights reserved

10 9 8 7 6 5 4 3 2

The views and opinions expressed in this book are the author's own and the facts
are as reported by him which have been verified to the extent possible, and the
publishers are not in any way liable for the same.

ISBN 9780143421146

For sale in the Indian Subcontinent only

Typeset in Bembo Roman by SÜRYA, New Delhi
Printed at Replika Press Pvt. Ltd, India

This book is sold subject to the condition that it shall not, by way of trade
or otherwise, be lent, resold, hired out, or otherwise circulated without the
publisher's prior consent in any form of binding or cover other than that in
which it is published and without a similar condition including this condition
being imposed on the subsequent purchaser.

www.penguinbooksindia.com

For Rukmini (Rinki) Banerji
Good Bihari, better Indian

If a modern Diogenes were to hunt out for Indians with his lantern in these days, he would be sure to come across fervid Hindus, bigoted Muslims and fanatical souls deeply engrossed with the problem of tirelessly finding out how unjustly their own particular community was being treated, and he would have to ask in sorrow: 'Where are the Indians?'

—Syed Abdullah Brelvi, editor of the *Bombay Chronicle*, writing in May 1926

~

By independence, we have lost the excuse of blaming the British for anything going wrong. If hereafter things go wrong, we will have nobody to blame but ourselves.

—B.R. Ambedkar, speaking to the Constituent Assembly of India, 26 November 1949

CONTENTS

~

PREFACE

THE CASE FOR POLEMICAL
MODERATION

~

I

I am a person of moderate views, these sometimes expressed in extreme fashion. This makes me an anomaly, an oddity even, for polemics are normally the preserve of the right and the left. My friend and teacher Dharma Kumar—whose shadow and example hangs over many of the essays in *Patriots and Partisans*—once complained in print that Indian liberals 'were a supine lot'. They did not fight their corner vigorously enough. Offering their views tentatively, hesitantly, liberals tended to be rolled over in public discourse by the more committed (in all senses) extremists of the left and right.

In the 1950s and 1960s, most Indian intellectuals and writers would have been happy to own the label 'liberal'. The characteristic features of their brand of liberalism were four. First, they believed in reform, not revolution; not in utopian schemes for upturning or rehauling society, but in incremental social change based on patient, steady hard work. Second, they urged, and often worked for, the creation of impersonal, rule-bound institutions within the state (as in universities and law courts), and in civil society (as in cooperatives or women's groups). Third, they kept their distance from political parties and (especially) from individual politicians.

Their allegiance was to the democratic ideals of the Indian Constitution, namely, a multi-party political system based on adult franchise, a secular state, a multilingual polity, equal rights for women, and special privileges for disadvantaged sections such as Dalits and tribals. It was not to any partisan rendering of these ideals. Finally, those Indian liberals practised an unselfconscious and understated patriotism. They loved this country and wished to leave India a better—or at least less discontented—place than it was when they entered it.

In the 1970s and beyond, there was a rise of illiberal tendencies in Indian society. The Indian Constitution had always been unpalatable to Marxist-Leninists, since it did not privilege a particular political party (their own); and to Hindu radicals, since it did not privilege a particular religious faith (their own). Ever since Independence, religious extremists and left-wing revolutionaries have made repeated attempts to impose their dogmas by force. In recent decades, a third threat to democratic functioning has manifested itself—namely, the corruption and corrosion of the constitutional centre, via the capture of public institutions, and of political parties, by individuals, families and caste groups.

Dharma Kumar had lived through the heyday—the complacent heyday—of Indian liberalism. As she grew older, she saw her fellow liberals wavering in the face of these three challenges. Some writers and scholars, out of weariness or opportunism, became courtiers of the Congress party. Others, out of disgust with this sycophancy, walked into the arms of the Bharatiya Janata Party (thus implicitly, at least, endorsing its ideal of the Hindu theocratic state). A third set of intellectuals, out of guilt or foolishness, became apologists for the revolutionary Maoists gaining influence in the forests and hills of central India.

It may be because I live in Bangalore, and not Delhi, that I have been able to maintain my independence from political parties. Specific essays in this book detail my disagreements with the Congress, the Sangh Parivar, and the parliamentary Left. The Maoists and their fellow travellers dislike me too—one of this ilk, writing on the website CG Net, attacked me for my 'anti-left views', claiming that I had 'strong ties to the Congress establishment' and 'stronger ties to the American establishment'.

In truth, the only 'establishment' that I count myself close to is that which runs Koshy's Parade Café in Bangalore. However, the fellow traveller was right in identifying me as a critic of the Maoists, whom I regard as being as great a threat to decency and democracy as the corruption of the Congress or the bigotry of the Sangh Parivar.

Whether writing of extremists of the left and right, or of opportunists and dealmakers at the Centre, I have sought to affirm my liberalism in ways that would not be considered 'supine'. I have followed my teacher's advice most faithfully in newspaper columns. And I have departed from it most radically in works of historical scholarship. When one has to state a case in a few hundred words one can, perhaps must, do so vigorously. When one has a few hundred pages to work with, it is best to let the depth of your research carry the burden of your argument.

These distinctions in tone are linked to the respective time horizons in which these genres operate. A column is written for the moment—the newspaper it is written for constitutes the next morning's rubbish. A book is written to endure; to be read—or so the author hopes—for months and years after it is published. One can be opinionated, even extravagantly so, in a column; one is obliged to be more careful, and restrained, in a book.

Intermediate between the column and the book is the essay. Here, one can be both passionate and substantial; thus to allow oneself into the narrative, while stiffening it with a core of new or at least little-known facts. In five thousand words (better still, ten thousand) one can develop the contours of an argument, rather than simply state it. Its nuances and complexities can be expanded upon. Its limitations and caveats can be underlined. And yet, since this is an essay and not one long, continuous book, the personality of the writer can—for good or for ill—still be allowed to exhibit itself.

The fifteen essays in *Patriots and Partisans* explore different facets of the Republic of India's heroic and flawed compact with nationhood and democracy. Some essays appear here in print for the first time; the others have all been revised, updated and, in several cases, substantially expanded for publication in this book. I have sequenced the essays so that they better convey the thrust of the larger argument as well as the author's presuppositions. Some essays, published originally in scholarly journals, carried footnotes and references; these have here been dispensed with.

The nine essays in Part I of this book deal principally with political matters; the six essays in Part II principally with the life of the mind. However, there are some reflections on scholars and writers in Part I, and much reflection on the practice of democracy in Part II. The essays—which range between three and thirteen thousand words in length—deal variously with individuals, institutions, and ideologies, these explored in and for themselves, and for what they might tell us about politics and society in modern India.

II

While introducing me to his class, an American law professor recently described me as a 'citizen of the world'. This was kindly meant, as a compliment; yet I immediately disavowed it. I was, I said, an Indian democrat, not a world citizen. I pointed my friend, and his students, to the words of the biologist J.B.S. Haldane, who said that one of the chief duties of a citizen was to hold his state to account. Since there was no world state, he had therefore to address his concerns—and complaints—to his own state, which was the Republic of India, of which Haldane had become a naturalized citizen. As a citizen of this country by birth, I can testify to the truth of Haldane's further observation that the Indian state has 'the merit of permitting a good deal of criticism, although it responds to it rather slowly'.

Patriotism is not to be confused with nationalism, still less with jingoism or xenophobia. The genius of Mahatma Gandhi was to disentangle love of one's country from adherence to a particular language or faith. The genius of Rabindranath Tagore was to show

how one could love one's country and yet have an open admiration
for other cultures and countries. In countries as different as Pakistan
and Israel, citizenship has been defined by adherence to a common
faith and common language, and identification of a common
enemy. To be a good Israeli means to be a Jew, speak Hebrew, and
disparage Arab culture. On the other hand, to be Indian one does
not have to be a Hindu, or speak Hindi. One does not even have
to hate Pakistan.

Tragically, the language of patriotism has in recent years been
appropriated by the Hindu right. In this they have been helped by
the Marxist left, whose Fatherland has always been some nation
other than their own—once Russia, then China, then Vietnam,
then Cuba (the current country of choice for the Indian Marxist
appears to be Venezuela). They have also been helped by liberals
and non-party leftists, who—dismayed on the one side by the
jingoism of the right and intrigued on the other by the high-
sounding talk of global citizenship in an increasingly inter-connected
world—have been too shy to think or speak of themselves as 'Indian'.

My own patriotism is inspired by the legacy of the great Indian
reformers of the past, whose work I have studied as a historian, and
by the example of some Indian democrats I have had the privilege
of knowing. Of these I may be allowed to single out three. I
therefore salute Shivaram Karanth and Mahasweta Devi, whose
patriotism was expressed in the work they did for their home state.
Acclaimed novelists—in Kannada and Bengali respectively—they
were deeply immersed in the life of their people. Karanth, almost
single-handedly, built an environmental movement in Karnataka
(along with reviving the Yakshagana dance–drama, promoting
widow remarriage, pioneering the Kannada novel, etc.). Mahasweta,
also almost single-handedly, has drawn wider attention to the plight
of tribals in general and of the communities stigmatized by the
British as 'criminal tribes' in particular.

Karanth was a good Indian and a better Kannadiga. Likewise,
Mahasweta's identification with adivasis has not come in the way of
affection for Bengal and for India. A younger writer who has

followed them in these respects is the brilliant, versatile and unstoppably energetic Uttarakhand historian Shekhar Pathak. Every ten years, he walks across the entire breadth of his home state—from Askot near the Nepal border to Arakot on the Himachal border—a journey of many weeks across high snowy passes and along rocky mountain paths. His walk is not uninterrupted—he stops sometimes to take photographs of rare plants, birds or animals, and oftentimes to speak to (or interview) Uttarakhandis of different castes, languages and genders. In between these epic padayatras he walks south–north rather than west–east, seeking to understand how his compatriots live (and labour) in the lower valleys and hills.

Shekhar Pathak has communicated the fruits of his journeys in several books, hundreds of articles and talks, and in twenty solid volumes of a periodical called *Pahar* that he (the phrase is unavoidable) single-handedly edits, produces, prints and distributes. (There is also his personal archive, of hundreds of interviews, thousands of letters, and tens of thousands of photographs, from which one day scholars who never met him will write their own social and ecological histories of the Himalaya.) His contributions to his state and to his country are incalculable.

It is because of these Indians—and others like them—that I do not call myself a 'world citizen'. In my opinion, that appellation carries a somewhat self-congratulatory ring. Those who avow it are generally well-educated professionals, who have the means to take up the citizenship of any country in the world. They can move with ease and success from one republic to another. On the other hand, the overwhelming majority of Indians have no such escape. They must necessarily live out their days (and nights) as citizens of the Republic of India. It is to their hopes (and fears) that the essays in this book, written by an Indian democrat, are addressed.

PART I

DEBATING
DEMOCRACY

chapter one

REDEEMING THE REPUBLIC

~

I

Let me begin with two epiphanies.

A few years ago, I visited a book fair held on the seafront in Kochi. The local publishers were represented, as were Indian and foreign firms. In between the stall of Oxford University Press and a shop stocking the works in Malayalam translation of Marx, Engels and Lenin, I came across a man selling, of all things, pickles from Bikaner. He had placed his wares in large open buckets, one containing *aam ka murabba*, another *shalgam ka achar*. I asked the young man how he had come from a northern desert to participate in a book fair in this southern port. '*Maine suna ki Keral mein mela lag raha tha*,' he answered, '*aur maine socha ki wahan ek dukan khol doon*.' (I heard that there was some kind of fair on in Kerala, so I thought, why don't I bid for a stall there?) Thus spoke a pickle man in a salad-bowl nation, adding his charmingly naïve logic to an apparently illogical country.

Some months after this encounter, I was travelling by car from Patiala to Amritsar. It was a hot day, and the countryside was monotonous. I fell asleep, and woke when the car slowed down. We were now in the market town of Khanna. I scanned the

3

buildings and their signs. One, particularly, caught my attention: it read, 'Indian Bank, Khanna Branch, Head Office, Rajaji Salai, Chennai'. I was charmed and uplifted, sentiments that (especially for the young) perhaps need explaining. For, 'Rajaji' was C. Rajagopalachari, the scholar–statesman who had been governor-general of India, chief minister of Madras State, founder of the free-market Swatantra Party, and author of bestselling versions of the Ramayana and Mahabharata. In his person he embodied all Punjabi stereotypes about the Madrasi; he was slight, wore thick glasses, had never played a single sport or consumed an alcoholic beverage, and was vegetarian. Yet here was evidence of his enduring legacy in the Punjab, where—as that sign informed me—there were many whisky-guzzling, chicken-eating Sikh farmers banking their savings in an institution headquartered in Chennai on a road named after a dhoti-wearing, rasam-drinking, austere Tamil scholar.

The writer Wallace Stegner once remarked that 'the tracing of ideas is a guessing game. We can't tell who first had an idea—we can only tell who first had it influentially, who formulated it in some form, poem or equation or picture, that others could stumble upon with the shock of recognition.' So it is with 'the idea of India'. Rabindranath Tagore used the phrase in a letter to a friend in 1921, writing that 'the idea of India is against the intense consciousness of the separateness of one's own people from others, which inevitably leads to ceaseless conflicts'. There may have been others who used the phrase before him. But it was only in 1997, when Sunil Khilnani used it as the title of his wonderful book, that his fellow citizens stumbled with a shock of recognition at what the idea of India represented.

As citizens, we ubiquitously use a humdrum manifestation of the miracle of India—namely, our currency notes, which have a portrait of Gandhi on one side and the national Parliament on the other, and its denomination written in seventeen languages, indeed seventeen different scripts, each encoding a distinct, sophisticated, ancient and proud literary culture. Since rupee notes are an artefact of everyday life, we do not see or sense their significance. However, in its own way our paper currency is as marvellous and strange as the Bikaneri achar-vendor in Kochi or the signboard of the southern bank in the Punjab.

II

The plural, inclusive, idea of India has three enemies. The best known is the notion of a Hindu Rashtra, as represented in an erratic fashion by the Bharatiya Janata Party (BJP) and in a more resolute (not to say more bigoted) manner by the Rashtriya Swayamsevak Sangh, the Vishwa Hindu Parishad, the Bajrang Dal, and other associated organizations. When Khilnani published his book in 1997, Hindutva appeared to be the major challenge to the idea of India. To the 'theoretically untidy, improvising, pluralist approach' of Gandhi and Nehru, he wrote, the Sangh Parivar offered the alternative of 'a culturally and ethnically cleaned-up homogeneous community with a singular Indian citizenship, defended by a state that had both God and nuclear warheads on its side'.

Living in north India between 1988 and 1994, I experienced this challenge at first- and second hand—by seeing my Muslim friends board trains under assumed Hindu names, by visiting Bhagalpur after the riots provoked by Lal Krishna Advani's rath yatra, by witnessing a more general polarizing of public opinion on religious lines. The poisonous residues of those years carried on well into the next decade, as illustrated by the pogrom against Muslims in Gujarat in 2002.

Shortly after the Gujarat riots, I was driving to the Mumbai airport from the south of the city, when I noticed the tricolour hanging out of every home on Muhammad Ali Road. As I proceeded northwards, beyond Parel into Dadar and Shivaji Park, the flags were not visible any more. The contrast puzzled me, till I reached the airport and saw a live telecast of an India-Pakistan cricket match. It remains one of the saddest memories of my life— the memory of how, intimidated by decades of harassment and violence at the hands of Hindutva bigots, so many of my fellow citizens had to shame themselves into a public display of patriotism solely on account of their faith.

One reason that Hindutva has been so successful is that it speaks in different voices. Arun Jaitley can be trotted out to calm the liberals; Narendra Modi to appeal to the hardliners. The BJP can distance itself from the RSS when it suits, but at other times can claim to be tied by an umbilical cord to it. The RSS in turn can opportunistically own or disown the trishul-waving goondas of the Vishwa Hindu Parishad and the Bajrang Dal.

Back in 1968, the scholar–statesman C. Rajagopalachari observed that the Jana Sangh (the predecessor of today's BJP) was a party which 'has quite a few good leaders'. Then he added: 'What is needed however is a broadmindedness that not just practises toleration but looks upon Mussalmans, Christians, Parsis and others as politically and culturally as good as Hindus.' Four decades later, Indians still wait for that broadening of Hindutva minds. Perhaps the wait has been in vain. For, in its origins and core beliefs, the Sangh Parivar is motivated by values and ideals that are antithetical to those of a modern, secular, liberal democracy.

Some commentators use the term 'Hindu nationalists' to characterize the members and leaders of the Sangh Parivar. It is a label that we must reject. How can they be called 'nationalists' when they would withhold full citizenship from those Indians who are Muslims or Christians or Parsis or atheists? One major Hindutva ideologue, Ashok Singhal, has long argued that India should emulate Pakistan by denying top jobs to the minorities and by making them vote in separate electorates. The Hinduvta cadres take this kind of thinking to the streets, as in their notorious slogan, shouted during communal riots, of 'Pakistan ya Kabristan' (go to Pakistan, or we will be off with your heads).

The Kannada writer U.R. Anantha Murthy adds an interesting caveat to this argument. He says that we should not call the Sangh Parivar the 'saffron brigade' either. For, saffron is a beautiful colour, the colour of wisdom and renunciation, with so many rich resonances in our myths and our history. Why should we then cede it to the hard, humourless men on the right? Let them not usurp the lovely colour 'saffron' nor, indeed, the inclusive term 'nationalist'. The correct characterization of the ideology of the Sangh Parivar, therefore, is 'Hindu chauvinist'.

To be fair, there are also other kinds of religious fundamentalisms lurking around in India. Some Christian and Muslim groups in India are as convinced of their theological superiority, as sure of their victory at the altar of history, as any bigot of the Sangh Parivar. The hold of the Muslim orthodoxy over the community is so strong that even liberal Muslim intellectuals are cowed down by them. As a Hindu, I do not need to refer to any religious text to attack Untouchability—I can merely point out that it is an inhuman practice impermissible in a civilized society. Regardless of what the Shastras might or might not say on the subject, the fact that the Indian Constitution abolishes Untouchability is good enough for me. But a Muslim asking for equal rights for women finds it far more difficult to argue from first principles. He takes refuge instead in one or other verse from the Koran, read or interpreted in a way most congenial to his argument. He tends to suppress or ignore the contrary evidence in other verses or sections.

There is, indeed, a reassertion of religious orthodoxy in all faiths in modern India—among Muslims and Christians as well as Sikhs and Hindus (and even, as it happens, among Jains). It is the illiberal tendencies in all these religions that, at the present juncture, are in the ascendant. The mullahs who abuse Sania Mirza or Taslima Nasreen, and the Sikh hardliners who terrorize the Dera Sacha Sauda, are also wholly opposed to the spirit of the Indian Constitution. But simply by virtue of numbers—Hindus are, after all, more than 80 per cent of India's population—and their much wider political influence, Hindu bigotry is indisputably the most dangerous of them all.

III

The threat to India from Hindutva bigotry was at its most intense from about 1989 to about 2004. When judged by political (and social) influence the threat appears to have receded, although the terrorist activities, recently exposed, of sundry sadhvis and swamis suggest that one should not be too sanguine on this score. At any rate, right-wing religious fundamentalism has now been matched in force and influence by a challenge to the idea of India from the extreme left—that posed by the Communist Party of India (Maoist). Anthropologists such as Nandini Sundar have documented in detail how the rise of the Maoists is linked to the dispossession of the tribals of central and eastern India. These tribals live in India's densest forests, along its fastest-flowing rivers, and atop its richest veins of iron ore and bauxite. As the country has industrialized, they have lost their homes and livelihoods to logging projects, dams, and mines which are directed by and benefit more powerful social forces.

Even when they are not dispossessed, the tribals are actively discriminated against. Demographically concentrated in a few hill and forest districts, they do not constitute a vote bank whose voice can, at least symbolically, be attended to by the political class. There is a contrast here with Dalits (as well as Muslims), who are more evenly distributed across India, and hence have a far greater impact on the outcome of state and national elections. Lacking adequate representation in the higher civil service, and without a political voice anyway, the tribals are subject to contempt and condescension by the officials of the forest, police, revenue, education and health departments, who are obliged by law to serve the adivasis but oriented in practice to harass and exploit them.

In the summer of 2006 I travelled through the district of Dantewada in Chhattisgarh state, as part of a group of independent citizens studying the tragic fallout of Salwa Judum, a vigilante army promoted by the state government. We found that the Judum had polarized adivasi society, fuelled very many murders and killings, and displaced tens of thousands of people from their homes.

In the most peaceful of times the state has often failed to uphold the law in tribal areas. Schedules V and VI of the Constitution provide for a substantial degree of self-governance in districts where adivasis are in a majority. Yet their clauses protecting tribal rights in land and forests, curbing the activities of moneylenders, and mandating the formation of village and district councils have been honoured only in the breach. These schedules provide for local councils to share in the royalties from minerals found on tribal land; what happens in practice is that the adivasis do not get to see or spend a paisa from mining, whose proceeds are shared between the contractors and the state-level (and usually non-tribal) politicians. Meanwhile, the criminal justice system is in a state of near collapse; as witnessed in the murder of Shankar Guha Niyogi, that selfless striver for the rights of adivasi workers in Chhattisgarh. It was widely believed that Guha Niyogi was killed by assassins hired by capitalists; yet those who planned and executed the murder have gone scot-free.

Even with this kind of record, Salwa Judum marked a new low. Bands of vigilantes roamed the Bastar countryside accompanied by the police and paramilitary, in search of Naxalite sympathizers, alleged or real. They attacked dozens of villages and burnt hundreds of homes. They killed many innocent people and terrorized many others. The Supreme Court of India has many first-hand testimonies of villagers who have suffered at the hand of these state-supported vigilantes. The residents of Pakela village, for example, recorded that twenty of their homes had been burnt by Salwa Judum cadres. 'Everything in the homes,' reads the English translation of their evidence, 'rice, clothes, utensils and money—got reduced to ashes.' Other villagers offered more precise accounts of the damage, listing the number of paddy sacks or hens or pigs seized or burnt from individual households. The collective sentiments of those targeted by Salwa Judum were expressed most poignantly by the residents of Korcholi village. They said:

> The frightened villagers of Gangaloor, Cherpal and Bijapur, seeing the Salwa Judum, have fled into [the] forests. The Salwa Judum burns the food stock, houses and clothes. They also break the cooking utensils. Raping women, slitting people's throat to kill, killing people by drowning them in water, robbing them, etc. are the main activities of the Salwa Judum leaders. Why is this happening in our country, why is this happening in Chhattisgarh?

Why has the Chhattisgarh administration been running this? Has our Chief
Minister been elected only for this?

When I visited Dantewada, I found that an atmosphere of fear and
insecurity pervaded the district. Families and villages were divided,
some living with, or in fear of, the Maoists, others in fear of, or in
roadside camps controlled by, the Salwa Judum. As many as fifty
thousand people were displaced from their homes. These tribal
refugees lived in a pitiable condition, in tents exposed to the
elements, and with no access to health care or gainful employment.
Thousands of others fled across the border into Andhra Pradesh.

Ironically, by arming civilians, the state had merely reproduced
the methods of the other side. For, tribal boys in their teens joined
Salwa Judum for much the same reason as other boys had previously
joined the Naxalites. Educated just enough to harbour a certain
disenchantment with labouring in field and forest, but not enough
to be absorbed with honour in the modern economy, these boys
were enticed by the state into a job which paid them a salary (albeit
a meagre one—Rs 1500 a month), and gave them a certain status
in society. Gun in hand, they strutted around the countryside,
forcing those without weapons to fall in line.

In this manner, the machismo of revolution was being answered
by the machismo of counter-revolution. Whether sangam organizer
or special police officer (SPO), the young men of Dandakaranya had
been seduced by their new-found—and essentially unearned—
authority. In the Dantewada district alone, there were several
thousand young males punch-drunk with the power which, as Mao
said, flows from the barrel of a gun.

In 2007, two Public Interest Litigations were filed in the Supreme
Court of India, asking for the disbandment of Salwa Judum. One
of the petitioners was Nandini Sundar, who in 1997 published a
landmark social history of the region, and has since regularly
returned to do fieldwork there. After many hearings spread over
several years, the court issued an order in July 2011, calling for the
disbandment of Salwa Judum and the filing of cases against those

guilty of arson, murder and rape. Justice B. Sudershan Reddy and
Justice Surinder Singh Nijjar observed that the Chhattisgarh
government appointed thousands of 'barely literate tribal youth as
SPOs', and then asked them 'to undertake tasks that only members
of the official and formal police ought to be undertaking'.

The creation of Salwa Judum, the apex court pointed out,
resulted in 'a miasmic environment of dehumanization of youngsters
of the deprived sections of the population, in which guns are given
to them rather than books, to stand as guards, for the rapine,
plunder and loot in our forests'. By arming poor and largely illiterate
adivasis, the Chhattisgarh government had installed 'a regime of
gross violation of human rights in a manner, and by adopting the
same modes, as [have] done Maoist/Naxalite extremists'.

The Supreme Court held that the creation of special police
officers violated 'the promise of equality before the law' assured by
Article 14 of the Constitution. It treated unequals as equals, asking
untrained adivasis to conduct tasks meant for trained policemen. It
also violated 'the dignity of life' promised by Article 21, since these
adivasi young men were wilfully exposed to the risk of death.

The court also expressed its disappointment with the cavalier
response of the government to questions and queries. Thus the state
and central governments repeatedly insisted 'that the only option for
the state was to rule with an iron fist, [and] establish a social order
in which every person is to be treated as suspect . . . and a Maoist'.
The judges were 'aghast at the blindness to constitutional limitations
of the state of Chhattisgarh, and some of its advocates, in claiming
that anyone who questions the inhumanity that is rampant in many
parts of that state ought necessarily to be treated as Maoists, or their
sympathizers, and yet in the same breath also claim that it needs the
. . . sanction, under our Constitution, to perpetrate its policies of
ruthless violence'.

The Supreme Court remarked that 'lawless violence, in response
to violence by the Maoist/Naxalite insurgency, has not, and will
not, solve the problems, and instead it will only perpetuate the
cycles of more violen[ce]'. The state of affairs in Chhattisgarh

reminded the judges of the state of nineteenth-century Africa, as described in Joseph Conrad's novel, *Heart of Darkness*. Thus, said the judges, the actions of both the state and the Naxalites manifest 'the darkness, represented by inhumanity and evil, to which individual human beings are capable of descending, when supreme and unaccounted force is vested, rationalized by a warped world-view that parades itself as pragmatic and inevitable'.

IV

Altogether, the tribals have gained least and lost most from six decades of democracy and development in independent India. This is not to say that Dalits and Muslims have not been discriminated against. However, their concerns have found powerful expression through democratically elected parties and politicians. The tribals have not even had that consolation. If there was no adivasi Ambedkar, there has been no adivasi Mayawati either. This is the vacuum that the Maoists have sought to fill, with increasing success, and also with increasing sympathy among sections of the Indian intelligentsia.

Metropolitan intellectuals have been fascinated by left-wing rebels for a very long time. From Mao through Ché Guevara and Fidel Castro, on to Subcomandante Marcos of the Mexican province of Chiapas and the late Comrade Kishenji of (as the news reports had it) 'somewhere on the Jharkhand-West Bengal border', guerrillas in the forest or highland have attracted admiring comment from writers and poets themselves living in the cities. The contrast, indeed, explains the intensity of their commitment. Because they themselves lead bourgeois lifestyles in a land where so many are so poor, these writers sublimate their guilt by an effusive and excessive endorsement of armed rebels who claim to speak on behalf of the deprived and disadvantaged.

My own trip to Dantewada in 2006 disabused me of any lingering romantic sympathies I may have had with the Naxalites. The state's policy of arming vigilantes was illegal and indefensible. At the same time, the Maoists had contributed to an escalating cycle of violence, by beheading alleged 'informers', assassinating village headmen, and setting off landmines which killed civilians as well as policemen. They had also blown up schools, transmission lines and railway tracks, and stopped paramedics from working in villages under their influence.

From its origins in the late 1960s, the Naxalite movement was riven by internal discord, by sharp and often bloody rivalries between different factions, each claiming itself to be the only true Indian interpreter of Mao Zedong's thought. However, by the end of the last century the People's War Group (PWG) and the Maoist Coordination Committee (MCC) had emerged as the two groups which still had a functioning organization and a devoted cadre of revolutionary workers. The PWG was very active in Andhra Pradesh, whereas the MCC's base was principally in Bihar.

The Naxalite movement gathered force after the merger in 2004 of the PWG and the MCC. The new party called itself the Communist Party of India (Maoist). That its abbreviation, CPI (M), mimicked that of a party that had fought and won elections under the Indian Constitution was surely not accidental. We are the real inheritors of the legacy of revolutionary Marxism, the new party was saying, whereas the power-holders in Kerala and West Bengal are merely a bunch of bourgeois reformists.

The new, unified party has been eight years in existence. In that time it has rapidly expanded its influence. The erstwhile MCC cadres have moved southwards into Jharkhand and east into West Bengal. Those who were once with the PWG have travelled into Orissa and Chhattisgarh. This last state is where the Maoists have made the most dramatic gains. Large parts of the district of Dantewada, in particular, are under their sway. On one side of the river Indravati, the Indian state exercises an uncertain control by day and no control at night. On the other side, in what is known as Abujmarh, the state has no presence by day or by night.

How many Maoists are there in India? The estimates are imprecise, and widely varying. There are perhaps between 10,000 and 20,000 full-time guerillas, many of them armed with an AK-47. These revolutionaries are conversant with the use of grenades, landmines, and rocket-launchers. They have maintained links with guerrilla movements in other parts of South Asia, exchanging information and technology with the (now-decimated) Liberation Tigers of Tamil Eelam and with the Nepali Maoists before the latter's conversion to multi-party democracy.

What we know of the leaders and cadres suggests that most Maoists come from a lower middle class background. They usually have a smattering of education, and were often radicalized in college. Like other Communist movements, the leadership of this one too is overwhelmingly male. No tribals are represented in the upper levels of the party hierarchy.

The general secretary of the now-unified party, the Communist Party of India (Maoist), calls himself 'Ganapathi'. He is believed to be from Andhra Pradesh, although the name he uses is almost certainly a pseudonym. Statements carrying his name occasionally circulate on the Internet—one, issued in February 2007, reported the 'successful completion' of a party congress 'held deep in the forests of one of the several Guerilla Zones in the country . . .' The party congress 'reaffirmed the general line of the new democratic revolution with agrarian revolution as its axis and protracted people's war as the path of the Indian revolution . . .' The meeting 'was completed amongst great euphoria with a Call to the world people: *Rise up as a tide to smash Imperialism and its running dogs! Advance the Revolutionary war throughout the world!*'

This chillingly straightforward credo was endorsed by a Maoist activist whom I met in Chhattisgarh in 2006. Working under the pseudonym of 'Sanjeev', this revolutionary was slim and clean-shaven, and soberly dressed, in dark trousers and a bush-shirt of neutral colours. Now thirty-five, he had been in the movement for two decades, dropping out of college in Hyderabad to join it. (The profile was typical—the leading Maoists in Chhattisgarh are all Telugu speakers from Andhra Pradesh.)

Speaking in quiet, controlled tones, Sanjeev soon showed himself to be both deeply committed as well as highly sophisticated. Their sangams, he said, worked to protect people's rights in *jal, jangal, zameen*—water, forest and land. At the same time, the Maoists made targeted attacks on state officials, especially the police. Raids on police stations were intended to stop the police from harassing ordinary folk. They were also necessary to augment the weaponry of the guerrilla army. Through popular mobilization and the intimidation of state officials, the Maoists hoped to expand their authority over Dandakaranya. Once the region was made a 'liberated zone', it would be used as a launching pad for the capture of state power in India as a whole.

Sanjeev's belief in the efficacy of armed struggle was complete. When asked about two landmine blasts which had killed many innocent people—in one case members of a marriage party—he said that these had been mistakes, with the guerrillas believing that the police had hired private vehicles to escape detection. The Maoists, he said, would issue an apology and compensate the victims' families. However, of other (and scarcely less brutal) killings he said these were 'deliberate incidents'; that is, intended as such.

I knew beforehand that the Naxalites were no Gandhians, but it took a conversation with a Muria tribal to see them in clearer light. This man, a first-generation graduate and former schoolteacher who had been rendered homeless by the civil war, explained to me how behind the macho image of an armed revolutionary lay a man who lacked any moral courage whatsoever. His words ring in my ears still—he said, in Hindi, '*Naxaliyon ko himmat nahin hai ki wo hathiyaron gaon ké bahar chhod ké hamare beech mein aake behas karé.*' (The Naxalites do not have the guts to leave their weapons outside our village and then come and have a discussion with us.) It was an arresting remark, deep in insight and understanding about the real meanings of democracy. Despite his machismo and certitude, the Naxalite was actually so fearful of his own self that he dare not engage in democratic debate—even with poor and unarmed villagers. If he really had confidence in his beliefs, why would he seek in the first instance to enforce them at the point of a gun?

The remark of the Muria teacher also allowed me to see that Maoist violence was not random or anarchic, but highly focused.

Schools were attacked because the revolutionaries did not want children to be exposed to a pedagogy other than their own. The Maoists regularly murdered panchayat members and leaders (including many women) because they saw electoral democracy, even—or perhaps especially—at the village level, as a threat to their vision of a one-party state.

In the short-term, the Maoists may sometimes provide the tribals succour against the exactions of the forest guard or the moneylender. In the medium- and long-term, they provide no real solution. For them, the tribals are essentially cannon fodder, a stepping stone in a larger war against the Indian state which will end—or so their ideologues claim—with the Red Flag being planted on the Red Fort in thirty or forty years' time.

This dream is a fantasy, but, since the Maoists are determined to play it out, a bloody war of attrition lies ahead of us. The Indian state will not be able to easily recapture the hearts and minds of the adivasis, nor able either to authoritatively reassert its control, by day and especially by night, in the territories where the extremists are now active. At the same time, if the Maoists try to move into the open country, they will be mowed down by the Indian Army. And so, in the hills and forests of central India, the conflict persists, without any side able to claim a decisive victory.

In the long run, perhaps, the Maoists might indeed make their peace with the Republic of India, and the republic might come to treat its adivasi citizens with dignity and honour. Whether this denouement will happen in my own lifetime I am not sure. In the forest regions of central and eastern India, years of struggle and strife lie ahead. Here, in the jungles and hills they once called their own, the tribals will continue to be harassed on one side by the state and on the other by the insurgents. As one adivasi in Bastar put it to me—'Hummé dono taraf sé dabav hai, aur hum beech méin pis gayé hain.' It sounds far tamer in English—'Pressed and pierced from both sides, here we are, crushed in the middle.'

V

The history of postcolonial India, like the history of interwar Europe, is one of an unstable democratic regime in the middle, challenged from the left and the right by absolutist ideologies that seek to replace it. In January 1948 Mahatma Gandhi was murdered by a Hindu fanatic; six weeks later, under the orders of Moscow, the then undivided Communist Party of India launched an armed insurrection against the Indian state. Through resolute leadership, the threats from left and right were contained, and a democratic Constitution put in place. However, ever since, the Hindu Rashtra and the Communist dictatorship have stood as sometimes recessive, sometimes aggressive, alternatives to the democratic idea of India.

A third challenge to the idea of India also goes back to the founding of the nation. This is the notion that the Indian Union is an artificial cobbling together of many rival nationalities that must, in time, break up into its constituent parts. In the summer of 1946, a section of the Nagas announced that when the British departed, they would form an independent nation of their own. In the summer of 1947, similar claims were put forward by (among others) the Dewan of Travancore, the Maharaja of Kashmir, and the Nizam of Hyderabad. The 15th of August 1947 was marked as a day of mourning by the Dravida Kazhagam, an influential Tamil party that likewise wished to strike out for an independent nation. Some Sikhs were upset by the division of British India into India and Pakistan, since they had hoped that a third nation, Khalistan, would also be brought into being.

Many British imperialists believed that an independent and united India would not survive. These sceptics included the former prime minister Winston Churchill as well as officials serving in the subcontinent at the time of the transfer of power. The Mizo Hills, then known as the Lushai Hills, were governed by a man named A.R.H. Macdonald. In March 1947, Macdonald wrote to his immediate superior that his 'advice to the Lushais, since the very beginning of Lushai politics at the end of the War, has been until

very recently not to trouble themselves yet about the problem of
their future relationship to the rest of India: nobody can possibly
foretell what India will be like even two years from now, or even
whether there will be an India in the unitary political sense. I would
not encourage my small daughter to commit herself to vows of
lifelong spinsterhood; but I would regard it as an even worse crime
to betroth her in infancy to a boy who was himself still undeveloped.'

In subsequent years, the infant developed sufficiently to persuade
or coerce its recalcitrant partners to unite with it. But the process
took time and money, and spilt a great deal of blood. Between 1947
and 1950 more than five hundred princely states were integrated
into the Union. In 1963 the Dravidian parties formally dropped the
plank of independence. The Mizos launched a rebellion in 1965;
two decades later, their leaders laid down arms and successfully
entered the democratic process. The 1980s witnessed a movement
for Sikh separatism in the Punjab; this was finally tamed, albeit with
considerable loss of life. The 1980s and 1990s also witnessed much
violence instigated by the United Liberation Front of Assam; this
too, has abated, with a vast majority of Assamese seeking a better
life within India rather than a separate homeland for themselves.

As I write this, three nationalist insurgencies retain their force and
relevance—those in Nagaland, Manipur and Kashmir. The first of
these has been led for more than three decades by a Thangkul Naga
named T. Muivah. In the late 1980s, the Dutch writer Bertil
Lintner trekked across the India–Burma border to meet the Naga
leader in his jungle hideout. Muivah told him that 'the only hope
the Nagas had to achieve their independence would be if India itself
broke up'. The Nagas had made contact with Sikh and Kashmiri
separatists, and Muivah 'fervently hoped a similar movement would
emerge among the Tamils of southern India—which would indeed
plunge the country into the anarchy he desired'.

The Tamils remain quite content to live within the Indian Union,
and (the recent reappearance of Bhindranwale posters notwithstanding)
the Sikh separatists are no longer active or influential. But the Valley
of Kashmir remains on the boil; Manipur is home to dozens of

armed insurgent groups; and despite fourteen years of ceasefire no agreement has yet been reached between the Government of India and Muivah's men.

The discontent in these three states has four major causes: their distance, geographical and cultural, from the Indian heartland; the power of the idea of national independence among young men; the impunity enjoyed by soldiers from arrest and prosecution, with their actions against civilians then leading to more discontent; and the support by the Centre to manipulative and corrupt local politicians. But the insurgents have their own crimes to account for, as for instance the expulsion of Pandits in the case of Kashmir, and the steady extortion of civilians by Manipuri and Naga rebels. They are also often funded by foreign nations. That said, the principal reason for the conflict remains the intense commitment of the rebels on the one side, and the excessive use of force by the state on the other.

Those with a detached, long-term view may point out that it took centuries for countries like Spain and the United Kingdom to successfully subdue the ethnic minorities that live on their borders. There is also the example of the American Civil War, and of China's troubles in Tibet and Xinjiang. These are all illustrations of the pain, the anguish, the bitterness and the brutality that often accompanies the process of nation-building. India, however, claims to be a modern democracy. The standards it sets itself must be different from those acceptable in aristocratic regimes of the nineteenth century or of totalitarian states of the present time. To reconcile the Kashmiris, Manipuris and Nagas to the idea of India must involve methods other than coercion or bribery.

The state's reliance on repression, and the rebels' insistence on full national sovereignty, has led (in Tagore's phrase) to 'ceaseless conflicts'. If the violence is to end, the Government of India must do far more to reach out to the people of Kashmir, Nagaland and Manipur. The notorious Armed Forces Special Powers Act must be repealed. Policemen and soldiers guilty of human rights violations must be punished. The constant interference with the functioning of democratically elected state governments must end.

At the same time, one should not romanticize little nationalisms, for they can be rather ugly themselves. The intolerance of Naga activists was on display in the summer of 2010, when they blockaded the Imphal Valley for more than two months, denying access to food, petrol and medicines intended for ordinary civilians. The narrow-mindedness (and perhaps paranoia) of Meitei insurgents is evident in their banning DVDs of Hindi films from being shown even in private homes. As for Kashmir, readers may wish to consult an essay by Yoginder Sikand in the *Economic and Political Weekly* laying out the reactionary, medievalist, world view of the Hurriyat leader, Syed Ali Shah Geelani.

There is also the question of viability. The small, hilly, land-locked independent homelands the radicals dream of will, in an economic and political sense, be unviable. (And an independent Kashmir will most likely become a receptacle for Al Qaeda.) If Tamils and Mizos can live within the Indian Union, there is no reason why the Meiteis and Nagas cannot. Educated, English-speaking and characterized by a high level of gender equality, these communities can access the best jobs in the whole of India (in fact, some of their members already do). Why then restrict oneself to a small, circumscribed piece of turf?

The idea of India is plural and inclusive. The Constitution of India is flexible and accommodative. As it stands, India incorporates a greater variety of religions (whether born on its soil or imported) than any other nation in human history. It has, among other things, a Sikh majority state (the Punjab), three Christian majority states (Mizoram, Nagaland and Meghalaya), a Muslim majority state (Jammu and Kashmir), Muslim majority districts in Kerala, Assam, Bihar and West Bengal, and districts dominated by Buddhists in Kashmir and Arunachal. India also has a greater variety of languages and literatures than any other nation, and a federal form of government. If flexibility is promoted more sincerely and accommodation implemented more faithfully, one can yet arrive at a resolution which allows for real autonomy, such that Manipuris and Nagas and Kashmiris have the freedom both to determine the pattern of their lives in their own state, and to seek, if they so wish, opportunities to work and live in the other states of the Union.*

VI

These three conceptual and ideological challenges (Hindu fundamentalism, Communist dictatorship, and ethnic separatism) all date to the founding of the nation. To these have more recently been added three more mundane and materialist challenges. These are inequality, corruption, and environmental degradation. In India today, there are gross and apparently growing inequalities of income, wealth, consumption, property, access to quality education and health care, and of avenues for dignified employment. These diverse disparities in turn run along diverse social axes, among them caste, religion, ethnicity, region, and gender. Upper castes (and Brahmins and Banias in particular) go to better schools and better hospitals, and are massively over-represented in the professional and entrepreneurial classes. In economic as well as social terms, Hindus, Sikhs and Christians are significantly better off than Muslims. The tribes of central India, as we have seen, may be even worse off than Muslims. Those who live in the west and south of the country have more regular sources of income than those who live in the north or east. All across India, per capita income is much higher in cities than in the countryside. Finally, in every social strata, men have easier access to education, health care, and employment opportunities than do women.

I am not a socialist, still less a Marxist. The history of Communism shows that those who seek by force to create a perfectly equal society only end up suppressing citizens, catalyzing violence, and creating a new class of *nomenklatura* who enjoy greater privileges and even greater immunity from public scrutiny than did medieval monarchs. The state of North Korea today is perfect proof of the idiocy and barbarity of the search for perfect equality.

*This theme, the reconciling of little nationalisms with the larger idea of India, is explored more fully in the last essay of Part I, 'The Beauty of Compromise'.

As that wise Indian, André Béteille, always points out, what we must strive for is reasonable equality of opportunity, not absolute equality of result. That we have plainly not achieved, hence the disparities noted above. The life chances of a Dalit remain grossly inferior to those of a Brahmin; of a Muslim to those of a Hindu; of a tribal to those of a Hindu or Muslim; of a villager to those of a city dweller; of an Oriya or Jharkhandi to those of a Maharashtrian or Tamil.

One consequence of market-led economic growth shall be to accentuate these differences. Since upper castes tend to have higher levels of education and greater mobility across India, they are likely to garner the most profitable jobs. Since well developed regions have a reputation for being rich in skills and open to innovation, the bigger investors will flock to them. Since cities have more resources and better infrastructure as compared to small towns and villages, they will continue to get the bulk of new investment. In this manner, the already substantial gap between (for example) Bangalore and rural Karnataka, south India and eastern India, city-dwellers and country-folk, will grow even larger.

These inequalities of income and status are made more striking by their magnification in the media, with its breathless worship of wealth and success. A leading newspaper routinely speaks of the India that wants to march ahead allegedly being kept back by the other India that refuses to come with them. There is a kind of Social Darwinism abroad, where the new rich promiscuously parade their wealth, while insinuating that the poor are poor because they deserve to be poor. The exhibitionism of the rich has reached its apogee in the construction of a twenty-seven-storey building in downtown Mumbai. Costing two billion dollars, and covering 400,000 square feet of interior space, this structure is meant for the exclusive use of a single nuclear family.

Rising inequalities have historically been part of the growth process all across the world. In the early phase of industrialization, the gap between the rich and the poor widens. Over time, however, these inequalities tend to come down. That, at any rate, was the experience of Europe and North America. Will later industrializers such as China and India also follow the same route? I cannot speak for China, but in India one cannot be unduly optimistic. One reason that inequalities tapered off in the West was because their governments worked effectively towards providing equality of opportunity. The contributions of the European Welfare State in providing decent health care and education to its citizens are well known. Less acknowledged, perhaps, is the part played in levelling inequalities by the outstanding system of public schools and publicly funded universities in countries such as Canada and the United States.

The situation in India is all too different. The inequalities in access to good education and health care are immense. The school my children went to in Bangalore is world-class; the school run by the state a few yards down the road is worse than third-rate. I can avail of top-quality health care, by paying (admittedly, through my nose); my house help must go to the local quack instead. To address these disparities, outstanding work has been done by social workers in the fields of primary education and health care. Brave, selfless, utterly patriotic Indians have worked 24 by 7 to get slum and low caste children into school, and to provide them protection against dangerous diseases. Ultimately, though, the scale of the problem is so immense that their work, heroic as it is, can only very partially make up for the apathy and corruption of the state. For, only a properly functioning state can equalize the life chances of all Indians, whether men or women, high, middle or low caste, Hindus or Muslims, northerners or southerners.

Social inequalities in India are also intensified by corruption, the diversion of public money meant to generate income and employment or to provide social services, into the hands of politicians and bureaucrats. In a novel written in the early 1950s, Verrier Elwin noted how homespun khadi, once 'the symbol of insurgence against British rule', had now become 'an almost official uniform, the sign of authority and power'. The rebel had become the governor; even so, the association of khadi with decency and honesty stayed on awhile. I am just about old enough to remember a time when

Indian politicians were, by and large, not selfish and narrow-minded, and not on the take. As prime minister between 1964 and 1966, Lal Bahadur Shastri presided over a Cabinet of largely honest men and women. His colleague, Gulzarilal Nanda, lived out his last days in a dark, poky flat in Ahmedabad, with no car, no fridge, etc. In those days, politicians of the left and right were often as upright (in financial terms) as those in the Centre.

There appear to have been three, overlapping, phases in the evolution of political corruption in India. The licence-permit-quota Raj of the 1950s and 1960s was the first stage. Favours were granted to particular individuals or firms in return for a consideration. The second stage, inaugurated in the 1970s, involved the ruling party taking a cut of large defence contracts. The third stage, which began at the same time but which really intensified only in the 1990s, has rested on the abuse of state power to allocate—or misallocate—land and natural resources to friends and cronies.

In a twelve-month period (roughly) beginning September 2010, the Union Cabinet was revealed to be complicit in a series of scams, the most serious of which related to the misappropriation of funds for the Commonwealth Games, and the underpricing of spectrum allocated to telecom companies. The loss to the public exchequer in these scandals ran into billions of rupees.

Investigations showed that, in both cases, the prime minister's office had been warned about the diversion of funds even as they were taking place. The men in charge of these schemes, Suresh Kalmadi (for the Commonwealth Games) and A. Raja (for the spectrum allocation) had been, if not on the take themselves, clearly in the knowledge that other people were on the take. For months on end, the prime minister, Dr Manmohan Singh, did not take any action against either man. Eventually, as a result of concerted pressure in the media, in the streets, and in the Parliament, and from the courts, Kalmadi and Raja were dismissed. By then the government run by Dr Singh was being spoken of as the most corrupt in Indian history.*

*The national debate on corruption, provoked and promoted in the latter half of 2011 by the Anna Hazare movement, is the theme of a later essay, 'The Professor and the Protester'.

The scams and scandals at the Centre have been accompanied by scams and scandals in the states. At the close of the last century, my home town, Bangalore, was a showpiece for the virtues of liberalization. Access to global markets had allowed the skilled workforce of the city to generate vast amounts of wealth, which in turn spawned a new wave of Indian philanthropy. At the beginning of the present decade, my home state, Karnataka, became a byword for the darker side of globalization. The loot of minerals and their export to China wreaked large-scale environmental damage, and polluted the political system through the buying and selling of legislators. A state once represented to the country and the world by N.R. Narayana Murthy was now being represented to itself by Janardhan Reddy.

The massive profits on mining are in part because of high international prices, but in greater part because the state charges a very low royalty on ore, allows many consignments to proceed to the ports without any royalty payments, and does not impose any environmental or labour standards on the mine operators. In October 2010, an attempt was made by the Opposition parties in Karnataka to unseat the government. According to news reports, individual MLAs were offered close to 50 crore rupees to change sides. Since many stayed where they were, it can safely be assumed that their party bid higher to retain them. Several thousand crores may have changed hands on this single transaction alone. It is a reasonable assumption that those who were willing to pay that amount were reckoning on making at least ten times as much money in the course of their government's tenure. One may further, and equally reasonably, assume that the commission paid to politicians by private entrepreneurs was one-tenth of the estimated proceeds. These are crude estimates, but it is clear that illegal and criminal profiteering on mining in Karnataka exceeds tens of thousands of crores annually.

Mining may have caused even more destruction to the fabric of democracy in other states, notably Goa and Orissa. Maharashtra appears to be next on the list. In the late autumn of 2010, I spent several hours in Puné with India's finest ecologist, Madhav Gadgil. Gadgil had just been on a tour of the Western Ghats. He found a thriving agrarian economy, based on the cultivation of fruits and spices, as well as on fishing. However, there was now a massive land grab afoot, with promoters of mines, power plants, and luxury resorts working with legislators and ministers to displace local residents and destroy forests and estuaries.

To suppress opposition to these projects, the district authorities routinely impose Section 144 of the Criminal Procedure Code, which prohibits public gatherings of more than five people. Himself followed (against his will) by a police escort, Gadgil found an atmosphere of terror and intimidation, which, as he recalled, 'struck me full in the face as I stood, for the first time in my life, flanked by policemen on three sides talking to Muslim fishermen of Nate village expressing their fear of total destruction of their livelihoods as the nuclear power plant comes up and swallows up their entire estuary as part of its security zone.'

As Gadgil and I spoke, there was a knock on the door. It was the postman, who was carrying, among other things, a sheaf of some sixty postcards from the residents of Ratnagiri and Sindhudurg districts. This was apparently an everyday occurrence. Since I do not read Marathi, I asked Gadgil to translate a letter for me. It was from a girl in high school, who urged the scientist to keep the marauders away and save the social and natural integrity of her district.

The mining and power sector boom is in part propelled by the fetish of achieving 9 per cent growth, which, it is said in some circles in New Delhi, is necessary for India to achieve superpower status. Those who most actively promote this ambition are a certain kind of Cabinet minister, a certain kind of corporate titan, and a certain kind of newspaper editor. They are all, I believe, beset with a deep inferiority complex, whereby they wish desperately to be placed on equal terms in international fora with the politicians, billionaires and editors of the West. Their hope is that India's democratic credentials and economic surge shall jointly ensure that at such places as the World Economic Forum in Davos, they are treated with as much respect—not to say reverence—as the leaders, entrepreneurs and editors coming out of Paris, Berlin, London and (especially) New York.

Willing along this superpower talk are Non-Resident Indians, particularly those resident in the United States. In the past, these had been somewhat embarrassed about their native country, its poverty and inequality especially. At the same time, by virtue of their colour and religious affiliation they had not been entirely at home in their adopted country either. Now, the expansion of the Indian economy and the listing on the New York Stock Exchange of some Indian companies has encouraged positive feelings about India, which—if articulated energetically enough—could perhaps get the Americans to treat them with greater seriousness and respect than in the past.

In truth, the superpower aspiration is as much a male, macho thing as Naxalism or Hindutva. It is likewise a fantasy, and an equally dangerous one. It has already spawned much conflict in its wake. With public policy overwhelmingly determined by the desire to achieve 9 per cent growth, we have handed over peasant and tribal lands for the most destructive forms of industrial and mining activity. By making that one number the *sine qua non* of national pride and honour, the central government has encouraged state governments to promote corruption, criminality, social strife, and massive and possibly irreversible environmental degradation.

To be sure, the Indian economy needs to grow at a steady rate to lift our people out of poverty. However, we must look more carefully at the components of that growth, at its distributive impacts across and between generations. We must assess different enterprises and sectors according to the kinds of employment they generate, and their varying impacts on nature. We must ensure that all processes of land acquisition and natural resource allocation are fair, just and transparent. The costs of a narrow-minded focus on GDP growth, and of a fetishization of a particular number—8, 9, 10 per cent—can be colossal. For, the GDP accounts do not subtract for the loss of water, and the pollution and destruction of land and vegetation caused by opencast mining.

The market can promote efficiency and productivity, but not ecological sustainability or social justice. The market does not value the needs of poor people who have no money; it does not value the future; and it does not value the right of other species to exist. It is thus in the rational interest of miners and industrialists to externalize the costs of degradation and pollution. (The laws to prevent this exist on the statute books, but, with a few spectacular exceptions, are not implemented.)

India today is thus an environmental basket case, characterized by falling water tables, dead rivers, massively high rates of air pollution and soil erosion, unregulated disposal of toxic wastes, and the decimation of forests and biodiversity. These processes are caused by a combination of inequality and corruption. Politicians in the Centre and the states, acting at the behest of the wealthy, pass on the costs of environmental damage to the poor and to future generations.

Eighty years ago, Mahatma Gandhi had pointed to the unsustainability, at the global level, of the western model of economic development. 'God forbid,' he wrote, 'that India should ever take to industrialization after the manner of the West. The economic imperialism of a single tiny island kingdom (England) is today keeping the world in chains. If an entire nation of 300 million took to similar economic exploitation, it would strip the world bare like locusts.'

These words come from an article published in the journal *Young India* in December 1928. Two years earlier, Gandhi had claimed that to 'make India like England and America is to find some other races and places of the earth for exploitation'. As it appeared that the western nations had already 'divided all the known races outside Europe for exploitation and there are no new worlds to discover', he pointedly asked: 'What can be the fate of India trying to ape the West?'

Along with India, China too is trying to ape the West, attempting to create a mass consumer society whose members can all drive their own cars, live in their own air-conditioned homes, eat in fancy restaurants and travel to the ends of the earth for their family holidays. Will these Chinese and Indian consumers collectively strip the world bare like locusts? Between them, they have set off a new scramble for Africa, stripping or at least strip-mining that unhappy continent to fuel their ever-growing appetite for resources. Between them, they also consolidated a military junta in Myanmar, putting their own selfish interests in minerals and energy ahead of the elementary human rights of the Burmese people.

The environmental challenges posed by the economic rise of China and India are of three kinds. First, at the global level, is the threat of rapid and irreversible climate change due to the accumulation of greenhouse gases. As the early industrializers, the West were the original culprits here; that said, the two Asian giants are rapidly making up for lost time. Second, at the regional or continental level, are the environmental (and social) costs of the ecological footprint of China and India outside their own national borders. The West has for some time worked to relocate its dirty industries to the Third World, passing on the costs to the poor and the powerless. In the same manner, the externalities of Indian and Chinese consumers will be increasingly borne by the people of other lands.

The third challenge is that posed to the environments of these countries themselves. Chinese cities have the highest rates of air pollution in the world. Rivers such as the Ganga and the Jamuna are, effectively, dead. India and China both have unacceptably high levels of air and water pollution. They have also witnessed, in recent years, the large-scale depletion of groundwater aquifers, the loss of biodiversity, the destruction of forests, and the decimation of fish-stocks.

There are two stock responses to the environmental crisis in India. One is to hope, or pray, that in time and with greater prosperity we will have the money to clean up our surroundings. The other is to see ecological degradation as symptomatic of the larger failure of modernity itself. The first response is characteristic of the consuming classes; the second, that of the agrarian romantic, who believes that India must live only in its villages, that, indeed, the majority of Indians are happy enough to live on in their villages.

Both responses are deeply wrong-headed. Contra the rural romantic, life among the peasantry can be nasty, brutish, and short. Most Indian villagers would cheerfully exchange a mud hut for a solid stone house, well water for clean piped water, kerosene lanterns for steady and bright tube lights, a bicycle for a motorcycle. The living standards of the majority of Indians can and must be enhanced. At the same time, the living standards of the most wealthy Indians must be moderated.

The demands placed on the earth by the poor and excluded are disproportionately low; the demands placed by those with cars and credit cards excessively high. A rational, long-range, sustainable strategy of development has to find ways of enhancing the resource access of those at the bottom of the heap while checking the resource demands of those in positions of power and advantage. This strategy has then to be broken down into specific sectors; so that, for example, we can design suitable policies for transport, energy, housing, forests, pollution control, water management, and so on.

Once, the mainstream media (in English and Indian languages) played a catalytic role in promoting environmental awareness. Through the 1970s and 1980s, journalists like Anil Agarwal, Bharat Dogra, Kalpana Sharma, Darryl D'Monte, Usha Rai, Shekhar Pathak and Nagesh Hegde wrote extensively on issues such as deforestation, species loss, water abuse, and sustainable energy policies. They drew in part on their own field investigations, and in part on the work of a whole array of Indian ecological scientists. However, when liberalization got underway and the economy began to show higher rates of growth, there was an anti-environmental backlash. Now, environmentalists began to be portrayed as party poopers, as spoilers who did not want India to join the ranks of the Great Powers of the world. In response to these criticisms, and sensible also of the pressures of commercial advertisers, most newspapers laid off their environment correspondents or perhaps sent them to cover the stock market instead.

Foolish or motivated newspaper editors damn environmentalists as anti-business and anti-enterprise. But, as the civil servant

E.A.S. Sarma points out, 'a small cultivator or a traditional fisherman represents as much of private initiative and enterprise' as a large corporation. Dams, mines and beach resorts (among other activities) often pit these two kinds of entrepreneurs against one another. Were it left to the market and to corrupt officials and politicians, the big guy would always win, and the small fellow (as well as nature itself) suffer.

The blindness (and perhaps malevolence) of the English-language media in this respect was manifest in the savage attacks mounted on Jairam Ramesh when he was environment minister. Trained in technology and economics, mentored by such visionaries as Lovraj Kumar and Sam Pitroda, and with wide experience of working in different parts of India, Ramesh infused vigour and energy into a once-moribund ministry. He was the first person to occupy that post who was both competent and honest. Previous environment ministers had broken rules and hastened clearances in deference to the whims of the corporate sector. Ramesh, however, made sincere attempts to streamline and make transparent the process of decision-making. He reached out to credible civil society groups, and involved India's finest ecological scientists in the activities and policies of the ministry.

Ramesh was merely doing his job, for which he was rewarded with a continual stream of abuse in sections of the English-language press. In October 2010 I spent some weeks doing research in New Delhi. I asked the boarding house I was staying in to send me a newspaper not printed in my home town, Bangalore. When I lived in Delhi, in the 1980s, this newspaper was known for the rigour of its grass-roots reportage and for the independence of its editorial views. It also had a strong tradition of environmental reporting. Now, however, it appeared that the same newspaper had become a sort of unofficial mouthpiece of the Confederation of Indian Industry.

In the short time I was in Delhi, this paper ran half a dozen stories vilifying Ramesh—stories that, unconsciously or consciously, revealed its own biases and interests. The Ambanis planned to build a new airport in Navi Mumbai, for which they were ready to destroy a

large swathe of mangrove forests. Ramesh sensibly pointed out that
with a slight realignment, involving the diversion of land from a
SEZ owned already by Reliance, the forests could be saved. The
paper, seeking to side with the promoters, approvingly quoted (of
all people) the Maharashtra industries minister Narayan Rane to the
effect that mangroves could be regrown anywhere and at any time.
(If this were indeed the case, Rane would get the world's top award
in ecological restoration.) Another story damned Ramesh as a
'maverick minister'; yet another accused him of 'cancel[ling] major
projects with worrying whimsicality'.

The ideology of this newspaper was most evident in successive
editorials it wrote on Arunachal Pradesh. After a visit to the state,
Ramesh had raised questions about the hasty clearances given to
large hydro-electric projects, built by private companies, that would
displace tribal people and destroy priceless forests and biodiversity.
He asked that public hearings be held, and local communities
consulted before these projects were approved. The newspaper now
ran an editorial accusing him of 'gadding about looking for more
fashionable causes to sponsor'. It claimed he wished to 'destabilize
an entire region's development'.

A few days later, another editorial on the same subject demanded
quick clearance of all schemes in the state. It claimed the 'environment
ministry has been careless and unwise in its approach to the various
relatively small (sic) projects that have been planned for Arunachal
in an attempt to increase the region's prosperity and integration into
the rest of the economy'. Warming to the theme, the editorial
insinuated that by keeping Arunachal 'backward', Ramesh was
merely playing into the hands of the Chinese.

In fact, it was the dams, rather than their stoppage, that threatened
to destabilize the region. Of all states in the North-east, only
Arunachal has not yet had an insurgency, in part because of sensible
policies designed by the anthropologist Verrier Elwin in the 1950s
and 1960s, which protected tribal rights in land and forests and kept
missionaries (of all faiths) out of the state. Ramesh's own proposals
made sound economic, social and political sense. The dams would
largely benefit cities in the plains, while displacing local farmers,

herders and fisherfolk. Besides, the Eastern Himalaya have India's richest reserves of biodiversity; they are also peculiarly earthquake-prone. Nature, as well as culture, mandated that proposals to build large dams be treated cautiously. Already there was growing popular discontent on the issue. Hence the suggestion that there be public hearings, so that the people of Arunachal, rather than some know-all editor in New Delhi, could decide what would best bring them 'prosperity' and 'integration'.

(As this book goes to press, in May 2012, *Mint* newspaper carries an article by Sudeep Chakravarti which speaks, among other things, of the dangers posed by unregulated dam building in Arunachal Pradesh. A reporter who knows the region well, Chakravarti observes that Arunachal 'has imported the worst practices from mainland India in land allocation for projects, and misuse of the doctrine of eminent domain. A recent case: In mid-April, the government violently dispersed protesters who had gathered to dissent against the private sector-led 2,700-megawatt Lower Siang Hydro Electric Project. Worse will follow.')

The one environmental story the media is happy to cover sympathetically has to do with the fate of large mammals such as the tiger. Yet, as Anil Agarwal once pointed out, one must move the environment debate 'beyond pretty trees and tigers'. In India, at least, the state and fate of the natural environment is intimately linked to livelihood and survival. Without sustainable irrigation practices, Indian farmers cannot assure themselves a long-term future. Without decent public transport and energy conservation, India will be beholden to the whims and fancies of countries with more oil than ourselves. Without clean air and safe drinking water, our children will be far less healthy than we want them to be.

However, in the eyes of the new, excessively market-friendly media, the environment is only about pretty trees and tigers. They wish their readers to have their cake and eat it too—to live resource-intensive lifestyles and yet be able to glory in the beauties of the wild. They cannot, or will not, see that the one imperils the other. Nor will they acknowledge the persistence and significance of more local, less glamorous, environmental issues—such as the state of the air and the water, the conservation of energy, the provision of safe and affordable housing. These issues affect the lives of hundreds of millions of Indians. However, by succumbing so readily to the cult of wealth and celebrity, the media can find no space for them.

VII

My focus on social disparities and environmental degradation must not be mistaken for a call to return to the licence-permit-quota-raj. In the early years of independence, Indian industry perhaps needed protection—it certainly demanded it. The Bombay Plan of 1944, endorsed by G.D. Birla and J.R.D. Tata among others, asked for both curbs on foreign investment and for an enhanced role for the state. India had once been colonized by a western multinational corporation—having, at last, gained its freedom, it intended to keep it. At the same time, Indian capitalists lacked the capital and knowhow to invest in sectors such as steel, power, roads and ports. They were thus content to focus on the manufacture and distribution of consumer goods, leaving capital goods and infrastructure to the state.

The time to liberalize the Indian economy was the late 1960s. A manufacturing base was now in place; so, too, was a steady supply of skilled technicians and engineering graduates. However, for reasons of political expediency, the prime minister of the day, Mrs Indira Gandhi, chose instead to strengthen the stranglehold of the state over the economy. Key sectors such as coal and petroleum were nationalized. The licensing procedure in sectors still open to the private sector was at once made more arbitrary and more stringent. Those industrialists who knew how to massage political egos or hand over bribes had an advantage over those who trusted their entrepreneurial abilities alone.

The 1970s was verily the lost decade, in a political as well as economic sense (this was also the decade of the Emergency, of the nurturing of committed judges and bureaucrats, and, on the non-Congress side, of the elevation of street protest over the procedures of democratic deliberation). Government policies became somewhat more business-friendly in the 1980s; and, at last, more market-friendly in the 1990s. The surge in economic growth is a direct consequence of this greater (if also greatly belated) trust placed in the capabilities of the Indian entrepreneur. Along with software, other sectors such as telecommunications, pharmaceuticals, motorized vehicles and air transport have also made impressive strides in recent years.

The reforms of the 1990s were therefore both overdue and necessary. They released the creative energies of the Indian entrepreneur, and thus increased incomes, generated jobs, and produced a 'multiplier' effect across the economy. Sectors that depended chiefly on innovation and knowledge prospered. This was capitalism at its most creative: generating incomes and jobs, satisfying consumer tastes, and also spawning a new wave of philanthropy.

More recently, however, some less appealing sides of capitalism have manifested themselves. The state retains control of three key resources—land, minerals, and the airwaves. As we have seen, these resources have become enormously valuable with the expansion of the economy, prompting sweetheart deals between individual politicians and individual entrepreneurs, whereby land, minerals, or spectrum are transferred at much less than market cost, and for a (quite large) consideration. This process rewards those entrepreneurs with the best contacts, rather than the best ideas. Creative capitalism has increasingly given way to crony capitalism, with dire consequences for society, for the environment, and for public institutions. Hence the 2G scandal, the spike in the Maoist insurgency due to the dispossession of tribals by mining companies, the killings of whistle-blowers by the land mafia, etc.

The first generation of reforms succeeded admirably in freeing India from the Hindu rate of growth. However, they should have been followed by a second generation of reforms, to enhance the capacity (and accountability) of state schools and public hospitals, and to create and properly staff the new, independent regulatory

institutions that were now required. These reforms might have
spread economic growth more evenly across regions and social
classes; and also checked the abuse of nature that the free rein
currently given to extractive industries (such as mining) has promoted.
Had this reform of public institutions taken place, it might have
prevented the polarizing social conflicts over land and other natural
resources. These reforms remain necessary, and overdue. Only then
might economic growth in India be made more inclusive and, in all
senses of the word, sustainable.

VIII

On the 4th of November 1948, B.R. Ambedkar introduced a draft
report in the Constituent Assembly. This, with a few modifications,
was to become the Constitution of India. Ambedkar said of the
document he had overseen that 'it is workable, it is flexible and it
is strong enough to hold the country together both in peace time
and in war time. Indeed, if I may say so, if things go wrong under
the new Constitution, the reason will not be that we had a bad
Constitution. What we will have to say is, that Man was vile.'

Sixty-four years later, the conclusion must be that in our failure
to fulfil the constitutional ideals of freedom, fraternity and equality,
one kind of man has been particularly vile—the kind mandated by
law to promote these ideals in office. For, the scale and ubiquity of
political corruption means *that perhaps the most powerful enemy of the
idea of India now is the Indian state.*

The Congress has played a leading role here. As the party of the
freedom movement, it helped define the idea of India. As the party
which, after Independence, promoted unity and democracy, it
deepened the idea of India. Its best leaders were genuinely committed
to inter-faith harmony, and deeply concerned with mitigating social
inequalities. However, over the past three decades the party and its
leaders have worked principally to damage and degrade the idea of
India. The terms that came to mind in characterizing an earlier
generation of Congressmen (and Congresswomen) were: patriotic,

efficient, social democratic, incorruptible. The terms that come to mind now are: selfish, nepotistic, sycophantic, on the make.

One may as well name names. Indira Gandhi, herself a child of the freedom struggle, schooled in the traditions of Tagore, Gandhi and Nehru, converted a decentralized, democratic party with robust district and state committees into a family firm; and destroyed the autonomy and integrity of the civil services by making loyalty to the leader the principal criterion for professional advancement. Rajiv Gandhi, a modern-minded man who said he was going to take India into the twenty-first century, opened the locks in the Ayodhya shrine and then, to please the bigots on the other side, annulled the progressive Supreme Court judgment in the Shah Bano case, thus catalyzing two decades of religious rivalry and rioting that left thousands of Indians dead and many more homeless (and also incidentally opened the space for Hindutva to move from the political margins to centre stage). Manmohan Singh, himself a man of personal integrity, presides over a political regime stinking with corruption, watching as thousands of crores illegally change hands as commission on the sanctioning of Special Economic Zones, infrastructure and communication schemes, and energy projects.

It is important to name the Congress leaders at the Centre, since chief ministers in the states have been encouraged by them to act likewise. Had Indira Gandhi not promoted the notion of the 'committed' bureaucrat, we would not have had such a large-scale subversion of the administrative machinery, with every state government assigning departments to civil servants on the basis of caste, ideology, and personal loyalty rather than competence. Had Rajiv Gandhi not so readily banned Salman Rushdie's *Satanic Verses* at the behest of reactionary clerics, Ashok Chavan would surely not have so obediently followed the instructions of another kind of bigot and withdrawn Rohinton Mistry's novel, *Such a Long Journey*, from the curriculum of Mumbai University. Had Manmohan Singh not been so reluctant to act against his tainted ministers, B.S. Yeddyurappa would not so easily have ridden out press exposure of his corruption and that of his Cabinet colleagues (when he was finally forced to resign, it was not by his party or his conscience, but by the courts). And had Sonia Gandhi not promoted a cult of her husband and mother-in-law, naming scheme after scheme after them, Mayawati could scarcely have launched her own extravagant projects of personal memorialization at public expense.

IX

To function moderately well, a democracy needs three sectors to pull their weight—the state, private enterprise, and civil society. In the 1950s and 1960s, when entrepreneurs were timid and risk-averse, and civil society was non-existent, the state performed superbly well. In 2012, it appears to be civil society which is performing best of all. There are hundreds of hard-working and selfless social activists, working in the fields of education, health, environment, women's rights, consumer protection, civil liberties, and more. The private sector, on the other hand, is marked by both visionaries and marauders; whereas ten years ago it was the technologically alert and public-spirited entrepreneurs who defined the trends, now it is the crooks and cronies who appear to enjoy more power and influence.

To restore faith in the idea of India, a more capable, focused and honest political class may be necessary. Meanwhile, we can take succour in the manifest intentions of the citizenry, who, despite the provocations of the extremes, continue to hold democracy and diversity in high regard. Outside of Gujarat, hard-line Hindutva has repeatedly been rejected by the electorate (as demonstrated most recently in Bihar, where keeping Narendra Modi out of their campaign helped the NDA to a spectacular victory in the state elections). The acts of Islamist terror in Mumbai, Delhi and elsewhere have not been followed by religious scapegoating or rioting. Likewise, peasants and adivasis in areas of Maoist influence regularly defy the rebels by participating enthusiastically in state and national elections, thus proving, incidentally, that ours is not a democracy for the bourgeoisie alone.

The decent instincts of the citizenry were also at display when they rejected, quietly and without any fuss, the campaign launched before the 2004 election campaign to portray the leader of the Congress party as a foreigner. By speaking of the dangers of a 'Rome Raj' led by 'Antonia Maino Gandhi', the xenophobes hoped to catalyse the base instincts of Indians in general and Hindus in particular. Outside the Hindutva faithful, the call found no resonance whatsoever. Voters made it clear that they would judge Mrs Sonia Gandhi by other criteria. Her birth in Italy and her Catholic upbringing were immaterial. By four decades of continuous residence on Indian soil she had claimed the right to be an Indian. To be sure, there remain many Indians who are unhappy with the promotion of a family cult, and many others who are critical of the Congress president's social and economic policies. But her European ancestry does not matter at all. Like the Rajasthani achar-seller in Kochi, she is free, as a citizen of India, to exercise her vocation where she pleases. We will assess her wares as they appear to us—and accept or reject them as we please.

It was, I think, Jawaharlal Nehru who pointed out that India was home to all that is truly disgusting as well as truly noble in the human condition. The nobility and the disgustingness were abundantly on display in his day, as they are in ours. Contemporary India is home to pluralists and democrats as well as to fanatics and sectarians; to selfless social workers as well as to greedy politicians; to honest and upright officials as well as to officials who are time-servers; to capitalists who distribute their wealth quietly and widely as well as to those who seek only to publicly and provocatively display it.

Six months after the demolition of the Babri Masjid, the historian Dharma Kumar wrote a short essay entitled 'India as a Nation-State'. Here, she took issue both with left-wing activists who thought the Indian state too strong, and with Hindu chauvinists who thought it too weak. One saw the state as an 'oppressive monopolist of power'; the other believed it lacked the will and the strength to stand up to the West or put its own minorities in their place. One seemed to welcome the possible disintegration of the country, in the belief that 'twenty countries, say, instead of one would leave the people of India less oppressed'; the other was 'terrified of the break-up of India', thinking that 'India has still not recovered from partition and any further secessions would lead to . . . Balkanization . . . This line of analysis leads to the perception of Muslims as the cause of national weakness.'

Dharma Kumar rejected both positions by affirming the inclusive and democratic idea of India upheld by its founders. As she put it, 'instead of deploring our lack of homogeneity we should glory in it. Instead of regarding India as a failed or deformed nation-state we should see it as a new political form, perhaps even as a forerunner of the future. We are in some ways where Europe wants to be, but we have a tremendous job of reform, of repairing our damaged institutions, and of inventing new ones.'

I have myself been fortunate in being witness to the work of many Indians who have sought to repair or redeem our institutions. I think of groups like the Association of Democratic Reform, which succeeded in making the criminal records and assets of politicians public; or like Pratham, which works closely with state governments in improving our public education system. I think of Ela Bhatt and Chandi Prasad Bhatt, respectively the grandmother and grandfather of modern social activism in India. Ela*behn* has challenged the state to be more alert to the rights of working women; Bhattji has forced it to move towards a more community-oriented (and ecologically sensitive) forest policy. I think of the scientists Obaid Siddiqui and Padmanabhan Balaram, who have nurtured world-class, non-hierarchical, research laboratories in a funds-scarce, anti-intellectual, and deeply inegalitarian society. I think, too, of my exact contemporaries and fellow PhDs Jean Dreze and Mihir Shah, who could have enjoyed comfortable careers as teachers and writers, but who chose instead to become full-time activists, and bent their expertise to making the Government of India more responsive to the lives and interests of the rural poor.

The groups and individuals mentioned in the preceding paragraph are, of course, merely illustrative. The work that they and others like them undertake is rarely reported in the mainstream media. For, the task of reform, of incremental and evolutionary change, is as unglamorous as it is necessary. It is far easier to speak of a wholesale, structural transformation, to identify one single variable that, if acted upon, will take India up and into the straight high road to superstardom. Among the one-size-fits-all solutions on offer are those promoted by the Naxalites, whose project is to make India into a purer, that is to say more regimented, version of Communist China; by the Sangh Parivar, who assure the Hindus that if they rediscover their religion they will (again) rule the world; and by the free-market ideologues, who seek to make India into an even more hedonistic version of the United States of America.

Based as it is on dialogue, compromise, reciprocity and accommodation, the idea of India does not appeal to those who seek quick and total solutions to human problems. It thus does not seem to satisfy ideologues of left or right, as well as romantic populists. To these sceptics, let me offer one final vignette. One Independence Day, I was driving from Bangalore to Melkoté, a temple town in southern Karnataka which incidentally also houses a celebrated Gandhian ashram. The first part of the drive was humdrum, through the ever-extending conurbation of Greater Bangalore. Then we turned off the Mysore highway, and the countryside became more varied and interesting. Somewhere between Mandya and Melkoté we passed a bullock cart. Three young boys were sitting in it; one wore a suit with spectacles, a second a *bandgala* with a Mysore *peta* atop his little head, the third a mere loin cloth.

The boys had evidently just come back from a function in their school, where, to mark Independence Day, they had chosen to play the roles of B.R. Ambedkar, M. Visvesvaraya and M.K. Gandhi respectively. Remarkably, none of their heroes were native Kannada speakers. Yet all spoke directly to their present and future. The boys knew and revered Ambedkar as the person who gave dignity and hope to the oppressed; knew and revered Visvesvaraya for using modern technology for the social good, as in the canals from the

Kaveri that irrigated their own fathers' fields; and knew and revered Gandhi for promoting religious harmony and leading, non-violently, the country's fight for freedom.

The vision of those young boys was capaciously inclusive. Ideologists may oppose Ambedkar to Gandhi; historians may know that Gandhi and Visvesvaraya disagreed on the importance of industrialization in economic development. Yet the boys understood what partisans and scholars do not—that our country today needs all three, for all were Indians of decency and integrity, all seeking sincerely to mitigate human suffering, all embodying legacies worthy of being deepened in our own age. What I saw that day was a spontaneous, magnificent illustration of the idea of India. To more fully redeem that idea would mean, among other things, matching the pluralism that those schoolboys articulated, with the democracy defended so precisely by the Muria schoolteacher in Dantewada.

chapter two

A SHORT HISTORY OF
CONGRESS CHAMCHAGIRI

~

I

One day in June 2005 I was forced away from my home town, Bangalore, to attend a meeting at the culture ministry in New Delhi. When I boarded the plane the outside temperature was 22 degrees Celsius; when I disembarked in Palam it was 45 degrees. I was muttering imprecations to myself through the ride into the city, through the meeting in Shastri Bhavan, through dinner at the boarding house where I was staying and, for all I know, right through my sleep as well. It was only the next morning that I cheered up. For one thing, before noon I would be winging my way back to Bangalore. For another, the newspaper that day printed a photograph of a group of young Indians who were much more under the weather than I was. And apparently quite willingly, too.

These were a band of Congress *chamcha*s who had gathered outside 10 Janpath, to greet Rahul Gandhi on his thirty-sixth birthday. Dressed in white, they were lined up in rows, the vanguard holding up, for the photographers to see, a cake weighing fifty kilograms which had been inscribed for their leader.

The chamchas had gathered around the Gandhi home early in the morning, and stayed on until dusk. My meeting had been rather dreary, but I noted (to my satisfaction) that these fellows had a duller day still. (As well as a much hotter one—at least my room was air-conditioned.) They had periodically sent messages through the watchmen asking their hero to step out, and periodically stirred themselves to shout: '*Desh ka neta kaisa ho/Rahul Gandhi jaisa ho.*' But however hard they tried, *Rahul bhayya* would not come, though whether it was out of embarrassment (justified) or fear of the heat (even more justified) the report did not say. By the time the chamchas departed, the remains of their cake were seen to be running a rather gooey line from 10 Janpath, quite a long way down in the direction of Connaught Place.

Not that the cake-carriers could ever bring themselves to refer to that part of New Delhi by its original name. Connaught Place and Connaught Circus is how I know those graceful rings, but these names were changed in an earlier Congress regime to 'Rajiv Chowk' (the inner ring) and 'Indira Chowk' (the outer one). In a tearful speech in Parliament, a Congress MP announced that this was done so that in death, as in life, Indira would forever hold Rajiv in her embrace. For the ordinary folk of Delhi, Connaught Place (and Circus) remain *de rigueur*, but for all members of the Congress those older names are, of course, *verboten*.

And the rush to name ever more places after the Family continues. Not long ago, I was a participant in a TV debate on the renaming of the new Hyderabad airport after Rajiv Gandhi. I suggested that one could name the airport after a genuinely great figure, such as the composer Thyagaraja, a choice that would be applauded across party–political lines. In any case, it was time we went beyond remembering only one family. Somewhere along the line, in response to a term I had used, the other member of the panel, a still-serving Union minister, said: 'We are happy to be Congress chamchas.'

II

The epithet the minister proudly owned is part of our political lexicon. I have myself used it here in the knowledge that readers

shall know exactly what I am referring to. Still, it might be helpful
to more precisely date and define it. 'Chamcha' is a Hindustani
word whose nearest English equivalent is 'sycophant'. There have
been chamchas since the birth of the Indic civilization—the lords
Rama and Krishna are alleged to have had countless such—but
there have been Congress chamchas only since about the year 1969.
Contrary to what the term might suggest, it does not connote
loyalty to the party in general but to the family which now leads
it in particular.

Most Indians are too young to know this, but the truth is that
until about 1969 the Congress was more or less a democratic party.
The great leaders of the freedom struggle—Gokhale, Tilak, Bose,
Gandhi and others—had followers and admirers, but these were not
publicly slavish in their sycophancy. The same was the case with
Jawaharlal Nehru, who kept his distance from courtiers and flatterers.

Nehru did not much like chamchas; and, contrary to a widely
accepted myth, Nehru did not start a 'dynasty' either. He had no
wish, nor desire, nor hope, nor expectation, that his daughter Indira
would ever become prime minister. In a book published in 1960,
the respected editor Frank Moraes wrote that 'there is no question
of Nehru's attempting to create a dynasty of his own; it would be
inconsistent with his character and career'. This was (and is) entirely
correct. When Nehru died in 1964, an otherwise bitter critic,
D.F. Karaka, nonetheless praised his resolve 'not to indicate any
preference with regard to his successor. This, [Nehru] maintained,
was the privilege of those who were left behind. He himself was not
concerned with that issue.'

True, in her father's lifetime Indira Gandhi was made President
of the Indian National Congress. But after a single term in this post
she retreated to domestic life. There she stayed for five years, with
no wish, nor desire, nor hope, nor expectation, that she would
assume a position of importance in Indian political life. Indeed, on
the 8th of May 1964, Mrs Gandhi wrote to her friend Dorothy
Norman that 'the whole question of my future is bothering me. I
feel I must settle outside India at least for a year or so . . .' Since both

her sons were then studying (after a fashion) in the United Kingdom,
it was to that country that Mrs Gandhi was thinking of moving.

Three weeks later, Nehru died. The new prime minister, Lal
Bahadur Shastri, now appointed Indira Gandhi the minister of
information and broadcasting, this being a gesture to the memory
of her father rather than an acknowledgement of merit or capability.
When Shastri died in January 1966, Mrs Gandhi was, to her own
surprise, catapulted into the post of prime minister. There were
other and better candidates for the job, but the Congress bosses
(notably K. Kamaraj) thought that they could more easily control a
lady they thought to be a *gungi gudiya* (dumb doll).

It turned out otherwise. In power, Mrs Gandhi displayed a streak
of ruthlessness few had seen in her before. She split the Congress,
threw out the bosses, and with the slogan of 'Garibi Hatao'
refashioned herself as a saviour of the poor. The once-democratic and
decentralized Congress party became, in effect, an extension of a
single individual. I recently came across an article entitled 'Mummy
Knows Best', published in the now-defunct New Delhi journal,
Thought, in October 1971. In recent weeks, Mrs Gandhi had sacked
two chief ministers. First it was Mohan Lal Sukhadia in Rajasthan,
then Brahmananda Reddy in Andhra Pradesh. As *Thought* wrote, it
mattered little who would succeed Reddy in Andhra; for, 'he that
ascends the gaddi will have to look for his survival to the lady in
Delhi rather than to the Legislators in Hyderabad or the Constituents
in Andhra at large'.

While she was growing into her new job, Mrs Gandhi's two sons
were trying out careers of their own. The elder boy, Rajiv, after
having followed his mother in having failed to complete a degree,
took a pilot's licence and joined Indian Airlines. The younger boy,
Sanjay, prudently chose not to go to university at all. He apprenticed
at Rolls Royce, where his lack of discipline provoked a flood of
anguished correspondence between his mother and the Indian high
commission in London, who were naturally worried about the
repercussions of the son's waywardness on the reputation of the
prime minister.

In time Sanjay returned to India, and sought to set up a car factory of his own. He said he would manufacture not limousines but a 'people's car' named Maruti. Despite the gift of cheap land (from a sycophantic chief minister of Haryana) and soft loans from public sector banks, the project failed to deliver on its promises. Another of Sanjay's chamchas, Khushwant Singh, then the editor of the *Illustrated Weekly of India*, claimed that his factory would roll out 50,000 cars a year. 'Soon little Marutis should be seen on the roads of Haryana and Delhi,' wrote the editor: 'and a month or two later they will be running between Kalimpong and Kanyakumari.'

As it happened, Sanjay Gandhi's factory did not produce a single roadworthy car. (The little Marutis that now run on Indian roads are based on the Japanese design of a standard Suzuki vehicle.) It seems that Sanjay anticipated this, for, in 1975, when his factory was yet to be completed, he went in search of another career. He had not to search very far—no further than his own home, in fact. Mrs Gandhi had just imposed the Emergency; to keep it going she needed support, and her younger son was happy to provide it. He soon showed that he enjoyed the exercise of authority even more than his mother did. Some of the more notorious events of the Emergency, such as the forced sterilizations and the demolition of homes in Old Delhi, were the handiwork of Sanjay.

By the time the Emergency ended, Sanjay Gandhi had discarded any pretence of being a maker of cars. Henceforth it was all politics for him. He fought two Lok Sabha elections, became general secretary of the Congress, and served as his mother's deputy on all matters concerning the party and (from January 1980) the government. But then in June of that year he died in an air crash. The mother, bereft, turned to her elder son to take Sanjay's place.

While Sanjay was alive, Rajiv Gandhi had shown no inclination to join politics. His greatest professional ambition was to graduate from flying Avros on the Delhi–Lucknow run to flying Boeings between Calcutta and Bombay. By June 1980 he had been flying for twelve years, but his record did not yet merit the promotion he so ardently desired. He was rather luckier in politics. Once he had answered Mummy's call, and changed his career, the rewards were swift. Within five years of joining the Congress, he had become prime minister of India.

No sooner had Rajiv joined politics than Congress members and ministers all across the country queued up to salaam him. He was asked to lay foundation stones for medical colleges, open electric lines to Harijan colonies, give speeches to Congress clubs on Nehru's birthday. This build-up of the future leader was the subject of a satirical column by the Bombay writer 'Busybee' (Behram Contractor), a still unparalleled commentary on the culture of sycophancy in India's oldest political party. Here is the column, reproduced more or less in full:

The Padayatra (Walking Tour) Programme

Apropos Sunday morning's padayatra through the Dharavi slums by Mr Rajiv Gandhi, the following is the programme (Congress-I volunteers to note):

7.30 a.m.: Mr Rajiv Gandhi arrives at Santa Cruz Airport, received by 20,000 party workers (trucks will be provided to transport them . . .) Garlanding ceremony. Workers to shout: 'Rajiv Gandhi ki jai!'

8 a.m.: Motorcade leaves airport and proceeds to Dharavi passing under welcome arches along the route . . .

8.10 a.m.: Housewives of the government housing colony at East Bandra to spontaneously halt the motor cavalcade and perform the arti ceremony for Mr Gandhi. Local Congress (I) councillors to organize the housewives.

8.30 a.m.: Arrive at Dharavi . . . Welcome speech by Dharavi councillor and MLA. Garlanding ceremony. Flag-hoisting of Congress flag by children of the Dharavi municipal school.

9 a.m.: Tea and refreshments in school hall. Mr Gandhi receives telephone calls from . . . chief minister . . . and deputy chief minister, welcoming him to Bombay. A special telephone line to be installed . . . to enable Mr Gandhi to receive the calls.

9.30 a.m.: Mr Gandhi changes his chappals for gym shoes . . . Padayatra begins. (Organizers to note: Mr Gandhi should be taken only along those lanes which have been specially swept and cleaned for the padayatra.)

10 a.m.: TV cameras in position to take special shots of Mr Gandhi talking to oldest resident of Dharavi. TV shot of Mr Gandhi inaugurating new public tap. (Note to organizers: Arrangements should be made to fly colour film back to Delhi in time for inclusion in national news same night.)

10.30 a.m. to 11.30 a.m.: Mr Gandhi makes four speeches at four different locations in Dharavi, preferably where pressmen are present. (Further note to organizers: cars to be kept ready for Mr Gandhi to travel from one padayatra spot to another. Arrangements to be made for a man to hold umbrella over Mr Gandhi's head.)

Noon: Padayatra ends. Mr Gandhi changes gym shoes for sandals.

Before he joined politics Rajiv Gandhi was known to be a gentle character. But after he joined politics he quickly took to the authoritarian ways of his mother and brother. I recall him visiting Bangalore in the late 1980s, and giving a press conference at the airport on his way out. At some stage a journalist summarized the views on some subject of the chief minister of Karnataka, Veerendra Patil, a veteran freedom fighter and first-rate administrator. Rajiv Gandhi's response was to say: if that is what Patel believed, he would no longer be chief minister. Within a day or two this indeed came to pass.

The greatly reduced majorities of the Congress nowadays mean that its leader cannot be anywhere near as arrogant. Yet crucial positions are still decided on the basis of personal loyalty rather than professional competence. To get their job and retain it, Union ministers and chief ministers belonging to the Congress have to depend on the will and whim of the First Family. But the culture of sycophancy percolates right through the party and into the wider world beyond. Thus high posts in the civil service and diplomatic corps, as well as prestigious academic positions, are often allocated on the basis of a candidate's closeness—real or imagined—to the Family. Say, you are a professor or judge who is keen on a particular job. Then, if you lobby A who is close to B who is friendly with C who is known to be in the inner circle of the First Family—then, if you work away and are fortunate, you might even get that assignment.

India has been called a 'dynastic democracy'. Perhaps it would be more accurate to call it a *darbari* democracy. Especially when the Congress is in power, the atmosphere in New Delhi resembles nothing so much as a medieval court. Intrigue and gossip are rife. Those who seek public office nudge themselves ever closer to the inner circle of the King, the Queen, or the Prince-in-Waiting. Those who already hold public office have one eye on their job and another on what needs to be done, sycophantically, to retain it.

Twice a year, on the birth and death anniversaries of Rajiv Gandhi, the sycophantic culture of the Congress party is put on public display in the pages of our newspapers. Thus, judging by the television news on the night of the 20th of May 2010, it was a day like any other—marked by natural disaster (a cyclone predicted for Orissa), violent rebellion (the blowing up of railway tracks by Maoists in Bihar), political partisanship (the insistence by Mamata Banerjee that the Union railway minister would be from her party even if she soon moved back to Kolkata to become, as she hoped, the chief minister of West Bengal), and corruption in sport (fresh allegations of match-fixing, this time against Pakistani cricketers). The next morning, however, the newspapers had given top billing to a man who had not figured in the news the past twenty-four hours, or the past week, or even the past month. In fact, as page after page of that day's newspaper indirectly and inadvertently reminded us, he had been dead a full nineteen years. The reason that he was yet commanding much space was that he was once India's prime minister, and, more importantly, was the husband of the most powerful living Indian, the chairperson of the United Progressive Alliance (UPA).

On this day, the 21st of May 2010, several pages of the daily newspaper were given over to printing the photograph, and extolling the virtues, of Rajiv Gandhi. A half-page advertisement taken out by the ministry of petroleum and natural gas printed a large portrait with the line: 'Remembering Rajiv Gandhi and following his path . . .' The ministry of information and broadcasting went further—they paid for a full page, and in colour too. 'Nation pays tribute to Rajiv Gandhi on his martyrdom day. Nation resolves to strengthen the spirit of unity', ran (part of) the text. Other half-page or full-page advertisements were taken out by (among others) the ministry of housing, the ministry of power, and the department of information technology. These were slightly more ecumenical in their worship—while a portrait of Rajiv Gandhi and an excerpt from his words dominated, smaller pictures of the prime minister, Dr Manmohan Singh, and of Mrs Sonia Gandhi were also inserted, along with a picture of the minister in charge of the department.

These advertisements were paid for from the public purse, but without the consent or concurrence of the public. So far as I could tell, with only one exception, all the ministries that had taken out ads were headed by Congressmen (or Congresswomen). The exception was also very partial—it pertained to the department of information technology, whose ad was dominated by a large portrait of Rajiv Gandhi, but which also contained photos of the three ministers in this ministry. Two of these were Congressmen. The third, A. Raja, was not, but in view of the controversies he was then embroiled in, may not have been entirely averse to being associated with a commemorative venture designed, above all, to please the head of his alliance.

The best, and perhaps only, way to understand these advertisements is that they are statements of loyalty and devotion on the part of men, and women, who owed their jobs to the wife of the man they were seeking to honour. The size of the advertisement may be taken as proportionate to the minister's insecurity—the larger the ad, the more he or she felt the need to signal his or her devotion to the First Family of Indian politics. As for those ministries which chose not to take out any ads on that day, it must be that their heads were completely secure in their jobs, or in their relationship with the Congress president. There is a third possibility—that they might simply have forgotten the significance, to their party, of 21st May.

The advertisements were carried in the several English-language newspapers I subscribe to. They were also printed in Indian-language periodicals across the country (I saw them, for example, in

the Kannada newspapers, and in the Bangalore edition of a Hindi
newspaper). What did this collective exercise in political sycophancy
cost the nation? A major national newspaper I checked with said a
full-page colour advertisement would cost Rs 1.38 crore. However,
by law, or custom, ads put out by government departments enjoy
a substantial discount. Still, the fact that so many ads were taken,
and in so many editions of so many newspapers, must mean that the
aggregate cost would have been very substantial indeed. A back-of-
the-envelope calculation suggests that on the 21st of May 2010,
perhaps sixty or seventy crore were spent by the taxpayer—without
his or her consent—on praising Rajiv Gandhi. Since the practice has
been in place since 2005, the aggregate expenditure to date on this
account is probably in excess of Rs 300 crore.

I wonder if the ministers who sanctioned those ads thought of
alternative, more constructive, and more enduring ways in which
the money could have been spent. How many villages might the
ministry of power have electrified had it chosen not to take out that
full-page ad in colour? How many government schools could have
been supplied computers by the department of information technology
if the ministers concerned had been more secure of their position
in party and government?

I cannot speak for Rajiv Gandhi, but as a student of Jawaharlal
Nehru and his times, I can confidently state that Nehru would have
been embarrassed by such flattery at the taxpayer's expense. For,
despite its handful of billionaires, India remains a poor country.
Despite its healthy foreign exchange reserves, the Government of
India operates at a large fiscal deficit (currently in excess of 10 per
cent of GDP). It really cannot afford to throw crores and crores at
assuaging the insecurities of individual ministers or indulging the
vanity of a particular family.

III

The dynastic principle has damaged the workings of India's pre-
eminent political party, and beyond, the workings of Indian

democracy itself. One manifestation as remarked above, is the filling of important positions on the basis of chamchagiri rather than competence. Another is that Mrs Indira Gandhi's embrace of the dynastic principle for the Congress served as a ready model for other parties to emulate. With the exception of the cadre-based parties of left and right, the CPM and the BJP, all political parties in India have been converted into family firms. The DMK was once the proud party of Dravidian nationalism and social reform; it is now the private property of M. Karunanidhi and his children (with *their* children in the wings, awaiting their chance). Likewise, for all his professed commitment to Maharashtrian pride and Hindu nationalism, when picking the next Shiv Sena leader, Bal Thackeray could look no further than his son. The Samajwadi Party and Rashtriya Janata Dal claimed to stand for 'social justice', but the leadership of Mulayam's party passed on to his son, and in Lalu's party to his wife. The practice has been extended down the system, so that if a sitting MP dies, only his son or daughter can be nominated in his place.

The cult of the Nehru–Gandhis, dead and alive, is deeply inimical to the practice of democracy. It has led to the corruption and corrosion of India's premier political party, whose own example in this regard has been eagerly followed by the regional formations. Travelling through Tamil Nadu some years ago, I was met at every turn by ever-larger cut-outs of the chief minister's son and heir apparent—cut-outs of M.K. Stalin smiling, Stalin writing, Stalin speaking into a cell phone. The only other place where I have felt so stifled by a single face was in the Syria of Bashar Assad.

For his part Jawaharlal Nehru, following Gandhi, tried to base his policies on procedures and principles, rather than on the force of his personality. Within the Congress, within the Cabinet, within the Parliament, Nehru worked to further the democratic, cooperative, collaborative ideals of the Indian Constitution. The judiciary, the bureaucracy and the press were given autonomy; there was no attempt to force them to do the Leader's bidding. In his long tenure as prime minister, Nehru did not impose chief ministers of his liking on Congress-ruled states; these were chosen by the local legislators alone. In all this, Nehru was working against the grain of history, against the deep-seated feudal and hierarchical tendencies in Indian society. Indeed, his own party, his bureaucracy, his press, would still tend to sometimes treat him as if he had the attributes of the divine.

Nehru might not have entirely succeeded in building a democratic, non-hierarchical culture in Indian politics. But it is notable that he tried. Which cannot, however, be said for his daughter Indira Gandhi or his grandsons Sanjay and Rajiv Gandhi. One cannot really say this about the current head of the Congress party, either. Thus, shortly after the United Progressive Alliance came to power in 2004, Sonia Gandhi's birthday was celebrated at a well-attended function in New Delhi as 'Tyag Divas'. Here, one speaker claimed that his leader embodied the virtues of the Buddha, Ashoka and Mahatma Gandhi. Were this an ordinary Congress chamcha one might perhaps have disregarded it, but the person making these outrageous comparisons was no less than the Union home minister, Shivraj Patil.

Loyalty to the Leader, in person, rather than to the policies of his or her government—such was the legacy of Mrs Indira Gandhi, to be furthered and distorted by her progeny, and by leaders of other parties too. What Indira Gandhi did at the Centre was exceeded in the provinces, where the likes of M.G. Ramachandran and N.T. Rama Rao created leadership cults that might have impressed Joseph Stalin himself. Their initiatives in this regard have been taken even further by Bal Thackeray and J. Jayalalithaa, who have used the bhakti of their followers in dangerously undemocratic ways. Those who disagree with them in public have every chance of being physically attacked, as has been the experience of journalists in Mumbai and lawyers in Tamil Nadu.

This essay is being written to deplore the dynasty's role in the degradation of Indian democracy, but also to clear Jawaharlal Nehru of the false and motivated charge that he had anything to do with its creation. It was Indira Gandhi who founded the dynasty—she brought her sons into the Congress, and made it clear to all, within and outside the party, that she expected them to succeed her.

There is another, and perhaps more consequential reason, to separate Nehru from later generations of the Family. For him, politics was a matter of commitment and sacrifice, whereas for his descendants, politics has served as a comfortable safety net. The Indian National Congress was Nehru's true and proper family. Neglectful of his wife, distant towards his daughter, it was the Congress that gave real meaning and purpose to Nehru's life. For nearly fifty years it was his primary affiliation and allegiance. In the years before Independence, he worked ferociously hard in building the party's profile in northern India. He also travelled extensively across Europe and Asia to take the message of Congress nationalism to the world. These activities were interrupted by periodic bouts of jail-going, which however afforded the opportunity of forging ever closer friendships with his fellow Congressmen and, it must be added, Congresswomen.

Nehru's attachment to the Congress comes out most vividly in his writings. His *Letters to Chief Ministers* contains frequent references to freedom fighters who had recently died, commending their work and example to those who were alive and still sought to serve India. His most famous book, *The Discovery of India*, is dedicated to 'my colleagues and co-prisoners in the Ahmadnagar Fort Camp'. These colleagues were, of course, all Congressmen, likewise jailed for their involvement in the Quit India movement. The preface builds on the dedication in these still moving words:

> My eleven companions in Ahmadnagar Fort were an interesting cross-section of India and represented in their several ways not only politics but Indian scholarship, old and new, and various aspects of present-day India. Nearly all the principal living languages, as well as the classical languages which have powerfully influenced India in the past and present, were represented and the standard was often that of high scholarship. Among the classical languages were Sanskrit and Pali, Arabic and Persian; the modern languages were Hindi, Urdu, Bengali, Guj[a]rati, Marathi, Telugu, Sindhi and Oriya. I had all this wealth to draw upon and *the only limitation was my own capacity to profit by it* [emphasis mine].

Nehru was not prone to false modesty, so we may take that last caveat as being wholly sincere. At any event, one cannot imagine Indira, Rajiv or Sonia writing in this fashion. This is so for at least three reasons: they lacked the literary ability, they did not have the good fortune (or otherwise) to spend extended periods in prison, and they did not think that they had much to learn from other members of the Congress.

Jawaharlal Nehru could have been a successful lawyer, or an internationally renowned writer; he chose to fight for the freedom of his country instead. The cases of Sanjay, Rajiv and Rahul Gandhi are all too different. After having failed to distinguish themselves in other fields, they took their mother's advice to enter the family business—where there was a place reserved for them at the very top.

IV

I would like to end this essay with a counterfactual question—what if Lal Bahadur Shastri had lived for another five years? If Shastri is at all remembered today, it is for his bold leadership during the war with Pakistan in 1965, when he opened a second front in the Punjab after the invaders threatened to overrun Kashmir. In fact, his contributions to the nation were more substantial. For instance, it was Shastri who laid the foundation of the Green Revolution. The first few Five Year Plans had neglected the agrarian sector, leading to a serious shortage of foodgrains. No sooner was he made prime minister than Shastri shifted his able colleague, C. Subramaniam, from the then prestigious steel ministry to the agriculture portfolio. With the prime minister's backing, Subramaniam set about reorganizing the system of agricultural research, orienting it towards the selection and promotion of high-yielding varieties. These moves were consistent with the stirring slogan coined by the prime minister—'Jai Jawan, Jai Kisan'. Meanwhile, Shastri had also initiated moves to free industrial enterprise from the shackles of state control.

In the first weeks of 1966 Shastri died of a heart attack in the city of Tashkent, which was then part of the Soviet Union. The Indian prime minister had gone there, at the invitation of the Soviets, to forge a peace treaty with Pakistan's Ayub Khan. There has been some speculation about whether Shastri died of natural causes—speculation that continues because the Government of India has (typically) refused to release the official report on his death. But perhaps there was no hanky-panky—perhaps it was just that his traditional apparel did him in, with a dhoti and kurta inadequate protection against the harsh cold of an Uzbek winter.

Shastri was only sixty-three when he died. The question one must ask is not how he died, but what if he had lived another five or ten years? His conduct during the war with Pakistan had greatly elevated him in the minds (and hearts) of his countrymen. Had he lived, he would have assuredly led the Congress to victory in the fourth General Elections in 1967. With a solid majority behind him, he might have undertaken to find a final resolution to the Kashmir dispute. A further five years in power would also have allowed him, and his colleagues, to deepen their programmes of economic reform.

In the event, Shastri died in 1966, and Indira Gandhi became prime minister—not because she was the most able and experienced member of the Cabinet, but because the Congress bosses thought they could control her. By the end of the 1960s India was beginning to achieve self-sufficiency in food production. Naturally, the credit accrued to the incumbent prime minister, rather than to her dead predecessor. Meanwhile, she had also enjoyed a success that could be more directly attributed to her own initiative and drive—namely, the victory over Pakistan in the war of 1971.

But what if Lal Bahadur Shastri had lived? Then it would have been he, not Mrs Gandhi, who would have been praised for the benefits of the Green Revolution; he, not she, who would have been given credit for any battles won against Pakistan.

Had Shastri continued as prime minister until the end of the 1960s, or beyond, the economic history of India might have turned out very differently. In the 1950s, under the direction of the state, India had nurtured a reasonably robust domestic industry. It was now time to allow for the freer play of market forces. In speeches made in 1965, Shastri clearly indicated that he would like to take the economy in that direction. Sadly, he died soon afterwards. Instead of trusting to the energy and enterprise of the private sector, his successor strengthened the control of the state over the economy. The consequences were the continuation of low rates of growth, a situation that began to change only after the reforms of 1991 and beyond.

Had fate given Lal Bahadur Shastri a longer innings as prime minister, then the Indian economy may now have been more robust and resilient. He was both a pragmatic reformer as well as a man of conscience. Had he freed the processes of production from state control, he would simultaneously have initiated welfare measures to ameliorate poverty. As a man of vision and integrity, he would also have sought to improve the performance of India's public institutions.

Had Shastri lived, Indira Gandhi may or may not have migrated to London. But even had she stayed in India, it is highly unlikely that she would have become prime minister. And it is certain that her son would never have occupied or aspired to that office. Had Shastri been given another five years, there would have been no Nehru–Gandhi dynasty. Sanjay Gandhi and Rajiv Gandhi would almost certainly still be alive, and in private life. The former would be a (failed) entrepreneur, the latter a recently retired airline pilot with a passion for photography. Finally, had Shastri lived longer, Sonia Gandhi would still be a devoted and loving housewife, and Rahul Gandhi perhaps a middle-level manager in a private sector company.

chapter three

HINDUTVA HATE MAIL

~

I

I was born in a home of broad-minded Hindus. My father, though by caste a Brahmin, never wore a thread. His own father's brother was a lifelong opponent of the caste system; a hostel he opened for Dalit students still functions in Bangalore city. My mother went from time to time to a temple, but was happy to eat with or make food for humans of any background or creed. Two of her brothers had married out of caste; a third had married a German.

When, in 1984, I got my first job, at the Centre for Social Studies in Calcutta, I had to fill in a questionnaire which, among other things, asked me to denote my religion. I wrote 'Hindu', immediately attracting the ire of a friend who worked at the same centre. He felt that a secular state had no business asking for a person's religion, and thus I should have left the answer blank. This friend was a Marxist, so (although he would not then recognize or admit it) he actually subscribed to a faith of his own.

As I saw it, I was brought up, if loosely, in the Hindu tradition. One could still be a Hindu and not believe in—indeed, militantly oppose—caste discrimination and the subjection of women. One could be a Hindu and still be respectful of other faiths and traditions.

That is what my reading of Gandhi had taught me. And if Gandhi, who in adult life did not enter a temple, and who was villified by Sants and Sankaracharyas, could yet call himself a Hindu, so—when pushed—could I.

Five years after this debate with a Marxist, I encountered a rather more direct challenge to my Hindu faith. I had gone with a team of scholars to investigate a communal conflict in and around the town of Bhagalpur, in Bihar. The riot was sparked by the brick worship ceremonies connected with the plans to build a Ram temple on the site of the Babri Masjid in Ayodhya. The ceremonies clashed with a Muslim festival, and violence broke out between young men of the two religions. The conflict spread outwards from the town into the countryside.

Nearly two thousand people died in the Bhagalpur riots. Many more were rendered homeless. Although Muslims were less than 20 per cent of the population, they constituted more than 70 per cent of those who had been killed. or displaced. We visited a once-flourishing village of Muslim weavers, or *julahas*, whose homes and looms had been totally destroyed by a mob of Hindus. The survivors were being taken care of by a prosperous Muslim merchant in Bhagalpur town, who had laid out tents in his garden. Other refugees were being provided food and shelter by a Muslim religious organization. Of government work in the resettlement and rehabiliation of the refugees there was not a sign.

I was shaken to see that my fellow Hindus would willingly partake of such savagery, and that my government would take no responsibility for the victims. Till then, the politics of religion had no place in my scholarly work or writing. My principal field of research was the environment. I had just published a book on the social history of the Himalayan forests, and had written scholarly essays on environmental conflicts in Asia and North America. However, I was now provoked to write an essay on the Bhagalpur riots for the *Sunday Observer*. That newspaper collapsed soon afterwards, but I remain grateful to it for publishing the first article I wrote on the bloody crossroads where religion and politics meet in modern India.

II

In the 1990s and beyond, as the religious right gained in strength and importance across the country, I was making the move from academics to becoming a full-time writer. I now published fortnightly columns in two different newspapers. My brief, in each case, was very broad; I could, and did, write on history and sport apart from politics. But since these were the years in which the Sangh Parivar moved from the magins to the centre of public life in India, naturally I wrote about their activities as well.

In the past two decades, I must have published some forty articles that have dealt with the politics or policies of the Bharatiya Janata Party and the Rashtriya Swayamsevak Sangh, or of state and central governments led or directed by them. This constitutes somewhat less than 10 per cent of my total output—that is to say, at least nine in ten of my articles have dealt with other subjects. However, it is always articles that touch on the philosophy and practice of Hindutva that attract the most attention (and anger). They have brought me into contact with a certain kind of Indian who gets up before dawn, has a glass of cow's milk, prays to the sun god, and begins scanning cyberspace for that day's secular heresies. If a column I write touches in any way on faith, Hinduism, Hindutva, Guru Golwalkar, Gujarat or Ayodhya, by breakfast I would have in my Inbox—or perhaps in the 'Comments' section of the newspaper's own website—mails which are hurt, complaining, angry, or downright abusive. A representative sample follows:

> I think you are living on other planet. As historian, if India's integrity is at stake from terrorist Islamic Shaitan Pakistan you are quiblling* on small matters ... So called pseudo historians like you besmirch India in Western media from whom you get sinecures and royalty.

> Ramachandra is very much a Hindu name. Please dont insult that name, and show your secularism by changing your name to rahim or rehaman.

---

*In quoting these letters, I have retained errors of spelling, grammar, and punctuation, as well as capitals and emphases, only indicating by the conventional three dots where words or sentences have been deleted.

ANYWAY . . . SANATANA DHARMA DOES NOT WANT COWARDS LIKE YOU!!! ESPECIALLY COWARDS WHO RAPE THEIR OWN MOTHER(LAND)!!!

It would be to your advantage if you get mentally treated before it is too late if you are suffering from a mental problem of distortions and if it is treable and can be cured. Good luck. When muslims got a land to live out of the land that belongs to hindus of india since 2000 B.C where is the need for muslims to continue to live in India and if they cannot go to there to the land given to them they should keep quiet and vote in Pakisthan elections not in India. You too can go with them to pakisthan and live there . . . I will be the most happiest man if a poison like you is not exist in this world. If so our country will be more safe with less one enemy.

Sometimes the mails are sent as letters to the editor of the journals where I write, with a copy mailed to me. These ostensibly impersonal rejoinders tend to be rather forceful as well. Consider these examples, where the historian is characterized as, respectively, a Naxalite sympathizer (but simultaneously a Nehru–Gandhi family loyalist), a newspaper sales agent, a covert Christian missionary, and as akin to a Swiss bank:

India has been one country not in the westophilian sense but in a Dharmic sense for the last thousands of years. He might not have heard about Adi sankara who was born in Kaladi but established Mutts in the four corners of India. For him Indian spiritual unity does not exist. Guha who is a Naxalite sympathiser has got permission from Sonia [Gandhi] to use the archives at Nehru Museum to write his book and so sing the songs of the Sonia Dynasty.

What your news paper want cheap publicity I can understand. Actually you want to increase sell of news paper that's why you published this type of anti India and anti RSS article because at least RSS people will buy your newspaper. I vow not to buy your news paper and will try to convince more and more people. The egoist people like Guha will be punished by masses along with you.

Any criminal in India can get his stupid views on every thing under the son published in any so called secular publication and even earn a very comfortable living provided he invariably starts his piece with a lamentation about the untold suffering the Christians have been undergoing in India since independence. But still, how could somewhat decent people like Mr. Vinod

Mehta [then editor of *Outlook* magazine] tolerate these fake intellectuals? It is advertisement income, stupid. The controlling share of almost all multinationals are held by church groups.

Mr.Guha was one of the historical cartels in India who brainwashed the young and impressionable students in India about how worthless ancient Indian heritage was . . . I think Ramachandra Guha's assets are liable to be proceeded against in a Class Action law suit either in India or the USA like the Swiss Banks' role in profiting from the Holocaust victims under Hitler by laundering the sufferings of Hitler's Jewish victims. The Swiss Banks received the gold from Hitler's Germany including those melted from the tooth fillings of his Jewish victims. I believe the Colonial victims of India and their descendants including those victimized by Mr.Guha censorship of ancient Indian Heritage for ideological reasons are on a similar standing to the Holocaust victims and their descendants!!!

Not all letters are angry or abusive. Some are written in a civil tone, yet reflect the same anxieties and (dare one say) paranoias of a certain kind of modern Hindu. A letter I received from an elderly gentleman now based in El Cerrito, California, feared that India was becoming a Muslim nation. In the 1940s, the leaders of what this man called a 'rogue religion' had intrigued with the British to create Pakistan; now, they sought by demographic means to convert the already Balkanized motherland into another Islamic state. Afghanistan, wrote my Californian correspondent, was once

a 100% Bodth [Buddhist] Country and entire poplation was converted to Islam by the terroristic tactics in the past many centuries. Now, the Madarsas of India are too churning out terrorists like Pakistan at the expense of Hindu taxpayers. . . . Soon the population explosion of Muslims will make them in Majority and the fate of Indian Temples will be the same as Bamyan Budha had faced . . . You may not be able to give such thoughts to the Indian Press because of certain reasons but these fears are real and felt thousands of miles away by Hindus who are living in United States . . .

Sometimes, the chastisement is gentle, offered in sorrow rather than anger, and outlining the hope that, despite my past errors and misdemeanours, I might yet come to respect and even represent the cause of the vulnerable and aggrieved Hindu. A correspondent with whom I had an extended exchange, asked:

I beg, please do a favour. Do not use every single opportunity to offend those
who speak for Hindus. We have no where to go. This is our fatherland /
motherland our spiritual land. The land of our gods. And we have only
welcomed every persecuted race on earth and given space here. Helped them
to flourish and now we are paying the price. There are bigger monsters to
fight. Please use your energy there. We need bright intellectuals like you
there, sir. For our great nation and its great civilisation. And like it or not,
the Hindu Civiilsation is the only glue that keeps our great nation together.
And if it dies we have no identity and India would not exist.

III

This was a selective but not unrepresentative sample of the mails I
have received over the years from the intensely chauvinistic tribe of
Internet Hindus. I have replied, as courteously as I possibly could,
to each email I received (a practice I still maintain), but discontinued
the correspondence if (as was often the case) the mailer proved
incapable of reasoned discussion or debate.

I have withheld the names of my correspondents. Notably, they
were all male. I do have one Hindutva-oriented mailer who is a
woman—but she is an exception, the only one I have encountered
in some fifteen years of such correspondence. Along with the
gender bias is a caste bias. Srivastava, Sharma, Shukla, Rao, Iyer,
Gupta—these kinds of surnames recur with regularity in my Inbox.
These are typically *dwija* names, denoting 'twice-born' castes who,
according to the tenets of orthodox Hinduism, can wear the sacred
thread. (My experience in this regard tends to confirm the
characterization of the BJP as a 'Brahmin–Bania' party.) Other
names I recognize are of Kayasth or Rajput origin, that is to say,
also upper-caste.

The age profile is harder to construct. It appears that a large
proportion of my mailers are in their twenties and thirties, but there
is a significant sprinkling of senior citizens as well. The former tend
to be impatient, seeking to overcome India's manifest weakness as
a nation and a state with an infusion of the right kind of *dharmic*
energy. The latter tend to be anguished or bitter, believing that

India threw away its chances of becoming a great and powerful nation because of the reliance of its leaders on the pernicious western ideology of secularism. Had India followed the example of Israel, they argue, and based its national unity on a shared religion, language, and sacred text (Hinduism, Sanskrit, and the Vedas, in this case), it would have stood tall among its neighbours, and in the world. For these despairing, defeatist nationalists, the one true moment of national pride was when India defeated Pakistan in the war of 1971, for them both revenge and consolation for centuries of humiliation at the hands of Muslim and Christian invaders.

The young profess to detest the West, too. But for all this love of the motherland and the ancestral faith, it is striking how, while this particular heretic lives in India, so many of his orthodox opponents are based overseas, in the prosperous and decidedly un-Hindu nations of Europe and North America. One of my regular mailers writes from his home in 1650 Voyager Avenue, Simi Valley, CA, USA. A second, who chooses rather to address the editors of the journals I write for, signs his name and then adds, by way of further identification, 'Out West, USA'. A third (the only woman in the pile) writes from Canada and always reminds me that she is a 'Ph D, Western Ontario'. A fourth, who likewise combines an admiration of indigenous culture with an almost unreasoning hatred for the modern West, nonetheless never fails to mention that he is the possessor of those very western certifications, 'M. D., Ph D'. A fifth ended a long and very angry mail with these oddly defensive sentences: 'I risk of being dismissed as a unemployed "Hindu fundamentalist" and would not be surprised at all if this mail is put in trash can. Hence I think it is appropriate that I introduce to you that I am a experienced Senior Management professional working with a MNC in India's sunshine industry.' A sixth first asked: 'Who cares about your opinion, man? You speak as if you are representing a billion plus Hindus! Dimwits and slaves like you sit in a corner of your dimly lit houses and pontificate to others'; and then offered his own, rather, better qualifications for speaking about the subject at hand: 'I am educated, young, well read (with 3 masters degrees) and residing in the west. Yet I have great pride and respect for my country, its culture, my Hindu religion, its Heroes, God and philosophies.'

The sociological background of the Hindutva hate mailer can be partially reconstructed from his name and background. His ideology is more directly manifested in his mails. This rests on a deep suspicion of and hostility towards those Indians who are not Hindus by religious background. Christians and especially Muslims come in for special animosity. And yet, as the historian Dharma Kumar once pointed out, the philosophy of Hindutva only mimics and reproduces the ideology of its major adversary. Its unacknowledged model is the Islamic state, where those who do not belong to the ruling faith are tolerated if they are obedient and subservient, but attacked if they seek to assert the rights of equal citizenship.

Hindutva*wadi*s thus want to construct what Dharma Kumar described as 'an Islamic State—for Hindus'. In medieval Muslim states, there was a category known as *dhimmi*, consisting of Jews and Christians, who, as people of the book, were treated somewhat more leniently than the *kaffir*s, the unbelievers. The *dhimmi* were barred from the top positions in the state and in the army. However, so long as they paid their taxes and did not challenge the ruler, they could live in peace and security. The *kaffir*s, on the other hand, were seen always and invariably as adversaries. In the same manner, if the RSS were to get its way, Muslims and Christians in modern India would live undisturbed, so long as they acknowledged their theological and political inferiority to the dominant Hindus. But if they sought equal rights of citizenship they would be punished as the *kaffir*s had once been.

Like all fanatics, the Hindutva hate mailer thinks in black-and-white. Although I am a liberal who has consistently stood against left-wing as well as right-wing extremism, the default reaction to my criticisms of Hindutva is that I must be a Communist. The mail that follows is characteristic:

> If the communist journalists thinking they can distroy an organization by writing few words against them, you are wrong sir. There was a time people

forced to belive what you wrote. But today there is mass Communication between people. Unlike earlier there are people now to respond against communist journalists immediately.

Today even your own media can not survive without supporting Hindutva. You see today your CPM channel in Kerala is live coverage (though it was sponsored) of a Mahayagam at Thirivananthapuram. 90% of the participants are Sangh Parivar leaders. I pity your CPM channel, they have no other alternative but to telecast the live coverage. Remember that our work is already spreads each and every corner of the country. Now we are engaged to increase our activitis more powerful. It is our challange we will dismantle Communist party in India. You wait and see what is going to happen in the coming time.

The extremist only recognizes other extremists. Since I carry a Hindu name, yet have distanced myself from the bigotry and chauvinism of the Hindutvawadi, I must be a crypto-Communist. Apart from thinking in black-and-white, the fundamentalist is convinced that he will, in the end, be victorious. This triumphalist rhetoric, however, is actually a product of paranoia and insecurity. Like the Marxist, like the evangelical Christian, like the Islamic fanatic, the Hindutvawadi needs constantly to reassure himself that he will win in the end. This mail I received from a young man of Gujarati extraction is both typical as well as rather sad:

Narendra Modi is the Chief Minster of my great state Gujarat. He is without doubt the greatest Chief Minster in the history of India. One day in the near future he may become the Prime Minster of India. You all third rate parasitical dhimmi toads who do nothing all your lives except lecture others and contribute not an ioata to the Indian economy can then take a permenant sabbitical to your natural abode Paki Stan. You can bark you can rant and you can use every conceviable weapon to villify and demonise Narendra Modi and us Gujaratis and every time we will show you envious scums of the earth two fingers and treat you like one treats sewage. We Gujus are no 1 and will always remain no 1 whether you like it or not and continue to contribute the highest to the Indian economy . . . You third rate filth we Gujus have nothing but contempt and disdain for your types. you can continue barking and ranting against my State,its Chief Minster and her people and everytime we will say Up yours!

To this deep suspicion of diversity and pluralism, this tendency to think in black-and-white, this insistent (if ultimately unconvincing) claim that they are history's inevitable winners, let me add one final characteristic of the Hindutva hate mailer—an utter lack of humour. The mails already quoted illustrate this in abundance, but consider also some responses to an essay I wrote criticizing the ministry for human resources development for proposing that the wife of the richest man in India be made a 'brand ambassador' for their adult literacy campaigns. I had pointed out that 'if one is thinking of a name to motivate poor women or men to learn their letters, no name could be more spectacularly inappropriate than Nita Ambani's. She is soon to be the resident of a 400,000 square feet house; she is already the recipient of a Boeing aircraft as a birthday gift. If this exhibitionism does not run contrary to our constitutional commitment to socialism and equality, I don't know what does. As for our other national commitment to secularism and the scientific temper— which I presume the HRD Ministry shares—how does one square that with Mrs Ambani's periodic visits to a southern hilltop to pray for, of all things, a cricket team?'

The article was published in a paper that does not have an edition in Bangalore. Downloading it the morning it appeared, I noticed that the boys weaned on cow's milk had come sniffing already. One mailer complained that 'the "Southern Hilltop" the journalist so callously refers to here is the much-revered Lord Balaji's temple. Where do these people get the nerve?? Will he say "People running to middle eastern desert" for Haj pilgrimage?? This is called "Proving one's secular credentials" by putting down the most revered Lord in India.' Another angrily asked: 'Would Mr. Guha have taken a swipe at a Muslim person, worthy or worthless in her own right, for praying five times a day or for doing Haz? Why this step-motherly treatment for visiting temples?'

Fortunately, these mailers had been put in their place by an Indian with a sense of proportion, who responded to their screeds as follows: 'There we go again, just drag religious sentiments into it, and finish off with a Hindu-Muslim comparison to highlight a

perceived bias. [Guha] was commenting on [Nita Ambani's] visits to
pray "for, of all things, a cricket team" . . . The point being she was
praying not for literacy, not for end of poverty, not for benefit of
fellow man, country or world but her commercial interests in a
cricket franchise.'

IV

The number and intensity of Hindutva hate mails in my Inbox has
varied over the past two decades. They have increased and become
more abusive at particular moments—after the Gujarat riots of 2002,
for example, or after the terror attack in Mumbai of 2008. Before
the General Elections of 1999, 2004 and 2009 I also got a flood of
mails warning me that I would be put in my place once the party
of the faithful would be elected or re-elected to power. The mails
fly thick and fast in times of political controversy, but they by no
means dry up in quieter periods in-between. For the hard-core
fundamentalist, the hunt for heretics is a full-time business.

I shall end this essay by quoting five very special mails, that, in
their individual and distinctive ways, illustrate the peculiarities and
pathologies of the *Homo Indicus Hindutvawadi*.

The first mail offers this apparently careful and close definition
of Hinduism:

> A Hindu is someone who believes in the native and natural traditions of
> India. These traditions include a lifestyle that is compatible with the natural
> bounties and limits of India. A belief in the multiple facets of spirituality and
> tolerance of diverse concepts of god(s) (incl. that it is Man who created god(s)
> - not the other way around!). By this token some Moslems or Christians may
> be better Hindus than those who were born Hindus. But in general Hindus
> are the backbone of India and give it its true character. Minority communities,
> no matter how large, are the unfortunate remnants of past invasions.
> Westernized seculars like Ramachandra Guha are mere third rate stool
> pigeons who could not move to the richer West on their own but would say
> anything to harm the core of India for a few dollars as baksheesh!

The definition was however undermined by the address of the
writer ('out west, United States')—although, as a patriotic Hindu,

perhaps he had demanded of his employer that he be paid in (saffron-coloured and lotus-shaped?) rupees.

My second example, coming also from a non-resident Indian, is notable for its capacious demonology, which included Muslims and Englishmen but privileged above all the Muslim-loving and English-loving renegade Hindu, Jawaharlal Nehru:

Dear Mr. Guha,

I have read some of your articles, the headings of your articles have nothing to do with body of your articles, every article is BJP/RSS and Hindu bashing.

But if you care to answer two questions which are asked by large number of Indians, the questions are:-

1. After British left India, all British invaders had left India, why Muslim invaders were not evicted? What right Nehru and Gandhi had to keep tens of millions of Muslims after giving them "homeland" (read Hindu land)?
2. If there are 150 million Muslims in India then why Pakistan was created and if Pakistan was created then why there are 150 million Muslims in India ?

Are you denying that before British took over Hindus were not fighting to get rid of Muslims ? It seems all the "historians" are on Saudi pay roll.

When I come to India I talk to rickshaw wallas, rail coolies, waiters and other real Indians, all ask the same questions. They talk to me because they know I live overseas and I am not a danger to them like journalists and people like you who immediately declare Hindus "anti-Muslim", "anti-secular", "chauvinists" etc and also let police and Congress goons let on them . . .

Nehru was a loafer, thug and a ruffian, he was only interested in Lady Mountbatten, can't you see the damage done by Nehru? Kashmir, Tibet, Aksai Chin and decimation of Hindu society ? About Gandhi, less said the better.

But coming back to my two question, do you have the courage, guts, IQ to detach yourself from white skinned lady and answer truthfully, not your general doble-de-gook . . .

The third example illustrates the hectoring and bullying typical of a certain strain of Hindutva. It was written from Maharashtra, after I had published an article in the *Telegraph* of Kolkata on the Maoist threat to Indian democracy. I here recalled a similar threat from the extreme right in the early days of Indian independence, and mentioned in passing that Gandhi's murderer, Nathuram Godse, had once been a member of the Rashtriya Swayamsevak Sangh. An angry mailer claimed that my article

> has nothing to do with facts and history also equating RSS with Maoist is sheer lie and hence court suit is inevitable against you if you doesn't tenders straightaway apology to RSS.
>
> We have successfully countered such type of blasphemous propaganda against RSS through court battle . . . So I am hereby demanding immediate apology from you and The Telegraph for the report or be prepared for legal battle,In case legal battle starts it is sure that your career as journalist would end abruptly,so it is not in your personal interest hence better to tender apology and end the matter here before reaching to the Court premises.

No apology was offered either by myself or the *Telegraph*—a libel suit is awaited.

My fourth example illustrates the streak of paranoid triumphalism I spoke of earlier. After I had published a long essay explaining why, given the social and political fault lines within, India would not and should not become a superpower, a reader wrote in to say that 'India is bound 2 be worldpower. Take my words. People like Mr Guha are agents of China and they also go to temple (though in the dark of night).'

Of all the hate mails that, over the years, have popped into my Inbox, my personal favourite came from a man (with a resoundingly Brahmin name, as it happens) living in the town of Ghaziabad, in Uttar Pradesh. This, in one single sentence, encapsulated the sentiments of his fellow fanatics and ideologues. 'It is suspected,' said my correspondent, 'that you are getting money through Hawala [the black market] from antiIndia forces or your mindset is communist or you are psychologically weak requiring treatment or modern time "Asura" [demon] wishing to destroy motherland.'

I think of myself as a patriot, who loves his country, and lives and works in it. I also think of myself as a moderate, middle-of-the-road, liberal democrat. But by the definitions of right-wing Hindus I was something else altogether. Since I found flaws in Hindutva thought, it was self-evident that I could not be a patriot. Since I criticized the practice of Hindu fundamentalist groups, I must be an extremist on the other side, that is to say, a Communist. Since I made these criticisms repeatedly, it was overwhelmingly likely that I was in the pay of foreign powers. And since I was published in a well-circulated Indian newspaper I was probably a demon in disguise, too. To be fair, the criticisms also allowed for a more benign interpretation of the words that appeared under my name— namely, that I was suffering from some kind of mental illness. If only I could see the right doctor, who would then prescribe me the correct medicines, the motherland would be saved.

Postscript: They say a writer is known by the enemies he makes. As this book was going to press, I was alerted to an attack on me on the website of the chief minister of Gujarat, Mr Narendra Modi. 'Ramachandra Guha's impotent anger,' wrote Mr Modi's website,

> is typical of a snobbish but vacuous intellectual who simply cannot tolerate a person from humble background attaining greatness by the dint of his own hard work, learning and persistence. But Ramachandra Guha, after more than 40 years of Dynasty history writing remains where he is while Narendra Modi has continues to scale up. Which is why Modi can speak about and implement well-considered policies on topics as diverse as governance, economy, environment, industry, infrastructure, solar energy, IT, and tourism while Guha is simply unable to look beyond the walls of 10 Janpath. (http://www.narendramodi.in/the-will-of-the-people-always-triumphs/ accessed 9th July 2012).

The attention was unexpected but not unwelcome, this notwithstanding the farrago of innuendoes, half-truths and outright falsehoods it conveyed. I have been a historian for a mere twenty-five years, and a political historian for only the last ten of those years. I have never entered 10 Janpath, nor met any of its occupants. Not that I would be permitted entry. For, I am a long-standing critic of the Congress party's First Family, and have (as a later essay in this book, 'In Nehru's House: A Story of Scholarship and Sycophancy', explains), suffered professionally because of this.

By my count I have, in the past decade, written two articles critical of Mr Modi (one for his handling of the 2002 riots and the other for an architectural monstrosity he has commissioned in Mahatma Gandhi's name), and at least seven or eight that detail the damaging effects on politics and public life caused by the culture of sycophancy and dynastic rule introduced by Indira Gandhi. On the other hand, I am an admirer of Jawaharlal Nehru, which is perhaps what sticks in the throat of Mr Modi's acolytes and cheerleaders, who, in their perfervid fantasies, presume their leader to be greater than Nehru and in the same league as the Mahatma himself. I shall let history, and a future generation of historians, be the judge of *that*.

chapter four

THE PAST AND FUTURE OF THE INDIAN LEFT

~

There was a great Marxist named Lenin
Who did two or three million men in.
That's a lot to have done in,
But where he did one in,
That great Marxist Stalin did ten in.

—Robert Conquest

I

In elections held in the summer of 2011, the Communist Party of India (Marxist) lost power in the state of Kerala, and, more damagingly, in West Bengal, where it had ruled for thirty-four years at a stretch. These defeats call for a detached, dispassionate analysis of the place of the party in the history of modern India. In what manner, and to what extent, did politicians committed in theory to the construction of a one-party state reconcile themselves in practice to bourgeois democracy? What were the sources of the CPI(M)'s electoral appeal in Kerala and West Bengal? How were its policies constrained or enabled by its ideology of Marxism-Leninism? How should this ideology be rethought or reworked in the light of the fall of the Berlin Wall and the manifest attachment of the people of India to multi-party democracy? How might the CPI(M) restore and reinvent itself after these electoral reversals in Kerala and West Bengal?

In seeking to answer these questions, I shall start with the analysis of a printed text. This is apposite, since Marxists are as much in thrall to the printed word, or Word, as are fundamentalist Muslims or Christians. True, their God had more than one Messenger, and these messengers wrote multiple Holy Books. Withal, like Christianity and Islam, Marxism is a faith whose practice is very heavily determined by its texts. Thus Communists the world over justify their actions on the basis of this or that passage in the works of Marx, Engels, Lenin or Mao.

It was the philosopher Alasdair MacIntyre who first drew attention to the parallels between a professedly secular belief system and a religious doctrine. In a book called *Marxism and Christianity* (originally published in 1953, and reissued in an expanded edition fifteen years later), MacIntyre observed that 'creedal uniformity, as in religion, often seems to be valued by Marxists for its own sake'. He further pointed out that this secular creed, like its religious counterpart, endowed its adherents with an emancipatory role denied to individuals who believed in more humdrum ideologies. To quote MacIntyre, 'both Marxism and Christianity rescue individual lives from the insignificance of finitude ... by showing the individual that he has or can have some role in a world-historical drama'. In this, Marxism and Christianity are akin to one another, and to Islam, whose devoted or dogmatic adherents likewise believe that their life, and death, find meaning and fulfilment in a pleasure-filled and enemy-free Utopia.

II

The text I shall here subject to scrutiny—the technical term may be 'exegesis'—was written not by Marx or Lenin, but by a *desi* deity so to say. One of the most influential of all Indian Marxists, his name was Balchandra Triambak Ranadive. He was known as

'BTR', these initials whispered with respect, or might we say reverence, by party members past and present.

The text that I am going to resurrect was written in 1978, a year after a Left Front government dominated by the CPI(M) came to power in the large and crucial state of West Bengal. It took the shape of an extended review of a book by the Spanish Communist Santiago Carrillo entitled *Eurocommunism and the State*. The review was published over thirty-three closely printed pages of *Social Scientist*, a Marxist monthly edited by scholars associated with the Jawaharlal Nehru University. Here, Ranadive attacked Carrillo as a renegade, the last in a shameful line of 'revisionists' who had abandoned the path of revolution in favour of the softer option of reform.

The Indian Communist charged his erstwhile comrade with six heresies in particular:

First, Carrillo thought that, at least in western Europe, socialists and Communists could now come to power via the ballot box rather than through armed revolution. In Ranadive's paraphrase, 'the central point of Carrillo's book is that there is absolutely no need for a revolution in the developed capitalist countries ... According to him socialism can be achieved peacefully, without violating any of the rules of bourgeois democracy ...'

Second, Carrillo claimed that Communist parties did not necessarily possess a monopoly on the truth. The Spanish Communist party, wrote Carrillo, 'no longer regards itself as the only representative of the working class, of the working people and the forces of culture. It recognizes, in theory and practice, that other parties which are socialist in tendency can also be representative of particular sections of the working population ...'

Third, Carrillo held that private enterprise had a role to play in economic growth, albeit in alliance with the state. As the Spaniard put it, 'the democratic road to socialism presupposes a process of economic transformation different from what we might regard as the classical model [of Marxism]. That is to say it presupposes the long-term co-existence of public and private forms of property.'

Fourth, Carrillo argued that in the Cold War, Europeans should keep their distance from the Americans and the Soviets alike. As he wrote, 'our aim is a Europe independent of the USSR and the United States, a Europe of the peoples, orientated towards socialism, in which our country will preserve its own individuality'.

Fifth, Carrillo believed that Marx, Engels and Lenin were not infallible, and that their views were open to correction with the passage of time and the evidence of history.

Sixth, Carrillo believed that the Communist party was not infallible either, that at least in non-political matters individuals should feel free to follow their own conscience. In the Spaniard's formulation, 'outside collective political tasks, each [party] member is master of his own fate, as regards everything affecting his preferences, intellectual or artistic inclinations, and his personal relations'. Significantly, he added: 'In the field of research in the sciences of every kind, including the humanities, different schools may co-exist within [the party] and they should all have the possibility of untrammelled confrontation in its cultural bodies and publications.'

Reading Carrillo through the quotes provided by Ranadive, one cannot help but admire his honesty, his overdue but nonetheless brave recognition that the bloody history of his country (and continent) mandated a radical revision of the Communist idea. But B.T. Ranadive saw it very differently. He spoke with contempt of Carrillo's faith in those 'miserable parliamentary elections', and with even more disdain of Carrillo's independence with regard to the Cold War. 'Can any Communist,' he fumed, 'put the enemy of mankind, the gendarme of world reaction, American imperialism, on the same footing as Soviet Russia?'

Carrillo's argument that other political parties should exist, indeed that these parties might even sometimes be correct in their views, was seen by Ranadive as 'giving a permanent charter of existence to non-Marxist, anti-Marxist and unscientific ideologies'. In fact, it amounted to nothing less than a 'liquidation of the Leninist concept of party'. Further, the encouragement of a diversity of thought outside the sphere of politics was 'the final denigration of the Marxist-Leninist Party in the name of freedom for all its members

to profess any opinion they like on any subject'. In contrast to the
heterodox Spaniard, Ranadive insisted that 'the Party's outlook and
the outlook of its members is determined by their firm allegiance to
Marxism-Leninism and must be consistent with it'.

Ranadive's own riposte to the renegade Carrillo rested heavily on
quotes from Marx, Engels and Lenin, the Holy Trinity whose works
and words he himself never questioned, emended, or—Heaven
forbid—challenged. The Indian Communist complained that 'Carrillo
turns a blind eye to Lenin's teachings'; worse, 'a large part of his
argument is lifted from bourgeois writers and baiters of Marxism'.

Carrillo's views, in fact, sound very much akin to those who
wrote the Indian Constitution, and who nurtured the infant republic
in its early years of existence. Parliamentary democracy based on
universal adult suffrage, the proliferation of political parties, a mixed
economy with space for both public and private enterprise, a non-
aligned and independent foreign policy, the freedom of creative
expression—these were the ideals that animated the Constitution
and Republic of India at its creation, and the ideals embraced by
Santiago Carrillo some three decades later.

These ideals, however, remained anathema to a prominent Indian
Communist. It is necessary to point out here that it was the self-
same B.T. Ranadive who, in 1948, led Communists in an insurrection
against the infant Indian state. At Independence, the general secretary
of the then undivided Communist Party of India (CPI) was
P.C. Joshi, a cultured, sensitive man who understood that freedom
had come through the struggle and sacrifice of hundreds of thousands
of ordinary Indians. A statement issued by the CPI thus acknowledged
that the Congress party, led by Jawaharlal Nehru and Vallabhbhai
Patel, was 'the main national democratic organization'. Under
Joshi's direction, the CPI said it would 'fully co-operate with the
national leadership in the proud task of building the Indian republic
on democratic foundations . . .'

However, by the end of 1947, P.C. Joshi found his line challenged
by the radical faction of the CPI. They claimed that the freedom
that India had obtained was false—'*Ye Azaadi Jhooti Hai*', the slogan

went—and asked that the party declare an all-out war against the Government of India. The radicals were led by B.T. Ranadive, who saw in the imminent victory of the Chinese Communists a model for himself and his comrades. A peasant struggle was already under way in Hyderabad, against the feudal regime of the Nizam—why not use that as a springboard for the Indian Revolution?

On the 28th of February 1948—four weeks after Gandhi's murder—the CPI leadership met in Calcutta, and confirmed that the revolutionary line would prevail. Joshi was replaced as general secretary by Ranadive, who declared that the Indian government was a lackey of imperialism, and would be overthrown by armed struggle. Party members were ordered to foment strikes and protests to further the cause of the revolution-in-the-making. Bulletins and posters were issued urging the people to rise up and 'set fire to the whole of Bengal', to 'destroy the Congress Government', and move 'forward to unprecedented mass struggles. Forward to storm the Congress Bastilles.'

The government, naturally, came down hard. Some 50,000 party members and sympathizers were arrested. These arrests forestalled Ranadive's plans to crystallize strikes in the major industrial cities of Bombay and Calcutta. It took some more time to restore order in Hyderabad, where a recalcitrant Nizam was refusing to join the Indian Union, egged on by militant Islamists (known as 'Razakars') who were making common cause with the local Communists. But in September 1948 the Indian Army moved into Hyderabad; slowly, over a period of two years, the areas where the Communists were active were brought back under the control of the state.

In 1950, the Ranadive line was formally abandoned, and the Communists came overground to fight the General Elections of 1952. In 1957, the Communist Party of India came to power in Kerala, via the ballot box. Seven years later, the party split into two factions, the newer and more numerous group calling itself the Communist Party of India (Marxist). In 1967, the CPI(M) were part of winning coalitions in both West Bengal and Kerala. Later, in 1977 and 1980 respectively, they came to power in these states more or less on their own.

Since 1957, then, parties professing a creedal allegiance to 'Marxism-Leninism' have been in power for extended periods of time in several states of the Union. And yet, these successes could not succeed in reconciling leading Communists to 'bourgeois' democracy. For, B.T. Ranadive's critique of Santiago Carrillo was really a warning to those among his comrades who might likewise think of revising the classical postulates of Marxism-Leninism. It is quite extraordinary, yet also quite in character, that Ranadive chose—so soon after his party had come to power by democratic means in the large and very populous state of West Bengal—to let loose this fusillade against parliamentary democracy, the mixed economy, freedom of expression, and non-alignment in foreign policy.

III

I have resurrected B.T. Ranadive's views here not simply out of a historian's interest in the strangeness of the past. For, the prejudices he held—and so vigorously articulated—are unfortunately still quite widespread in the CPI(M) today. In practice the party's ideologues seem somewhat reconciled to parliamentary democracy, but they retain an aversion to private enterprise, are still hostile to intellectual debate and dialogue, and cling to a faith in their party's infallibility.

I have long held that the central paradox of Indian Communism is that its practice is vastly superior to its theory. Where other kinds of politicians have eagerly embraced the Page Three culture, many Communists still do mix and mingle with the working people. Communist leaders and activists are probably more intelligent than their counterparts in other parties, and—by and large—more honest. (To be sure, there have been allegations of corruption in recent years against some Kerala CPI(M) leaders, but the amounts they are said to have pilfered are pitiful in comparison with scams associated with politicians in other parties.)

It may be that of all the major parties in India, it is only the leaders of the CPI(M) who do not have Swiss bank accounts. (Some do not even have Indian bank accounts.) Their views may be out of date, and even bizarre, but in their conduct and demeanour most major leaders of the CPI(M) are—the word is inescapable—gentlemen. As a bourgeois friend of mine puts it, they are the kind of people in whose home she can safely permit her teenaged daughter to spend the night.

That Communist leaders are less greedy and corrupt, that they do not live or endorse luxurious lifestyles, is one very important reason why, despite their irrational and often antediluvian beliefs, they have enjoyed power for such long stretches in the states of West Bengal, Kerala and Tripura. In these three states they built their strength from the bottom up, by working with the poor and the excluded. They have organized landless labourers, poor peasants, slum dwellers, industrial workers, and the refugees of Partition, in fighting for better wages, greater access to land, better housing facilities, and the like.

Decades of patient and often selfless work with subaltern groups has resulted in success at the ballot box. In Kerala and Tripura this success has been episodic, with Communists alternating with Congress-led regimes. In West Bengal it has been continuous. Here, they held power uninterruptedly from 1977 to 2011. (In terms of size and influence, Tripura does not compare with West Bengal and Kerala. I shall therefore exclude it from the rest of this essay, only noting that its CPI(M) chief ministers—Nripen Chakraborty, Dasarath Deb and now Manik Sarkar—have exemplified the unostentatious lifestyles and personal integrity characteristic of the best Indian Communists.)

In thirty-four years in power, the Left Front in West Bengal had but two chief ministers—Jyoti Basu and Buddhadeb Bhattacharjee. So far as I know, neither was personally corrupt. As men of culture, both appealed to the bhadralok, or middle class. Yet their record as administrators is something else altogether. Under their leadership, West Bengal has performed poorly on conventional indicators of social and economic development. As the 2011 Annual Survey of Education Report showed, the quality of teaching in schools in West Bengal is worse than in Bihar and Uttar Pradesh. Meanwhile, in terms of per capita income, West Bengal ranks sixteenth among the twenty-eight states of the Indian Union. Development economists place it in the 'backward' rather than 'forward' group of states in India. This classification runs counter to the self-image of the Bengali bhadralok and of the Marxist, with the former claiming the legacy of India's first modernizers, and the latter claiming to constitute the vanguard of humanity itself.

The vanity and self-regard of the bhadralok does, or did, have a concrete basis. Bengal was once ahead of the rest of India. India's first modern social reformers, first modern entrepreneurs, first scientists of world class, first globally influential writers and film-makers, all came from Bengal. On the other hand, Marxism's sense of its own superiority is less hard to accept. Our scepticism is mandated not so much by the fall of the Berlin Wall, or by the barbarism and brutality of Communist regimes before the Wall fell, but by domestic and provincial events. If, after all the advantages that West Bengal started with, it still lags behind the more advanced parts of India, surely the blame lies to a large extent with the party that ruled the state continuously for three-and-a-half decades?

The Left Front, dominated by the CPI(M), came to power in West Bengal in 1977. In the first decade of its rule, it launched Operation Barga, a programme to protect the rights of sharecroppers and tenants. This was mostly successful, and widely applauded. Yet it was not followed by reforms in other spheres. There was no effort to improve the school education system; in fact, by discouraging the teaching of English, the Communists gave the children of the state a grave handicap (from which they are yet to recover). The state of public health remained as shambolic as before. The building of rural roads and bridges was not a priority.

If, apart from Operation Barga, rural development was largely given the go-by, the urban and industrial sectors suffered even greater neglect. Fear of working-class militancy led to the flight of capital to other states of India. The hatred of the West, so much a part of Indian Communist discourse, turned off foreign investors. When the middle class reacted by voting against the Left Front, the latter responded spitefully, by relegating urban renewal further down their list of priorities.

One of the more unpleasant things about Communists in general (and Leninists in particular) is their desire to capture and control public institutions. It was a desire the Bengal Communists fully shared, and which they enacted on a large scale, in both city and countryside. The police came under the control of the party cadres, helping them fix local elections and capture the panchayats. The appointment of senior bureaucrats, and of vice chancellors, was in the hands of the party.

The control of the bottom from the top ensured control of the middle as well. The history department of Calcutta University, once India's finest, was turned into a loyalty parade of the CPI(M). One had to be a member or sympathizer of the party to be appointed to a professorship. Thus scholars as fine and productive as Gautam Bhadra, Lakshmi Subramaniam, Sekhar Bandyopadhyay and Rudrangshu Mukherjee were pushed out of a department they had studied and taught in. Ironically, these were all left-wing historians; but they were all independent-minded academics for whom scholarship always superseded party loyalty. Conditions were made so difficult for them that they had no option but to leave. This experience was entirely typical. What happened here, in a particular department of a particular university, occurred in dozens of other departments, universities, offices and corporations across the state.

In 2006, after decades of demonizing capitalism and capitalists, the Left Front in West Bengal decided to bring in the demons themselves to develop their state. The Salim Group of Indonesia was allotted 40,000 acres to create a 'Special Economic Zone'. The major Indian industrial house, the Tatas, were invited to start a car factory. These projects, in Nandigram and Singur respectively, became controversial, since local peasants were not consulted about them, nor were they given any meaningful stake. Rather, their land was abruptly notified and taken over by the state; when the peasants protested, the police, aided by party cadres, attacked them, often brutally.

Forcible acquisition of agricultural land had been resisted in other parts of India. The Left Front in West Bengal could have forged a new model of industrialization, by paying a fair market price for land, or by not buying land outright but paying a substantial annual rental, or by training and educating peasants beforehand, so that they could get well-paying jobs in the factories built on their land. Instead, both projects were implemented in an authoritarian, top–down manner. The violence in Nandigram, in particular, deeply scarred the image of the CPI(M).

The one notable success of the CPI(M) in West Bengal has been the relative lack of communal violence. In 1984, when Sikhs were being butchered all across North India, the Sikhs of Kolkata—many of whom were turban-wearing taxi drivers, and hence very visible and vulnerable—were barely touched. The ripples of the Ayodhya movement never reached the state. Unlike in Orissa and Gujarat, missionaries in remote outposts have not been attacked. Sikhs, Muslims and Christians have felt safe in Communist-ruled West Bengal—and have been made to feel safe.

What then of Kerala? Unlike West Bengal, this is a state that has an outstanding record in social development. Its literacy rates are comparable to, and its health services better than, the world's richest and most powerful country. What share of the credit for this must go to the Communists?

The short answer is a fair amount, but not as much as that commonly accorded them by party followers or fellow travellers. The definitive account of the Kerala miracle is Robin Jeffrey's *Politics, Women and Wellbeing*. In this and other books, Jeffrey shows that the progress in education, health, gender and caste emancipation in Kerala is owed to a complex interplay of several factors, which include: (1) The fact that one very numerous caste, the Nairs, are matrilineal; (2) The fact that another very numerous caste, the Ezhavas, were organized by the remarkable Sree Narayana Guru (1855–1928) to fight against Brahminical orthodoxy and liberate themselves through education. Notably, Narayana Guru's influence was not restricted to Ezhavas alone. He was emulated by upper-caste and Muslim reformers, who likewise urged their followers to engage with and adapt to the modern world; (3) The fact that Kerala had progressive maharajas who built schools and sent brilliant students of all castes (and both genders) on scholarships abroad; and (4) The fact that the state also had very active Christian institutions which emphasized the importance of education, including women's education.

I do not want to apportion percentages, so will not say that for the admirable performance of the Malayalis in the social sector, the Communists should get exactly 20 per cent of the credit, the balance being equally distributed among the other contenders. So let me put it qualitatively: their contribution has been more than modest, but less than definitive. In the absence of caste reformers, missionaries, maharajahs, matriarchs, etc., the human development record of Kerala may have been closer to that of West Bengal's. It must also be said that the Congress in Kerala has been more socially progressive, and less morally corrupt, than the Congress in other states. When they are in power, they have maintained the quality of schools and hospitals, for example.

Where the Kerala Communists perhaps deserve more credit (as in West Bengal) is in their energetic promotion of land reforms. On the other side, and like their Bengali comrades again, they have packed universities and other state institutions with party loyalists, and promoted a culture of mindless militancy among organized workers, scaring off investors and entrepreneurs.

In economic terms, Kerala, unlike West Bengal, shall be placed with the forward rather than the backward states of the Union. The official state government website claims that the per capita income of Kerala is the highest in the country; more objective assessments place it at sixth or seventh. Unlike West Bengal, there is no desperate poverty in Kerala. A key reason for this is the mass migration of Malayalis to the Gulf. The economy of Kerala has for some decades now been kept afloat by remittances. This is not a sustainable model—what happens when the oil runs out? With the state's very high literacy rates, Kochi and Thiruvananthapuram, rather than Bangalore and Hyderabad, should really have been in the forefront of the software revolution. One reason why this has not happened is the anti-industrialism and anti-westernism of the CPI(M).

IV

In an essay published on the eve of the 2009 General Elections, I had hoped for the emergence of one or more of four alternatives to the identity politics of the present. These alternatives were: a Congress that was not beholden to the dynasty; a Bharatiya Janata Party that was not remote-controlled by the Rashtriya Swayamsevak Sangh; a united and reform-oriented Left; and a new party altogether, this based on the aspirations of the expanding middle class.

Despite six decades of democracy and development, India remains a deeply inegalitarian country. Across cities and within states, there are large and perhaps growing inequalities of income, status, education, and access to health care. However, the concerns of the underprivileged are rarely reflected in the media and rarely acted upon by the major political parties.

India needs a Left—as, perhaps, do most Indians. A romantic may pin his hopes on the Naxalites, who seek to overthrow the bourgeois order by force of arms. The realist knows this dream is a (blood-soaked) fantasy. In that case, what kind of Left must an Indian democrat hope for? Shortly after coming overground, the Nepali Maoist leader Prachanda said that 'multi-party democracy was the political system of the twenty-first century'. This admission, or acknowledgement, has not yet come from the Indian Maoists— nor even from the CPI(M), who fight parliamentary elections, but do still somewhere believe in a one-party state controlled by themselves. It is this dogma that stopped them from joining governments at the Centre, such as those led by the Janata Dal in 1996 and by the Congress in 2004.

From the point of view of the national interest, the Left's decision to keep away from these coalitions is undoubtedly to be deplored.

For, they would have provided a much-needed stiffening to the central government. The Communist ministers would have been among the most articulate and intelligent members of the Union Cabinet, and certainly the most honest. They would have shown a commitment to maintaining communal harmony. They would have acted as a stable counterpoint to the sectarian elements in the Janata Dal, and to the corrupt allies of the Congress.

Indeed, I believe that from their own point of view as well, the decision of the Communists to stay away from central governments has been a mistake. Here was a chance to put their own pet concerns—agrarian reform, political decentralization, labour-intensive industrialization—on the national agenda. Here was an opportunity to make their talented leaders known and admired outside their bases in Kerala and West Bengal. By participating actively and creatively in government, the Communists could have become, in both senses of the word, a properly *national* political formation.

A modern Left must also stop playing, or replaying, the battles of the Cold War. Consider our relationship with the United States of America. The view of the CPI(M) (expressed in *People's Democracy* and in the editorial pages of *The Hindu*) is that one must always be suspicious of American intentions and always give the Chinese government the benefit of doubt. Neither position is tenable. We should examine our relationship with both countries on a disaggregated basis. With both China and the USA, India has interests that converge and interests that conflict. What we do, or which side we take, depends on the sector, policy, controversy, or case in question.

While Marx himself was a great champion of modern technology, Indian Marxists are technophobic. Their hostility to private enterprise is combined with a suspicion of innovation in general. In the 1980s and 1990s, they resisted the computerization of banks and railways. In protecting the interests of a relatively small constituency, the organized working class, they disregarded the tens of millions of ordinary consumers who benefited from computerization.

But a modern Left must also appeal to the middle class. This class will grow further in numbers and influence in the coming decades.

Most middle-class people are revolted by the company kept by the leaders of the major parties, by their proximity to crooks and moneybags. Many are further disenchanted with the sycophantic tendencies of the Congress; many others detest the bigotry of the BJP. But they have nowhere else to go. Those disgusted by the First Family vote by default for the BJP; those who cannot abide Hindutva vote reluctantly for the Congress. If the Left can modernize, and present itself as a party of reform, a party that is inclusive and outward looking, a party committed to social welfare but not opposed to economic growth, and yet (or also) a party whose leaders are honest and hardworking, it could capture a vote bank that is far more numerous than represented by its own current special interest, the organized working class.

Finally, the CPI(M) must abandon the Leninist dogma that it alone understands and represents the interests of the poor and the excluded. This dogma has set them in opposition to activist groups that work outside the party's framework. In the 1980s, the CPI(M) made the foolish (and possibly tragic) mistake of dismissing Indian environmentalists as reactionary and anti-progress. I remember a CPI(M) friend telling me that the Chipko movement had to be opposed since it was against the working class. The felling of the Himalayan forests was, in his view, objectively necessary to create the industrial proletariat that would lead the revolution. That deforestation economically ruined hill peasants, or that it caused floods which destroyed villages in the plains, was of no matter to him.

The environmentalism of Chipko and the Narmada Bachao Andolan is an environmentalism of the poor. It defends the rights to livelihood of peasants, artisans, pastoralists, fisherfolk and tribals. It has also outlined sustainable alternatives to development practices that deplete and destroy the basis of human life on earth. Yet the CPI(M) opposed this environmentalism of the poor; it also stood apart from groups such as the Self Employed Women's Association, which have enhanced the dignity and economic security of women working in the informal sector.

In 1985, the current general secretary of the CPI(M) published an extraordinary attack on these civil society groups, calling them fronts for American imperialism. The polemic had its roots in an ideology whose twin, complementary, attributes are certitude and paranoia—only the Party knows the Truth, and anything undertaken outside the Party's auspices must necessarily be False. Farcical in all situations, the attitude is especially so in India, a land so varied and diverse that no single ideology or doctrine can contain or explain it.

These dogmas have cost the party dearly, and inhibited its expansion into parts of India and among social groups whose predicament cannot be adequately understood through the lens of a philosophy developed in another continent in another century. And they have driven away the idealistic youth, who wish to work with and for the poor, but currently see greater possibility of realizing this hope in the company of Ela Bhatt and Medha Patkar, rather than under the leadership of Prakash Karat and Buddhadeb Bhattacharjee.

V

When the Soviet Union collapsed, the critic George Steiner wrote that this left a 'black hole in the history of hope'. Steiner was by no means a Marxist, but he had some appreciation of what that ideology had meant to the best and brightest of his generation. I have myself been, for some thirty years now, an anthropologist among the Marxists. I arrived in Kolkata in 1980, shortly after the CPI(M) came to power. I stayed six years in that city, and still write a column for the *Telegraph*. I know the work of the Marxist activists of Kerala reasonably well, and know, probably too well, the work of the Marxist intellectuals of the Jawaharlal Nehru University.

I am an unaffiliated liberal by choice, and a student of Marxism by habit. How must I view the defeat of the CPI(M) in Kerala and, especially its rout in West Bengal? It is certainly a defeat for dogmatism and close-mindedness. I suppose that, as a critic of that dogmatism and close-mindedness, I should feel vindicated and even triumphant. I know that they had to go. Thirty-four years in power was too long. But one must not be tempted to write an epitaph. In Kerala, they will be back in five years. In West Bengal, the bhadralok intelligentsia were nostalgic about them after five months of Mamata Banerjee assuming office as chief minister.

Will their recent electoral defeats make the cadres and leaders of the CPI(M) vengeful and even more dogmatic? Or will it chasten them, such that they look inwardly, at the prejudices which have bound and damaged them for so long now? Can they become modern and, in all senses of the word, democratic?

Karl Marx himself welcomed and celebrated change, perhaps excessively and uncritically. For, under capitalism and even feudalism, human beings fashioned ideas and institutions whose value and relevance transcends those modes of production. To construct a more just social order it is not necessary that all that is solid must melt into air. But some things must change. For all their talk of transforming and shattering the system, however, Marxists—and more particularly Marxist-Leninists—are conservative in their attachment to past ideas and ideologies. To quote Alasdair MacIntyre again: 'Originally a negative, sceptical, and subversive doctrine in liberal society, Marxism acquired, as it became a positive doctrine, precisely that kind of attachment to its own categories which it had already diagnosed in liberal theory as one of the sources of liberalism's inability to view society except through the distorting lens of its own categories.'

In terms of its attachment to its own categories, Communism worldwide, and in India too, has been deeply conservative. A modern, democratic, and even properly *Indian* Marxism, needs a strong dose of robust revisionism. Who or where will it come from? Who, now, will step up to be the Indian Eduardo Bernstein (who abandoned the dogma of one-party dominance in Germany), the Indian Deng Xiaoping (who embraced the market in China) or the Indian Santiago Carrillo (who spoke in favour of multi-party democracy, the mixed economy, an independent foreign policy, cultural pluralism, and the autonomy of intellectual work—all at once)?

In the past, Indian Marxists have been chastised for their dependence on foreigners. The party congresses of the CPI(M) still feature portraits of four men—Marx, Engels, Lenin and Stalin, that is to say, two nineteenth-century German intellectuals with two twentieth-century Russian autocrats. No women, nor, more crucially, no Indians. In the 1960s, the Naxalites insisted that 'China's Chairman is our Chairman'. Their descendants, who now control a large swathe of hill and forest in central India, still call themselves the Communist Party of India (Maoist).

It may be too much to hope that the CPI(M) shall replace their foreign icons with (shall we say) Gandhi, Nehru and Ambedkar. Those thinkers have been appropriated by other parties anyway. What they can and should do, if they wish to renew their party and make it a force in Indian politics again, is to retain Marx (who was undoubtedly a thinker of genius), and find ways of incorporating the ideas, if not the images, of socialist thinkers who are far more relevant to India today than Lenin and Stalin.

The revisionism that is now called for would also mean, if not a formal burial, at least an unspoken disavowal, of the desi leaders who took them along those self-destructive paths in 1948, 1977, 1996, 2004, etc. I note that the Delhi headquarters of CITU, the party's trade union, is named after B.T. Ranadive. I also note that the Communist head of the BSNL employees union writes that 'Com. BTR was one of the brilliant theoreticians as well as a mass leader of the toiling masses who analysed each and every situation critically and stood like a rock against all attacks from the ruling classes.'

The word that sticks and stands out here is 'critically'. Piety and ancestor worship may demand it, but plain English and the facts of history suggest that this allegedly brilliant man tended to analyse complex political situations mechanically. In 1948 he thought he would become the Indian Mao, and come to power via the barrel of a gun; in 1978 he fancied himself as the Indian Lenin, who would vanquish the renegades and heretics. The first time, he disregarded the social history of his own country; the second time, he disregarded the commitment of his compatriots to incremental reform under the conditions of multi-party democracy. Had the party the wisdom and the courage to support P.C. Joshi after Independence, instead of taking the adventurist line advocated by B.T. Ranadive, by now the Communists would not be known for their insularity, both geographical and intellectual, but for having a visible and largely beneficial presence in India as a whole. Had Ranadive himself accepted and endorsed the sagacious advice offered to Communists by Santiago Carrillo in the late 1970s, he would have been thirty years behind the Indian Constitution. But he might have saved his party from thirty mostly wasted years nevertheless.

Postscript: The above essay was published (under a different title) in the June 2011 issue of *Caravan* magazine. It prompted a long rejoinder by the general secretary of the CPI (M), Prakash Karat, which was published in the November issue of *Caravan*. It was gracious of Karat to respond to a writer he characterized (not inaccurately) as a 'bourgeois liberal'. It was also gratifying to see that, unlike the overwhelming majority of Indian public figures, Karat acknowledged some of his party's mistakes, as in the lack of women in top positions in the Communist movement, the excessively long time that Marxists took to understand that environmental degradation in India affects the poor, and the insensitive and arrogant manner in which land was acquired for industry in West Bengal.

On the other hand, Karat defended his party's decision not to participate in coalition governments at the Centre. He claimed that his party does not have a doctrinal opposition to coalitions, adducing the 'Left Fronts' in Kerala, Tripura and West Bengal. However, in those fronts the CPI(M) was in a position of dominance, with the smaller parties in the alliance allotted minor ministries and having little say in government policy. The CPI(M) does not join coalitions where it is not Big Brother—which is why it stayed away from multi-party governments at the Centre in 1996 and 2004.

The decision, both times, cost the party, and perhaps cost the people of India too. Back in 1977, the socialist Madhu Dandavate, after decades in Opposition, decided to join the first non-Congress Government in New Delhi. Allotted the railway ministry, he added two inches of foam to the hard, wooden sleepers of third-class compartments. He also introduced the computerization of railway bookings. These two innovations made railway travel more bearable for the labouring poor as well as for the middle class. In 1979, Dandavate had to demit office; but in two years he had perhaps done more for the ordinary citizen of India than any other Union minister past or present. Who is to say that if some likewise intelligent, honest, and public-spirited leaders of the CPI(M) had joined the Union Cabinet in 1996 or 2004, they would not have brought about reforms that might have enhanced human dignity and diminished social suffering?

Another example of the good that leftists can do while collaborating with 'bourgeois' parties in government comes from Prakash Karat's own state of Kerala. In his response to my essay, Karat claimed that 'the land reforms [in Kerala] that Guha mentions would not have been possible without the first Communist ministry headed by the "Stalinist" EMS [Namboodiripad]'. In fact, these land reforms were taken further and deeper by a later government, which governed Kerala between 1969 and 1975, and which had as its constituents the Congress, the Communist Party of India, and some smaller parties. The government was led by the outstanding CPI leader C. Achutha Menon. This multi-party government (with a significant 'bourgeois' component) is widely acknowledged to be the best that Kerala has had.

In his response to my essay, Karat complained that I 'idealize the bourgeois democratic system'. In fact, I am a sceptic and anti-utopian, who does not idealize anything or anyone (not even Sachin Tendulkar). However, my historical studies have made me keenly aware of the deficiencies, in theory and especially in practice, of left-wing as well as right-wing alternatives to liberalism. Hence my simultaneous aversion to Hindutva and to Maoism. To be sure, liberal regimes are subject to corrosion and corruption from within, as is certainly the case with the Congress-led central

government today. What is needed is a renewal of liberalism, its
infusion (or re-infusion) with democratic ideals, not its abandonment.
I am a liberal who inclines (slightly) to the left, hence my
admiration for democratic socialists like Madhu Dandavate and
Kamaladevi Chattopadhyay, and hence my desire, or hope, that the
CPI(M) will finally follow a path laid down by the German Marxist
Eduard Bernstein more than a century ago, when he rejected armed
revolution in favour of incremental social change by using the
instruments of constitutional democracy. Bernstein was vilified by
Lenin, but he was admired by left-wing democrats in France,
England, and Scandinavia, who, in the succeeding decades, built
socialist movements and welfare states that helped moderate the
inequalities created by unbridled capitalism without sacrificing personal
freedoms and individual liberties.

chapter five

THE PROFESSOR AND THE PROTESTER

~

I

The Republic of India has a billion (and more) citizens who, at any given time, are involved in a thousand (and more) controversies. Knowing which controversy is the most significant is always hard, and often impossible, to judge. Even so, we can be fairly certain that 2011 will go down in Indian history as the year of the Great Lokpal Debate, just as 1962 was the year of the war with China, 1975 the year of the Emergency, 1991 the year the licence-permit-quota-raj was first undermined, and 1992 the year the Babri Masjid was demolished.

Vigorous arguments still rage on the causes and consequences of the China war, the Emergency, economic liberalization, and the Ramjanmabhoomi movement. How then does one judge the import of events as they are still unfolding? It may be decades before a proper historical judgement is passed on the characters and events in the Great Lokpal Debate. What follows is very much a provisional, *interim* assessment. It focuses on two principal actors: the Cambridge-and-Oxford-educated, former university professor, Manmohan Singh;

and the high school dropout and one-time army *jawan*, Anna Hazare. Through what Dr Singh did and did not do, and Mr Hazare did and did not say, I explore the implications for Indian democracy of the debate over a new all-purpose ombudsman for the nation.

II

Soon after the General Elections of 2004, I heard a sociologist and an economist exchange stories about the new prime minister. Back in the early 1990s, the sociologist was asked to write a recommendation for one of Manmohan Singh's daughters. Since he knew (and admired) her work, he agreed readily. When the young lady's CV reached him, he found that she had gone to some considerable trouble to hide the fact that her father was finance minister of India. She was staying with her parents in their large Lutyens bungalow; yet had chosen to use as her mailing address a friend's flat in East Delhi.

The economist said he had a better story. In the late 1970s, when Manmohan Singh was a secretary in the finance ministry, the two had lunch at the India International Centre. After the meal, the economist asked Dr Singh: 'Do you mind if after dropping you at South Block, your car drops me at my office on Ring Road?' 'Do you mind if it didn't?' answered Dr Singh, a brush-off as gentle as has ever been delivered or received.

When he assumed office in 2004, Dr Singh was by some distance India's best educated prime minister. He was the most widely travelled since Jawaharlal Nehru. He was the most honest since Lal Bahadur Shastri. He had a wide range of experience in government, having served as, among other things, deputy chairman of the Planning Commission, governor of the Reserve Bank, and finance minister.

There were great hopes of Dr Singh as prime minister. Some thought that the co-author (with P.V. Narasimha Rao) of the first generation of economic reforms would further free entrepreneurs from state control. Others looked forward to the experienced administrator modernizing the civil service by encouraging the lateral entry of professionals. Still others believed that the former secretary of the South-South Commission would adopt a foreign policy independent of American pressures. And everyone expected that a person of rectitude and personal honesty would promote probity in politics and administration.

To those who knew him or knew of him, Manmohan Singh appeared to be a throwback to the age of the honest and intelligent politician: the age of a Jawaharlal Nehru whose main income was the royalty from his (well written and finely argued) books; of an E.M.S. Namboodiripad, who, after serving three terms as chief minister of Kerala, had his house broken into, the thief escaping with 800 rupees and a gold sovereign.

And yet, in a twelve-month period (roughly) beginning September 2011, the government which Dr Singh headed was revealed to be complicit in a series of scams, the most serious of which related to the misappropriation of funds for the Commonwealth Games (CWG), and the underpricing of spectrum allocated to telecom companies. The loss to the public exchequer in these scandals ran into billions of rupees.

Investigations showed that, in both cases, the prime minister's office had been warned about the diversion of funds as they were taking place. The men in charge of these schemes, Suresh Kalmadi (for the Commonwealth Games) and A. Raja (for the spectrum allocation) had been, if not on the take themselves, clearly in the knowledge that other people were on the take. However, Dr Manmohan Singh did not take any action against either man. Eventually, as a result of concerted pressure in the media, in the streets, and in Parliament, and from the courts, Kalmadi and Raja had to leave their respective posts.

III

About twenty years ago, I found myself in the same room as Anna Hazare, at a meeting organized by the Centre for Science and Environment in New Delhi. Mr Hazare was becoming known in environmental circles for the work he had done in his native village, Ralegan Siddhi, which is located in Ahmednagar district of Maharashtra. His successful programmes of watershed conservation and afforestation stood in stark contrast to the efforts of the state forest department, which had handed over vast tracts of virgin forests to industry. Moreover, whereas the forest department was hostile to community participation, identifying villagers as 'enemies of the forest', Hazare had energized peasants to care for and renew their natural environment.

When Anna Hazare came into that Delhi meeting room of the early 1990s he wore the same dress as he does now—white kurta, white pyjamas and white Gandhi cap. He exuded the same simplicity. But, as I recall, he spoke softly, even with some diffidence. He was not entirely at home in a hall filled with urban folks whose cultural, albeit not moral, capital was far greater than his.

It is said that power and wealth make men younger. So, apparently, does the attention of television. As we become older, the rest of us grow less alert, less energetic, less combative. In the summer and autumn of 2011, Anna Hazare defied this law of biology. For the man Indians then saw on their television screens was not the man I once saw in that seminar room in New Delhi. He challenged and taunted the central government and its ministers, wagging his finger at the cameras. Once, Hazare was the voice and conscience of the village of Ralegan Siddhi; now he demanded that he be seen as the saviour of the nation itself.

In August 2011, while Anna Hazare was fasting in Ramlila Maidan, television channels claimed that Anna Hazare represented the overwhelming bulk of Indians. Print, cyberspace and soundings on the street suggested a more complicated picture. Liberals worried about the dangers to policy reform contained in street agitations led by men whose perfervid rhetoric undermined constitutional democracy. Dalits and backward castes saw it a reprise of the anti-Mandal agitation, led and directed by *savarna* activists.

To these political reservations may be added the caution of the empirical sociologist. The population of the Delhi metropolitan area is in excess of ten million; yet at their height, the crowds in the Ramlila Maidan never exceeded 50,000. In May 1998, 400,000 residents of Kolkata had marched in protest against the Pokharan blasts. No one then had said that 'India stands against Nuclear Bombs'. Now, however, as television cameras endlessly showed the same scenes at the same place, we were told that 'India is for Anna'; even, at one stage, that 'Anna is India and India is Anna'.

That said, it would be unwise to dismiss the resonance or social impact of the campaign led by Anna Hazare. It came on the back of a series of scandals promoted by the UPA government—CWG, 2G, Adarsh, et al. The media coverage of these scandals had led to a sense of disgust against this government in particular, and (what was more worrying) against the idea of government in general. It was this moment, this mood, this anger and this sense of betrayal, that Anna Hazare had ridden on. Hence the transformation of a previously obscure man from rural Maharashtra into a figure of— even if fleetingly—national importance.

Hazare had previously campaigned against corruption in Maharashtra. His fasts in New Delhi in April and August 2011 massively expanded his reach and reputation. The fasts were conducted to compel the central government to create a Lokpal, an ombudsman with the powers to arrest and convict corrupt officials. In another time the solution would have been seen as simplistic. But with the prevailing atmosphere of disgust with the government, Hazare's programme acquired a compelling appeal. For, 2G and CWG were (admittedly colossal) symbols of a far more pervasive problem. Large-scale scams notwithstanding, at an everyday level the citizen was met with grasping policemen, tax inspectors, electricity and ration shop officials, et al. From registering your child's birth to registering your father's death, to getting a gas connection or a building permit, citizens knew that what was by law their right would only be granted if currency notes were transferred from them to an official of the state.

There were therefore, twin, complementary sources of Hazare's appeal—his own sincerity and simplicity (he had no bank account and slept in the village temple) and the fact that more or less all Indians knew the impact of corruption at first-hand. Now, as he fasted in Delhi, the movement led by Anna Hazare gathered resonance and force. Lawyers and human rights activists clustered around him. Film stars turned up to show their support. In cities and towns across India, citizens gathered in markets and parks and street corners, discussing, mostly with admiration, the character of the saint who had come to cleanse the nation. Marches and candle-light vigils were held to show solidarity with 'India Against Corruption', the title now adopted by Hazare and his movement. The young people who participated in these marches had not previously heard of the miracle worker of Ralegan Siddhi; now, however, he had become the symbol and leader of a countrywide fight against corruption.

Hazare's success, at least among the middle classes, was in part because he appeared to be everything the prime minister and his ministers were not—courageous, independent-minded, willing to stake his life for a principle. In an otherwise sceptical piece—which, among other things, called Anna Hazare a 'moral tyrant' presiding over a 'comical anti-corruption opera'—the columnist C.P. Surendran remarked that 'a party that can't argue its case against a retired army truck driver whose only strength really is a kind of stolid integrity and a talent for skipping meals doesn't deserve to be in power'.

It was precisely these two strengths—honesty and the willingness to eschew food, and by extension, the material life altogether—that shone in comparison with the dishonest and grasping men on the other side. The contrast was then stoked and inflated by the electronic media, which repeatedly showed a split screen of Hazare on one side and the prime minister on the other. This was a face-off with only one winner.

IV

During Anna Hazare's first fast in New Delhi in April 2011, he was often compared, in the media and beyond, to Jayaprakash Narayan, who, in the mid-1970s, had led a countrywide movement against the corrupt and authoritarian regime of Prime Minister Indira Gandhi. During his second fast, in August, Hazare was elevated further. Now, in news reports, columns, and chat shows, he was compared to Mohandas K. Gandhi, the Father of the Nation himself.

Let us take these comparisons in turn. Once a hero of the Quit India Movement, then a founder of the Socialist Party, Jayaprakash Narayan (known familiarly as 'JP') abandoned politics for social work in the 1950s. Two decades later, he returned to politics at the invitation of students disenchanted with corruption in Bihar. At first, JP focused attention on his own state; then, much as Hazare did three decades later, his struggle moved outwards to embrace the whole of India.

In the late summer of 1974, as his movement was gathering ground, JP went to Vellore for a surgical operation. While he was recovering, his associate Acharya Ramamurti kept him up to date with the struggle. Ramamurti's communications noted, with some alarm, the entry of a political party into a professedly 'apolitical' movement. While JP was away, wrote his colleague, 'the leadership of the movement at least at local levels, is passing into the hands of the Jana Sangh'. Ramamurti also worried that 'the common man has yet to be educated into the ways and values of our movement, whose appeal to him continues to be more negative than constructive'.

After some weeks in hospital, JP returned to Bihar. In September 1974, he invited his friend R.K. Patil to come observe the situation at first-hand. Patil was in his own way a considerable figure, who had quit the Indian Civil Service to join the freedom struggle, and later worked in rural development in Maharashtra. He now travelled through Bihar, speaking to a cross section of JP's supporters and critics, and to many bystanders as well.

On his return to Nagpur, Patil wrote JP a long letter with his impressions. He appreciated 'the tremendous popular enthusiasm generated by the movement'. However, he deplored its disparaging of political parties in particular and of constitutional democracy in general. As a man of intelligence and principle, Patil was 'well aware of the patent drawbacks of the Government presided over by Indira Gandhi'. But he did not think it 'wise to substitute for the law of "Government by Discussion", the law of "Government by Public Street Opinion"'. Patil reminded JP that 'there is no other way of ascertaining the general opinion of the people in a Nation-State, except through free and fair elections'.

The materials of history thus suggest that the parallels between JP and Anna Hazare are less comforting than we might suppose. Front organizations of the Jana Sangh's successor, the Bharatiya Janata Party, played an increasingly active role in 'India against Corruption'. While Anna Hazare was perhaps not to be blamed for the infiltration of his movement by partisan interests, he certainly stood guilty, as did JP, of suggesting that the street—or the maidan—should have a greater say in political decision-making than a freely elected Parliament.

As for Gandhi, the distance between Anna Hazare and the Mahatma in terms of moral courage and political understanding is roughly equivalent to the distance, in terms of cricketing ability and understanding, between this writer and Sachin Tendulkar. To see how far from Gandhi Anna Hazare is, one need only read, first, Louis Fischer's classic *The Life of Mahatma Gandhi*, and, after that, Mukul Sharma's recent book, *Green and Saffron*. Sharma is an admired environmental journalist, who did extensive fieldwork in Hazare's village of Ralegan Siddhi. He was impressed by much of what he saw. Careful management of water had improved crop yields, increased incomes, and reduced indebtedness. On the other hand, he found the approach of Anna Hazare 'deeply brahmanical'. Liquor, tobacco, even cable TV were forbidden. Dalit families were compelled to adopt a vegetarian diet. Those who violated these rules—or orders—were tied to a post and flogged.

Sharma found that on Hazare's instructions, no panchayat elections had been held in the village for the past two decades. During state and national elections, no campaigning was allowed in Ralegan Siddhi. The reporter concluded that 'crucial to this genuine reform experiment is the absolute removal from within its precincts of many of the defining ideals of modern democracy'.

During those fevered few days in New Delhi, when Hazare fasted with an image of Mohandas K. Gandhi behind him, a young journalist told me that 'while Gandhi became a Mahatma through his own efforts, we in the media have made a village patriarch a Gandhi'. In fact, Hazare is not even a 'Gandhian'. He has both preached and practised violence, and has never seriously pursued such quintessentially Gandhian projects as the abolition of caste distinctions, women's emancipation, and Hindu–Muslim harmony. The distance between Hazare and Gandhianism can be judged if one visits the cooperatives and banks run in Gujarat by the Self-Employed Women's Association, whose founder, Ela Bhatt, has successfully nurtured ideals of caste and gender equality, and religious pluralism, among lakhs and lakhs of previously sectarian and narrow-minded Indians.

In the last week of August 2011—after the ending of Hazare's second fast in New Delhi—I received a mail from a friend who lives in Maharashtra, and has three decades of experience as a researcher and administrator in that state. 'That Anna Hazare is personally honest and frugal,' he wrote, 'is beyond question.' He added:

> What has really changed over the years is that probably because of the build-up by those in proximity to him, he has started seeing a larger, world changing role for himself. Unfortunately, this has not been accompanied by an enlarged world view or by access to advisers who could articulate such an enlarged world view. His seeming successes in getting Maharashtra to adopt an RTI act (admittedly weak) years before the Central Act and campaigning against certain Ministers in the then Congress–NCP Government in Maharashtra have imbued him not only with a sense of purpose but also probably with a sense of infallibility in the rightness of his approach to public issues. However, Anna's ability to attract [people with] his standards of rectitude is in question. From personal experience, I can say that a number of those in different talukas and districts who have been nominated by him to man the local Corruption Eradication Committees were themselves of highly dubious quality. Some of them were even caught indulging in corrupt activities. While Anna did remove such persons as and when instances were brought to his notice, it does highlight the dangers of entrusting responsibilities on a large scale to persons whose integrity it would be difficult to vouch for. A

similar question could arise in the context of the present agitation: can he
vouch for the integrity and motives of even those closely associated with him?

The assessment was astute, as well as prophetic. Hazare's limited
world view was manifest during his agitation, as when he said that
senior government ministers did not understand India because they
had taken degrees at foreign universities. As it happens, among those
educated abroad were the two greatest social reformers of modern
India, M.K. Gandhi and B.R. Ambedkar.

Meanwhile, Hazare's judgement of whom to trust was also
quickly called into question. One close adviser was found not to
have honoured a financial agreement made voluntarily to his
employer; another to have regularly fudged her travel bills. The
amounts unpaid or pilfered were trifling compared to those stolen
by government ministers. Still, the fact that activists of an 'anti-
corruption' movement were found guilty of deceit, even petty
deceit, should have been reason enough for Hazare to dispense with
them. But he did not, perhaps because he thought that they were
necessary to act as intermediaries between him and the New Delhi
television channels who had helped make him a national figure in
the first place.

V

Shortly after Dr Manmohan Singh was sworn in for his second term
in office, Khushwant Singh wrote that he was the best prime
minister India has had. Khushwant is reliable on some matters: such
as the history of the Sikhs, the attractions of Scotch whisky, and the
poetry of Mohammed Iqbal. He is a man of enormous charm, with
a large fund of good and bad jokes. But in so far as politicians go,
he has a disastrous track record. He once saw in the ruffian Sanjay
Gandhi the redeemer of the nation.

Even at the time, Khushwant's praise of Manmohan Singh
seemed excessive. But why has this honest, intelligent, experienced
man been such a disappointment as prime minister? Here are four
reasons, roughly in order of importance:

1. His timidity, bordering at times on obsequiousness, towards the president of the Congress party. Dr Singh was evidently so grateful to Sonia Gandhi for having made him prime minister, that he yielded to her on matters which were within his preserve rather than hers—such as the appointment of ministers, governors and ambassadors; and the framing of public policies and laws. In truth, Mrs Gandhi needed Dr Singh almost as much as he needed her. She did not become prime minister in 2004 because she knew she was plainly unqualified—never having worked in government, how could she conduct Cabinet meetings, have official meetings with visiting presidents and prime ministers, participate in international conferences on climate change, etc.? Mrs Gandhi had bestowed on Dr Singh an unexpected gift; however, by accepting it, he had done her a favour, too. He should have made more of this reciprocity— by, for example, insisting that incompetent or malevolent ministers be replaced.

2. His timidity in not contesting a Lok Sabha seat. Dr Singh was, by my count, the fifth person to be sworn in as prime minister while in the Rajya Sabha. The other four sought election to the Lower House at an early date. Surely in the 2009 elections at least, he should have asked for a Lok Sabha seat, from a safe constituency if need be? This was a major source of the prime minister's weakness, of his inability to assert his authority over the Cabinet, or garner respect from the Congress party, from its coalition partners, and, perhaps above all, from the Opposition.

3. His lack of judgement when it came to choosing key advisers. The two principal secretaries in the prime minister's office were a notorious intriguer and a Gandhi family loyalist respectively. Unlike their predecessors, neither commanded respect within the civil service at large. His two media advisers were PhDs turned editorial writers, with little experience of on-the-ground reporting, and scant understanding of the power of television to make and unmake images. A less intellectual media manager might have insisted that the prime

minister go out often into the countryside, to meet and mingle with the *aam admi*.

4. His keenness to win good chits from western leaders. Dr Singh was reluctant to travel to most states of the Indian Union, but always happy to fly between continents for G–20 meetings and the like. As is well known, the one time he asserted himself was when canvassing for the Indo–US nuclear agreement. This treaty shall do little to meet our energy needs in an efficient or sustainable manner. And Indo–US relations were on an even keel anyway. But, as when he told George W. Bush that 'the people of India love you', his campaign for the nuclear deal suggested that when it came to his standing in the North Atlantic world, Dr Singh could act quickly and decisively.

In his first term as prime minister, Dr Singh did not notably enhance his reputation; nor, however, did he seriously diminish it. After the riots in Gujarat in 2002, and their tacit endorsement by the Union government as well as sections of the intelligentsia, the first UPA government had succeeded in calming communal tempers. The second term of the UPA, on the other hand, has been truly disastrous. It will be remembered, if at all, for the never-ending wave of corruption scandals; the slowing down of economic growth and the wider mismanagement of the economy (resulting in double-digit inflation and a precipitous fall in the rupee); the steady degradation of public institutions; the sense of drift and hopelessness—all under the watch of a prime minister who is a professional economist, and has decades of experience behind him in working in government.

Had Dr Singh retired from office in 2009, history would have judged him more kindly. He would have been remembered as one of the two main architects (the other being Narasimha Rao) of the liberalization of the Indian economy, and even as a moderately successful prime minister, whose government had stemmed the rise of Hindutva and initiated some progressive social policies.

If, however, Dr Singh thought himself able to carry on, then he should have sought election to the Lok Sabha. He did neither; to find his credibility steadily eroding. It was still possible, in the winter of 2010–11, for Dr Singh to have retrieved some lost ground: by sacking Suresh Kalmadi and A. Raja as soon as the scale of the scandals they oversaw became evident, and by insisting that the Congress break its ties with the DMK in Tamil Nadu, even if that meant the fall of the UPA government in New Delhi.

In the popular imagination, the prime minister was now seen as indecisive and self-serving; his fellow septuagenarian Anna Hazare, as courageous and self-sacrificing. It is a mark of how disappointing Manmohan Singh's second term has been that it allowed an authoritarian village reformer with little understanding of what Mohandas K. Gandhi said, did, or meant, to claim the mantle of the Mahatma.

VI

In the year 2011, aided on the one side by a frenzied media and on the other side by an incompetent (and occasionally malign) government, Anna Hazare brought the matter of state corruption to countrywide attention. However, to convert attention to action, one must radically depart from this particular activist's preachings. For instance, at the height of the movement of which he was the symbol and rallying point, Hazare claimed that the last sixty-four years of political freedom have been utterly wasted ('*chausutt saal mein humko sahi azaadi nahin mili hai*'). The fact is that had it not been for the groundwork laid by the first generation of nation-builders—Nehru, Patel, Ambedkar, Kamaladevi Chattopadhyay, etc.—Dalits and women would not have equal rights under the law, nor would elections based on universal franchise be regularly and freely held.

Dalits and women were less-than-equal citizens in the Raj of the British, and in the Raj of Anna Hazare's much-admired Shivaji Maharaj as well. Nor did those other regimes have constitutional guarantees for the freedom of movement, combination and expression. To be sure, there remains a large slippage between precept and practice. I have elsewhere called India a 'fifty-fifty democracy'. The jurist Nani Palkhivala once said the same thing somewhat differently: India, he suggested, is a second-class democracy with a first-class Constitution.

In the years since Palkhivala first made this remark, India may have become a third-class democracy. But the ideal remains, to match which one needs patience and hard work on a variety of fronts. Anna Hazare once claimed that the creation of a single Lokpal will end 60 to 65 per cent of corruption. That remark confused a village with a nation. A benign (and occasionally brutal) patriarch can bring about improvements in a small community. But a nation's problems cannot be solved by a Super-Cop or Super-Sarpanch, even (or perhaps especially) if he is assisted (as the legislation Hazare's team envisaged) by thousands of busybodies and themselves corruptible inspectors.

Improving the quality and functioning of democratic institutions shall require far more than a Lokpal, whether Jan or Sarkari. Democratically minded Indians have to work for, among other things, changes in the law to make funding of elections more transparent, and to completely debar criminals from contesting elections; the reform of political parties to make them less dependent on family and kin; the use of technology to make the delivery of social (and civic) services less arbitrary and more efficient; the insulation of the bureaucracy and the police from political interference; the lateral entry of professionals into public service; and more. In striving for these changes one must draw upon the experience, and expertise, of the very many Indians who share Anna Hazare's idealism without being limited by his parochialism.

chapter six

GANDHI'S FAITH AND OURS

~

I

In or about the year 1980—when I was a young doctoral student
in sociology—I had an argument with the philosopher Ramchandra
(Ramu) Gandhi about his grandfather's faith. I had always admired
the Mahatma, but my secular–socialist self sought to rid him of the
spiritual baggage which seemed unnecessary to his broader message.
Could we not follow Gandhi in his empathy for the poor and his
insistence on non-violence while rejecting the religious idiom in
which his ideas were cloaked? Ramu Gandhi argued that the
attempt to secularize Gandhi was mistaken. If you take the Mahatma's
faith out of him, he told me, then Gandhi would not be the
Mahatma. His religious beliefs were crucial to his political
philosophy—in this respect, the man was the message.

Gandhi was born a decade after the publication of Charles
Darwin's *The Origin of Species*. This was a time of widespread
scepticism among the educated classes in England and Europe, a
sentiment captured in the title of Thomas Hardy's poem, 'God's
Funeral'. But outside the continent, this was also a time of
heightened missionary activity. In their new colonies in Africa and
Asia, European priests sought to claim the heathen and the pagan

for Christianity. In reaction, Hindus in India started missionary societies of their own, as in the Arya Samaj, which sought to make Hindus more unified in facing the challenges of Islam and Christianity.

The distinctiveness of Gandhi's faith was that it simultaneously rejected the atheism of the intellectuals as well as the proselytizing of the missionaries. The home he grew up in was devout without being dogmatic. His mother, who was a profound early influence on him, was a Pranami, a member of a syncretic sect whose Hindu founder admired the Koran and is said to have visited Mecca. As a young adult, Gandhi learned the virtues of austerity and non-violence from his Jain preceptor Raychandbhai. His upbringing was ecumenical; so, too, was his personal orientation. He had close Muslim friends in school, and even closer Jewish and Parsi friends while working in South Africa. For most of his adult life his best friend was a practising Christian priest, Charles Freer Andrews.

Through the 1980s, as I read more by Gandhi and more about Gandhi, I became persuaded that religion was central to the Mahatma's personal life and to his political practice. My change in orientation was not unconnected to the fall of the Berlin Wall, which had knocked a hole in my socialist beliefs (or pretensions); and to the rise of the Ayodhya movement, which had made more urgent the relevance of a Hinduism such as Gandhi's, that was not intolerant of other faiths.

My conversion—if you could call it that—was hastened by my reading, c. 1996, of a book manuscript by an Australian scholar called J.T.F. Jordens. It was the product of prodigious scholarship, worn lightly. The author's approach was biographical as well as analytical. He knew the vast secondary material on Gandhi and Indian nationalism; and he had read, more than once, the ninety and more volumes of the *Collected Works of Mahatma Gandhi*.

Through his erudition (and industry), Jordens had located the evolution of Gandhi's religious thought in the context of the changing contours of his life as a whole. Reading his marvellous book put an end to my youthful project of de-spiritualizing Gandhi by making him into a Karl Marx *sans* a belief in violence as the midwife of social change.

II

Joseph Teresa Florent Jordens, the author of *Gandhi's Religion: A Home-Spun Shawl*, was born in Belgium in 1925. He joined the Jesuit order after finishing high school. Later, he studied Sanskrit at the University of Louvain, writing a doctoral thesis on 'The idea of the Divine in the Bhagavadgita'. In 1953, his doctorate in hand, he took a boat from Rotterdam to India. He spent several years in the subcontinent, studying Hindi and Sanskrit in Calcutta and Ranchi. He also played a great deal of football with his Indian friends; because of his tall frame, he was usually placed in the goal.

Befriending Hindus and Muslims led Jordens to rethink the idea of spending a lifetime as a Jesuit priest. He left the Order, and, recognizing that English—and scholarship in English—was the wave of the future, moved to Australia, taking up a job at Melbourne University, where he established a Department of Indian Studies in collaboration with Sibnarayan Ray, a writer and scholar known for his work on the Bengali revolutionary, M.N. Roy. Jordens later moved to the Australian National University in Canberra, where he came under the influence of the great historian of ancient India, A.L. Basham.

In the 1970s, Jordens returned to India, to research and write the first rigorous, scholarly, Life of the founder of the Arya Samaj, Dayananda Saraswati. His book drew on a wide range of source material in Hindi, English, Marathi and Gujarati. Combining biography and social history, Jordens traced the arc of Dayananda's life, from his early years in Kathiawar through his time studying with teachers in the Doab, to his subsequent founding of the Arya Samaj and his proselytizing work in Bombay, the United Provinces, Rajputana, and, not least, the Punjab. The interplay between man and environment was fascinatingly sketched, the narrative exploring what Dayananda learned from the various places he lived in, and what he gave them in return. Dayananda's studies, teachings, writings and speeches were analyzed in depth, the work of the reformer set against the background of the rapidly changing world of late nineteenth-century India.

Dayananda Saraswati: His Life and Ideas was published by Oxford University Press in 1978. Three years later the same publisher brought out Jordens's next book, entitled *Swami Shraddhananda: His Life and Causes*. This explored the complicated career of one of Dayananda Saraswati's most influential followers. Born Munshiram, this man overcame a youth spent in indolence and hedonism to emerge as a major leader of the Arya Samaj in north India. Munshiram founded a famous seminary, Gurukul Kangri, that turned out a stream of students who took the Samaj's message to the farthest corners of the land.

In 1917, at the age of sixty, Munshiram took *sanyas* and assumed the name Shraddhananda. He renounced his family, his office, and his possessions, but remained active in the workaday world. He joined the national movement and came into close touch with Gandhi, whom he admired, with reservations. Shraddhananda was also deeply committed to the abolition of Untouchability, if somewhat less so to the Mahatma's platform of Hindu–Muslim unity. In the event, it was a Muslim fanatic who assassinated the Arya Samaj leader in 1926.

Jordens's career mirrors that of his close contemporary W.H. (Hew) McLeod, a New Zealander who came to the Punjab in the 1950s as a Christian missionary, but was instead converted to the study of Sikhism. His books on Sikh history and scripture are classics. Jordens and McLeod were both anticipated by Verrier Elwin, an Anglican priest who, after meeting Mahatma Gandhi, left the Church and became the foremost scholar of adivasi culture and religion. Coming to India as convinced Christians, these three men soon immersed themselves in the scholarly study of faiths rooted in India instead.

Through the research for his first two books, Jordens acquired a profound knowledge of the sacred texts of Hinduism, and of how they had been reshaped by their modern interpreters. Writing about the travels and struggles of Dayananda and Shraddhananda deepened his understanding of the geography and social structure of India. Notably, Dayananda, like Gandhi, was born and raised in Kathiawar.

And, as Jordens remarked in an autobiographical essay, his book on Shraddhananda drew his research 'into the twentieth century, particularly the period in which the Indian National Congress developed. Overshadowing all was the giant figure of Mahatma Gandhi.'

Dayananda and Shraddhananda were both substantial figures; exploring their lives and causes was excellent training for the study of a Hindu social reformer who was even more radical and important than they.

III

As he narrates in his autobiography, Gandhi was not especially attracted to rituals and idol worship in his youth. In his native Kathiawar, he befriended very many non-Hindus, before proceeding to London, where his encounters with Christians and especially Theosophists 'had sown in his mind the idea that various religions have very fundamental things in common'.

Jordens identifies Gandhi's early years in South Africa as key to the evolution of his religious thought. Gandhi was greatly shaped by his correspondence with the Jain poet and thinker Raychandbhai, whom he had first met in Bombay in 1891. In June 1894 Gandhi posted Raychand a letter with as many as twenty-seven queries regarding religion. Raychand, in reply, counselled Gandhi against the idea of seeing God either as a personal Saviour or as an impersonal Absolute. Moksha, or liberation from the cycle of birth and rebirth, was not hastened by worship of mythological figures like Krishna or Vishnu either. Rather, argued the Jain thinker, the path to spiritual liberation lay through greater knowledge and ethical action.

Raychand's teachings were reinforced by two books by heterodox Christians that Gandhi read in 1894 and 1895—Tolstoy's *The Kingdom of God is Within You*, from which the young lawyer got the idea that service was the major obligation of a religious person; and *The Perfect Way* by Anna Bonus Kingford and Edward Maitland, which rejected the idea of Christ the Saviour and instead stressed self-improvement and self-purification (including the practice of asceticism).

The faith towards which Gandhi was moving during his South African years was, as Jordens shows, not dissimilar to Advaita. God did not take the shape of avatars whose idols or biographies should be worshipped, and who would distribute rewards or punishments according to the devotion (or lack thereof) of the worshipper. Rather, God was *nirakar, nirgun*, without form, without qualities. He dwelt everywhere, including within the individual human being. By the same token, Gandhi did not ascribe much importance to what was said (or not said) in the Hindu scriptures. Liberation depended not so much on knowledge of these texts as on living a truthful and compassion-filled life.

In South Africa, Gandhi was part of a tiny community of diasporic Indians. He returned to his homeland for good, in 1915, with some clear if unorthodox views on religion in general, and on one religion in particular. As Jordens remarks, he was immediately confronted with 'people who claimed to be experts in Hinduism, to know its holy books and its sacred language, and to have a right to give authoritative statements on matters of ethics, doctrine, and scriptural interpretation'. A lesser being would have been intimidated by these experts and their (professed) expertise. Not Gandhi. Although he was a Bania rather than a Brahmin, knew little Sanskrit, and had only a cursory acquaintance with the Vedas and the Upanishads, Gandhi was yet willing—and able—to defend his distinctive interpretation of the Hindu tradition.

Over the next thirty years, Gandhi clarified and refined his religious faith, while keeping in mind the social (and political) challenges facing Hindus and India. Jordens justly pays close attention to Gandhi's long, heroic campaign against Untouchability. 'I believe that all men are born equal,' said Gandhi in a speech in Tanjore in 1927. Five years later, he persuaded his fellow Congressmen to adopt a resolution stating that

> henceforth, amongst Hindus, no one shall be regarded as an untouchable by reason of his birth, and those who have been so regarded hitherto, will have the same right as other Hindus in regard to the use of public wells, public schools, public roads and other public institutions. This right will have

statutory recognition at the first opportunity and shall be one of the earliest
acts of the svaraj parliament.

In this paragraph lie the roots of the revolutionary sections in the
Constitution of India which mandated equal citizenship in a soil and
social climate so massively steeped in caste (and gender) inequality.

When some conservatives justified the pernicious practice of
Untouchability by saying they were sanctioned by the scriptures,
Gandhi replied:

> If I discovered those scriptures which are known as Vedas, Upanishads,
> Bhagavadgita, Smritis, etc, clearly showed that they claim divine authority for
> untouchability . . . then nothing on this earth would hold me to Hinduism.
> I should overthrow it overboard as I should overthrow a rotten apple.

Elsewhere, Gandhi remarked that 'every religious principle claiming
authority from the Shastras should be tested on the anvil of truth
with the hammer of compassion'. Truth and compassion led Gandhi
to promote campaigns of temple-entry, so as to demonstrate that all
were equal in the eyes of God; and, in time, to advocate inter-
marriage between Dalits and savarnas, thereby undermining a crucial
building block of the caste system.

While serving time in the prisons of the Raj, Gandhi had made
himself better acquainted with the Vedas and the Puranas. However,
the one sacred text he seriously read and identified with was the
Bhagavad Gita. With characteristic originality, Gandhi ignored or
finessed the element of bhakti in the Gita—as in its call to venerate
the avatar Krishna—in favour of an action-oriented understanding
of its message. He focused on some select verses of Chapter II of
the Gita, which spoke of ethical conduct, and which celebrated
(in Jordens's paraphrase) the stable, serene human being 'who has
gained a complete mastery over feelings of attachment, aversion,
love, lust, and hate, who cannot be swayed by his outer senses or
his imagination, who has an attitude of total indifference to all that
may please or displease him'.

Many Hindus have a transactional attitude towards religion, going
to temples and shrines to pray for the birth of a (male) child, for

good grades in their examinations, etc. Gandhi himself meditated in
the mornings and evenings, and held communal prayer meetings in
his ashrams. Prayer and the singing of hymns were for him an aid
to acquiring composure and serenity. He emphatically rejected the
idea that one should, or could, beg or demand favours from God.
'Divinity is in everyone and everything,' he once remarked, 'and
the meaning of prayer is that I want to invoke that Divinity within me.'

For Gandhi, chastity and fasting were practices that were the core
components of the ethical—and religious—life. Jordens traces, with
sympathy but not uncritically, Gandhi's experiments with celibacy,
from his abandonment of sexual relations with his wife in South
Africa in 1906 to his late, controversial experiments in sleeping
naked beside young women in the 1940s. He also closely studies
Gandhi's resort to fasting at times of personal or political crisis.
When confronted with dissidence (or worse) within his ashram, or
with caste and religious violence in society at large, Gandhi
undertook fasts that some saw as coercive but which he himself
claimed were acts of self-purification. Fasting, he said, 'quickens the
spirit of prayer'; a fast was a 'spiritual act and, therefore, addressed
to God'. Some of his fasts were remarkably efficacious, and not just
for him, accomplishing what the long arm of the law and the massed
power of the state could not—namely, persuade (or shame) warring
hordes of Hindus and Muslims to put down their weapons and
make peace with one another.

Gandhi's interpretation and practice of his ancestral faith was
unorthodox, heterodox, and even perhaps heretical. To achieve and
realize his peculiar, even unique, form of Hinduism, he had to wage
a series of arduous struggles: against orthodox Hindus, who hated
him, and even sought to assassinate him for daring to challenge the
practice of Untouchability; against his fellow Congressmen, who
wondered why Gandhi did not focus exclusively on political
freedom instead of taking these—to them—unnecessary detours into
temple-entry and the like; against his closest followers in the ashram,
who erratically and sometimes sullenly followed his teachings with
regard to sex, diet, health, and manual labour; and against himself,

as he tested the limits of his physical and emotional endurance through his experiments with celibacy and through his fasts. Gandhi's independence and courage in this regard were to some others merely stubbornness and pig-headedness. But in his pursuit of what he saw as the truth, he was never to be shaken by criticism, even that offered by his family and his closest friends. He was always, in the words of the Tagore song, prepared to walk alone.

Gandhi's religious faith was hard-won—the result of his own exertions and experiences, rather than of received wisdom or ancient texts. In an illuminating passage, Jordens says that while the teachings of a learned philosopher, such as Shankara, could be compared to a 'beautifully woven tapestry, extremely complex, where every colour and every thread takes its proper place in a symphonic whole', the spiritual synthesis Gandhi arrived at was more 'like a large, bulky, woollen shawl. At first it looks very plain to the eye, but we can detect the beauty of the strong patterns and the contrasting shades of folk art. With its knots and unevenness, it feels at first rough to the touch; but soon we can experience how effective it is in warming cold and hungry limbs.'

Among the conventional or traditional Hindu, religious devotion is expressed through the scrupulous observance of rituals, the loving and intense adoration of a personal or family God, or a deep knowledge of the scriptures—or all of the above. On the other hand, the essence of Gandhi's faith consisted of a commitment to truth, chastity, non-violence, and, especially, service. As Jordens writes, 'no school of sect [within Hinduism] did ever elevate the activity of service itself into one that caused the realisation of moksha'—which is what Gandhi did.

In 1936, Gandhi moved to a small hamlet in central India which he renamed Sevagram—the Village of (and for) Service. Gandhi told a friend that he had come here to find

self-realisation through the service of these village folk. Man's ultimate aim is the realisation of God, and all his activities, social, political, religious, have to be guided by the ultimate aim of the vision of God. The immediate service of all human beings becomes a necessary part of the endeavour simply because the only way to find God is to see Him in His creation and to be one with it. This can only be done by service of all . . . I am part and parcel of the whole, and I cannot find him apart from the rest of humanity . . . If I could persuade myself that I should find Him in a Himalayan cave, I would proceed there immediately. But I know that I cannot find Him apart from humanity.

For all his departures from scripture and his battles with the orthodox, Gandhi still called himself a Hindu, indeed even a 'sanatani' Hindu. Why was this? Was this out of sentimental attachment to an ancestral faith, or for tactical reasons, since positioning himself as an outsider would make it harder to persuade other Hindus of his arguments? Be that as it may, aspects of Gandhi's faith resonate closely with spiritual (or intellectual) traditions that are other than 'Hindu'. The stress on ethical conduct brings him close to Buddhism, while the avowal of non-violence and non-possession is clearly drawn from Jainism. The exaltation of service is far more Christian than Hindu. The emphasis on the dignity of the individual echoes Enlightenment ideas of human rights.

Gandhi had lived in the West, been mentored by a Jain, and had close friends who were Christian or Buddhist. His faith synthesized these varied encounters and experiences. If he still insisted on seeing himself as a 'Hindu', we should respect his self-assessment, noting only that his was a Hinduism that was massively individual and decidedly idiosyncratic, in a word, 'home-spun'.

IV

If Jordens's study is the best book-length work on Gandhi's place in the history of modern Hinduism, the most original short treatment of the subject is the last chapter of a now-forgotten primer published in 1962 by a now-forgotten (but in his lifetime very well-known) scholar named R.C. Zaehner. Zaehner was Sarvepalli Radhakrishnan's successor as Spalding Professor of Eastern Religions at All Souls College, Oxford. Like his predecessor he was a polymathic non-specialist who wrote prodigiously on very many topics and themes.

The last chapter of Zaehner's *Hinduism* is called 'Yudhisthira's Return'. This innovatively—and to my mind, convincingly—compares the great leader of Indian nationalism to the eldest of the five Pandava brothers. Gandhi, writes Zaehner, was 'in history what King Yudhisthira was in myth, the conscience of Hinduism that hungers and thirsts after righteousness in defiance of the letter of the law of gods and men'.

Gandhi is hailed as the Father of the Nation; yet, as Zaehner reminds us, he 'did not see himself primarily as the architect of Indian independence from British rule but as the liberator of the Indian spirit from the fetters of greed and anger, hatred and despair'. Gandhi was 'the greatest reformer Hinduism has seen'. He transformed his faith, and very many of the faithful, by defining dharma, or righteousness, in terms of conscience and compassion, rather than by what was said in the sacred texts. Thus in his battle against Untouchability, Gandhi was moved, inspired and directed not by 'the *dharma* of the law-books and Brahmans, but the *dharma* that rests on *ahimsa*, truth, renunciation, passionlessness, and an equal love for all God's creatures . . .'

Both Yudhisthira and Gandhi, notes R.C. Zaehner, saw themselves as failures for being unable to prevent fratricidal warfare, between Pandavas and Kauravas in the one case, and between Hindus and Muslims in the other. Yet 'both were yet triumphant, for both had been true to themselves, to conscience, to Truth, to the *sanatana dharma* as they saw it in themselves, and therefore to God'.

V

Jordens and Zaehner both focus on how Gandhi understood, refined and revised Hindu thought and practice. They trace, with sympathy and insight, his career as a heterodox/unorthodox/reforming/radical interpreter of his own religious tradition. In this concluding section, I shall stress rather what Gandhi's faith meant for, or means to, those who are themselves not Hindus. Here, one might foreground five crucial elements of Gandhi's religious ecumenism:

First, Gandhi rejected the idea that there was one privileged path to God. Second, he believed that all religious traditions were an unstable mixture of truth and error. From these two beliefs followed the third, which was that Gandhi rejected conversion and missionary work. Fourth, Gandhi advocated that a human being should stick to the religion he or she was born into, and seek to improve its 'truth content'. Fifth, Gandhi encouraged inter-religious dialogue, so that individuals could see their faith in the critical reflections of another.

Gandhi once said of his own faith that he had 'broaden[ed] my Hinduism by loving other religions as my own'. One of his notable innovations was the inter-faith prayer meeting, where texts of different religions were read and sung to a mixed audience. At an International Fellowship of Religions, held at Sabarmati in January 1928, he said, 'We can only pray, if we are Hindus, not that a Christian should become a Hindu, or if we are Mussalmans, not that a Hindu or a Christian should become a Mussalman, nor should we even secretly pray that anyone should be converted [to our faith], but our inmost prayer should be that a Hindu should be a better Hindu, a Muslim a better Muslim and a Christian a better Christian. That is the fundamental truth of fellowship.'

What does it mean to be a better Hindu, or Muslim, or Christian? The sacred texts of all religions have contradictory trends and impulses; sometimes sanctioning one thing, at other times its opposite. Gandhi urged that we recover and reaffirm those trends that oppose violence and discrimination while promoting justice and non-violence. The Shankaracharyas claimed that Untouchability was sanctioned by the Shastras; Gandhi answered that in that case the Shastras did not represent the true traditions (or real intentions) of Hinduism. Islamic texts might speak of women in condescending or disparaging terms in one place and in terms of reverence and respect in another; surely, a Muslim committed to justice would value the second above the first? Likewise, a Christian must privilege the pacifism of Jesus's life above the passages in the Bible calling for revenge and retribution against people of other faiths.

While he lived, there were three groups of Indians that most vocally opposed Gandhi's religious views. First, there were the secular socialists, who saw Gandhi's faith as superstition, as a throwback to a backward, medieval age. Second, there were the Muslim politicians, who saw his talk of religious harmony as a cloak and cover for his essentially Hindu interest. Third, there were the extremists of his own religion, who saw Gandhi's talk of inter-faith dialogue as a denial of the Hindu essence of the Indian nation. It was a member of this third tendency, Nathuram Godse, who murdered the Mahatma on the 30th of January 1948.

There was, in Gandhi's life and work, an inseparable bond between non-violence and religious pluralism. When, in the late 1930s, violent conflicts erupted between Jewish settlers and Palestinian peasants, with both sides claiming to act in the name of their faith, Gandhi remarked that 'a religious act cannot be performed with the aid of the bayonet or the bomb'. A decade later, aged seventy-seven, Gandhi walked through the riot-torn districts of eastern Bengal, healing the wounds. When independence came to India the following August, Gandhi refused to celebrate, for political freedom had come on the back of sectarian violence. Since the violence would not abate, Gandhi began a fast-unto-death in Calcutta. His act shocked and shamed the people of the city, who came around, slowly. A group of representative Hindus and Muslims met him with a written promise 'that peace and quiet have been restored in Calcutta once again'. The undertaking added: 'We shall never again allow communal strife in the city. And shall strive unto death to prevent it.'

Gandhi now called off his fast, and proceeded to Delhi. The Muslims of this city had been savagely attacked by Hindus and Sikhs, themselves inflamed by pogroms against their co-religionists in Pakistan. Gandhi abhorred this politics of revenge and retribution. He went on another fast in protest. His health rapidly declined. He was persuaded to break his fast after an all-party delegation pledged that 'we shall protect the life, property and faith of Muslims and that the incidents which have taken place in Delhi will not happen again'.

An old, frail man had, by the force of moral example, helped bring peace to two very large cities. He now wished to proceed to the Punjab, where the rioting had been especially fierce. Before he could go, he was murdered by a religious fanatic. But his example, and achievements, lie before us. For, like the late nineteenth century, the early twenty-first century has also seen a renewal of an arrogant atheism on the one side and of religious bigotry on the other. Bookshops are awash with titles proclaiming that God does not exist; and the streets are muddied and bloodied by battles and wars between competing fundamentalisms.

Thirty years after I argued with him, I can see that Ramu Gandhi was even more right than he knew. One cannot, as the philosopher cautioned me, understand the Mahatma without paying proper attention to his religious beliefs and practices. But Gandhi's faith was and is relevant not merely to himself. It may be of vital assistance in promoting peace and harmony between people who worship different Gods or no God at all. Back in 1919, while seeking to forge an entente cordiale between India's two major religious groupings, Gandhi asked them to collectively take this vow:

> With God as witness we Hindus and Mahomedans declare that we shall behave towards one another as children of the same parents, that we shall have no differences, that the sorrows of each will be the sorrows of the other and that each shall help the other in removing them. We shall respect each other's religion and religious feelings and shall not stand in the way of our respective religious practices. We shall always refrain from violence to each other in the name of religion.

It only remains for me to add: what Gandhi asked of Hindus and Muslims in India in 1919 should be asked again of them today; asked also of Jews and Arabs in Palestine, of Buddhists and Hindus in Sri Lanka, and of Christians and Muslims in Europe, North America, West Asia, and West and East Africa.

chapter seven

VERDICTS ON NEHRU: THE RISE AND FALL OF A REPUTATION

~

I

The first photograph I remember seeing was of Jawaharlal Nehru. He was wearing a white Gandhi cap, and a white waistcoat with a red rose over its left pocket.

The photo hung over my parents' bed in our home in Dehradun. My mother worshipped Nehru. When he visited our town in the aftermath of the China War of 1962, she went to hear him speak, and was so moved by his words that she donated her gold bangles to the National Defence Fund, an act of spontaneous patriotism that was derided, for years afterwards, in our extended family. That was exactly how pragmatic, prudent Tamil Brahmin women were *not* supposed to behave.

A decade before the China War, Nehru was speaking in another town roughly the size of Dehradun, albeit in a very different part of the country. Seeking votes for his Congress party in the first-ever General Elections, Nehru came, in January 1952, to Kharagpur, a railway town in West Bengal with a very mixed and diverse population. In the crowd to hear him speak were a group of Telugu-speaking women. As Nehru sonorously urged his fellow

citizens to place their faith in his party, which was the legatee of the
freedom movement and all that it stood for, one of the Andhra
women began to experience labour pains. At once, her colleagues
formed a protective ring around her. With one ear cocked to what
their leader was saying, they successfully delivered the baby. The
sources don't say what the sex of this new Indian citizen was; were
it male, odds-on that it was named Jawaharlal.

Women adored Jawaharlal Nehru—Brahmin women, working-
class women, Hindu and Muslim and Christian and Parsi women.
When Nehru was in his pomp, very many Indian men admired him
too. Take your mind further back a decade, to the early days of that
momentous year in Indian history, 1942. Mahatma Gandhi had
convened a meeting of the Congress Working Committee at his
ashram in Wardha. These were very troubled times, with the world
at war, and India still denied its freedom. After the meeting ended,
Jawaharlal Nehru prepared to catch the train back to his home
town, Allahabad. As he turned to leave, Gandhi's wife, Kasturba,
wished him Godspeed. (The account we have of this encounter is
in English—she probably said, in Hindustani, '*Ishwar tera saath dé.*')
At the mention of the Almighty the socialist and radical exploded.
What kind of God is this, said Nehru, who allows a barbarous war,
who permits the gassing of the Jews, who encourages the predations
of imperialism and colonialism? There was a hushed and appalled
silence all around. For, no self-described follower of Gandhi had
ever spoken so harshly to the revered old lady, who was, in a
manner of speaking, the Mother of the Nation-in-the-Making. The
situation was retrieved by the Mahatma. 'Let Jawaharlal be, Ba,' he
remarked, 'despite what he has just said, he is closer to God than
any of us.'

Once more, it must have sounded better in its original Hindustani.
(Here is a try: '*Usko rehné do*, Ba, *wo hum sabsé Ishwar ké nikat hai.*')
It sounds evocative enough in English. What Gandhi meant was
that as a person of decency and charm, a patriot of integrity and
commitment, Nehru more closely approximated the moral virtues
that men of faith often profess but less often practise.

II

It is safe to say that no modern politician had anywhere near as difficult a job as Jawaharlal Nehru's. At Independence, the country he was asked to lead was faced with horrific problems. Riots had to be contained, food shortages to be overcome, princely states (as many as five hundred) to be integrated, refugees (almost ten million) to be resettled. This, so to say, was the task of fire-fighting; to be followed by the equally daunting task of nation-building. A Constitution had to be written that would satisfy the needs of this diverse and complex nation. An election system had to be devised for an electorate that was composed mostly of illiterates. A viable foreign policy had to be drafted in the threatening circumstances of the Cold War. And an economic policy had to be forged to take a desperately poor and divided society into the modern age.

No new nation was ever born in less propitious circumstances. Fortunately, Nehru had on his side a set of superbly gifted colleagues. His Cabinet included such men of distinction as Vallabhbhai Patel, B.R. Ambedkar and C. Rajagopalachari. They were helped by the remaining officials of the Indian Civil Service—the steel frame that was one of British colonialism's unquestionable gifts to free India. They were also helped by the social workers; by women such as Kamaladevi Chattopadhyay, Mridula Sarabhai, Anees Kidwai and Subhadra Joshi, who resettled refugees, reunited families, and gave the Muslims who stayed behind in India a sense of safety and security.

For all the assistance he got, Jawaharlal Nehru was, as the elected prime minister, most responsible for the success or failure of his government's policies. In the popular mind, it was Nehru who was most directly identified with the philosophy of the new nation state; with ideas such as democracy, non-alignment, socialism and secularism, ideas to which, in his writings and speeches, he gave such eloquent expression.

At this time, the mid-1950s, Nehru's domestic reputation was as high as high can be. He came as close as anyone has, or ever will, to becoming the People's Prince. He was Gandhi's chosen political heir, and free India's first freely elected prime minister. After the death of Vallabhbhai Patel in 1950, he towered among his colleagues in the Congress party. His vision of an independent, self-reliant India fired by steel plants and powered by dams was widely shared. He was seen as a brave man, who fought religious chauvinists; as a selfless man, who had endured years in jail to win freedom; and above all, as a good man. His appeal cut across the conventionally opposed categories of man and woman, low caste and high caste, Hindu and Muslim, north Indian and south Indian. Representative here are the recollections of a now-distinguished Tamil diplomat who grew up in the capital in the fifties. He told me that 'to us Pandit Nehru was a great golden disc shining in the middle of New Delhi'.

A spectacular demonstration of the Indian people's love for Jawaharlal Nehru was on display during the General Elections of 1952. In campaigning for candidates of the Congress party, Nehru covered the country from end to end. He travelled 25,000 miles in all: 18,000 by air, 5,200 by car, 1,600 by train, and even 90 by boat. A breathless party functionary later described this as comparable to the 'imperial campaigns of Samudragupta, Asoka and Akbar' as well as to the 'travel[s] of Fahien and Hieun Tsang'.

In the course of the campaign, Nehru 'travelled more than he slept and talked more than he travelled'. He addressed 300 mass meetings and myriad smaller ones. He spoke to about 20 million people directly, while an equal number merely had his darshan, flanking the roads to see him as his car whizzed past. Those who heard and saw him included miners, peasants, pastoralists, factory workers and agricultural labourers. Women of all classes turned out in numbers for his meetings.

This is how a contemporary account describes the interest in Nehru:

Almost at every place, city, town, village or wayside halt, people had waited overnight to welcome the nation's leader. Schools and shops closed; milkmaids and cowherds had taken a holiday; the kisan and his helpmate took a temporary respite from their dawn-to-dusk programme of hard work in field

and home. In Nehru's name, stocks of soda and lemonade sold out; even
water became scarce . . . Special trains were run from out-of-the-way places
to carry people to Nehru's meetings, enthusiasts travelling not only on foot-
boards but also on top of carriages. Scores of people fainted in milling crowds.

No leader in modern times has enjoyed quite this kind of veneration.
Thus, as Escott Reid, the Canadian high commissioner in New
Delhi in the 1950s, remarked, Nehru was for his people the
founder, guardian, and redeemer of the Indian nation state—
Washington, Lincoln and Roosevelt all rolled into one. Even the
most hard-boiled sceptics were swayed by his charm and charisma.
Consider this now-forgotten encomium by Nirad Chaudhuri,
published in the *Illustrated Weekly of India* in the second week of
May 1953, a year after Nehru and his Congress had won a
comfortable victory in the first General Elections. The writer was
(by this time) a moderately well-known Indian, but his subject still
towered over him, as well as everybody else. Nehru's leadership,
remarked Chaudhuri, 'is the most important moral force behind the
unity of India'. He was 'the leader not of a party, but of the people
of India taken collectively, the legitimate successor to Gandhiji'.
However, if 'Nehru goes out of politics or is overthrown, his
leadership is likely to be split up into its components, and not pass
over intact to another man. In other words, there cannot, properly
speaking, be a successor to Nehru, but only successors to the
different elements of his composite leadership.'

As Chaudhuri saw it, the Nehru of the 1950s helped harmonize
the masses with the classes. 'Nehru is keeping together the
governmental machine and the people, and without this nexus India
would probably have been deprived of stable government in these
crucial times. He has not only ensured co-operation between the
two, but most probably has also prevented actual conflicts, cultural,
economic, and political. Not even Mahatmaji's leadership, had it
continued, would have been quite equal to them.'

'If, within the country, Nehru is the indispensable link between
the governing middle-classes and the sovereign people,' continued
Chaudhuri, 'he is no less the bond between India and the world.'

He served as 'India's representative to the great Western democracies, and, I must add, their representative to India. The Western nations certainly look upon him as such and expect him to guarantee India's support for them, which is why they are so upset when Nehru takes an anti-Western or neutral line. They feel they are being let down by one of themselves.'

Nirad Chaudhuri always prided himself on his independence of mind, on being above (and ahead) of the herd. But even he could not escape the glow of the great golden disc then shining in the middle of New Delhi. It is noteworthy that Chaudhuri never allowed this essay to be reprinted, a fact which adds to the delight with which I excerpt it here.

Such, then, was Jawaharlal Nehru's reputation at its zenith; it is time now to move on to its nadir.

III

In my early days as an academic, I made the mistake of defending Jawaharlal Nehru in the smoky seminar room of the Centre for Studies in Social Sciences, off Lansdowne Road in south Calcutta. I was then very young, and my defence was weak and confused anyway. I can't even remember what form it took (I most likely said that Nehru was a decent man, as politicians go). But it was enough to bring the roof down. I got snarls and dirty looks in the seminar room itself, and afterwards was set upon by my immediate boss, then a coming political scientist in his mid-30s (and now a scholar of world renown). This gentleman called a colleague into his study and, pointing to me, said: 'Ei shala Jawaharlal Nehru shapotaar!'

To be a supporter of Nehru in a Marxist stronghold of those days is much like someone now defending the emperor Babar in a *shakha* of that hard-core Hindu organization, the Rashtriya Swayamsevak Sangh. For the Left, Nehru was a confused, weak-kneed idealist, full of high-flown rhetoric but without the will or wherewithal to take revolutionary action against the ruling classes. Indeed, the political scientist who chastised me had just then published an essay making this case at some length—here he also compared Nehru, unfavourably of course, to Lenin.

Truth be told, the first prime minister of free India was not exactly popular among non-Marxist circles in Calcutta either. The intellectuals mocked his second-class degree from Cambridge, while the brown sahibs pointed out that, unlike his close contemporary the Yuvraj of Cooch Behar, he had not even made the cricket First Eleven at Harrow. And of course, Bengalis of all stripes and ideologies lamented the accident of history which had placed Nehru, rather than their adored Subhas Bose, at the helm of the government of free India.

What Bengal thinks today, India thinks tomorrow. An old cliché, which in this case turns out to be surprisingly true. For, Nehru has been, for some time now, the least liked of Indian politicians, dumped on from all parts of the political spectrum, in all parts of the land. As I know from experience, it is as risky a business to defend Jawaharlal Nehru in Delhi or Mumbai in 2012 as it was to defend him in Calcutta back in 1982.

A future historian, assessing the decline and fall of Nehru in the Indian imagination, might reckon 1977 to be the watershed, the year in which the delegitimization of an icon began gathering pace. That was when the Janata government came to power, after thirty long years of Congress rule (and misrule). The Janata Party was forged in the prisons of northern India, by men jailed under the Emergency imposed by Prime Minister Indira Gandhi. It brought together three disparate political groupings, united in the first instance by their opposition to Mrs Gandhi. These were the Hindu chauvinist Jana Sangh, the non-Communist (or Socialist) left, and the old style, so to speak, 'Gandhian' Congressmen.

The Janata Party is long dead, and its constituents have each gone their separate ways. Yet an examination of their political styles in the years since reveals that aside from the Emergency and Mrs Gandhi, these three political groupings (as well as the intellectuals who have supported them) were, and are, also united by their hatred of Jawaharlal Nehru.

Each of the Janata fragments has had its reasons for opposing Nehru and his legacy. The Jana Sangh, now metamorphosed into the Bharatiya Janata Party (BJP), takes its cue from its mother organization, the Rashtriya Swayamsevak Sangh (RSS), which seeks to build a Hindu state in India. Following the RSS, the BJP trains its fire on Nehru's philosophy of secularism, which they claim rests on the 'appeasement' of the minorities. Nehruvian 'pseudo-secularism' is said to have shown grave disrespect to Hindus while wantonly encouraging Muslims, this resulting in a wave of communal and ethnic conflict, not least in Kashmir.

By contrast, the non-Communist left takes its cue from the work of the brilliant, maverick intellectual Ram Manohar Lohia. Lohia took a PhD in political science from the University of Berlin, fleeing the city just as Hitler came to power. After his return he worked ceaselessly to root socialism in the cultural soil of India. Like Lohia, his modern-day followers—who exercise considerable influence in north India—have seen Nehru as the symbol of the upper-caste, upper-class, English-speaking intelligentsia that has held sway since Independence. This elite, they contend, has manipulated both political and economic power to its advantage, but to the detriment of the low-caste, non-English-speaking majority, whom the Lohiaites themselves seek to represent.

If for the BJP Nehru could not represent the 'spirit of India' because he did not subscribe to the right religion (indeed, to no religion at all), for the Lohia Socialists his unfittedness to rule was proven by the fact that he stood apart, in class, culture and language, from those he ruled over. The Gandhian critique takes a different line altogether. It argues that despite being the Mahatma's acknowledged heir, Nehru ultimately betrayed his legacy. Where Gandhi fought for a free India based on a confederation of self-sufficient village republics, Nehru is said to have imposed a model of industrial development that centralized power in the cities by devastating the countryside. Those who attack Nehru in the Mahatma's name have forcefully argued that planned industrialization has fuelled both environmental degradation and social conflict,

outcomes that could have been avoided if India had instead followed
a decentralized or 'Gandhian' approach to economic development.

To the Hindutva, Lohiaite and Gandhian critiques has now been
added a fourth. This comes from the supporters of economic
liberalization, who point an accusatory finger at Nehru for insisting
that the state play a dominant role in economic life. Without
Nehru's folly, they say, India would have long since become the
biggest of the Asian Tigers. As a passionate free-marketeer remarked
recently, Professor Rajkrishna's derisive phrase, the 'Hindu rate of
growth', should be renamed the 'Nehru rate of growth'.

The criticisms of Jawaharlal Nehru now are vast and varied, so
varied indeed that they contradict each other without fear of
recognition. Just before the General Elections of 2004, the Delhi
monthly *National Review* interviewed two stalwarts of the political
firmament: Lal Krishna Advani, then home minister and deputy
prime minister in the Government of India, for many years now the
leading ideologue of the Hindu right; and Dr Ashok Mitra, the
former finance minister of the Government of West Bengal, and a
still-serving ideologue of the Marxist left. This, without first
checking with one another, is what they said about Nehru's practice
of secularism:

Lal Krishna Advani: 'We are opposed to Nehruvian secularism. We
accept Gandhian secularism. Nehru started off with the assumption
that all religions are wrong. For Gandhi, all religions are true, and
they are different paths to the same goal. We thought many of
Gandhi's political policies were not sound, but we accepted his idea
of secularism.'

Ashok Mitra: 'Nehru turned the meaning of secularism upside
down. Secularism, he thought, was embracing each religion with
equal fervour. And which he exemplified by frequent visits to
mandirs and mosques, to dargahs and gurdwaras, to churches and
synagogues. But once you embark on this slippery path, you end up
identifying the state's activities with religious rituals such as *bhumipuja*
and breaking coconut shells to float a boat built in a government

workshop. This was inevitable because since Hindus constitute the
majority of the state's population, Hindu rituals came to assert their
presence within state premises.'

Which of these assertions is correct? Did Nehru hate all religions
equally, as Mr Advani suggests? Or did he love all equally, as
Dr Mitra claims? Perhaps it does not really matter. Perhaps these
statements tells us less about Nehru's actual beliefs (or policies), and
more about the political preferences of his contemporary critics. On
the one side, there is Mr Advani, who considers 'Hindutva' the
most promising political movement in modern India—and worries
why it has not progressed further. Whom does he blame? Nehru.
On the other hand, Dr Mitra considers Hindutva to be the most
pernicious political movement in modern India—and is angry that
it has progressed so far. And whom does *he* blame? Nehru.

It would be intriguing to develop the Advani/Mitra contrast in
other directions. Consider thus their likely views on economic and
foreign policies. Mr Advani probably thinks that the Nehruvian
epoch was characterized by excessive state intervention; Dr Mitra
certainly believes that the state did not intervene enough.
Mr Advani holds that, in the formative decades of the 1950s, India
aligned too closely with the Soviet Union; while Dr Mitra thinks
that we did not cosy up to Moscow enough. Mr Advani must
believe that Nehru did not do enough to promote the cause of the
Hindi language; Dr Mitra most likely holds that he did too much.

For both Mr Advani and Dr Mitra, their political project is best
defined negatively: as the repudiation of the economic and social
philosophy of Jawaharlal Nehru. Lifelong political adversaries though
they may be, the left-wing Indian and the right-wing Indian are
joined in a lifelong fight against a common enemy—Father.

IV

Jawaharlal Nehru's posthumous reputation brings to mind a remark
of the nineteenth-century British radical, Edward Carpenter.

Carpenter claimed that 'the Outcast of one Age is the Hero of another'. He clearly had himself in mind, an environmentalist and prophet of sexual liberation ahead of his time. But the case of Jawaharlal Nehru shows that the opposite can equally be true. That is, the Hero of one age can very easily become the Outcast of another.

Why has Jawaharlal Nehru's reputation fallen so far and so fast? One reason is that as the first and longest-serving prime minister, he was in a unique position to shape his nation's destiny. He did a great deal, but there is always the feeling that he should have done more—*much* more. And modern middle-class Indians are, as a rule, very judgemental, especially when it comes to passing judgement on dead politicians. As his biographer S. Gopal once pointed out, Nehru's 'very achievements demand that he be judged by standards which one would not apply to the ordinary run of Prime Ministers; and disappointment stems from the force of our expectations'.

Allied to this is Nehru's nearness to us in time. We live in a world shaped by him and his colleagues. And no modern man has had such an authoritative influence on the laws and institutions of his country. Adult suffrage, a federal polity, the mixed economy, non-alignment in foreign policy, cultural pluralism and the secular state—these were the crucial choices made by the first generation of Indian nation-builders. The choices were made collectively, of course, but always with the consent and justification of one man above all—Jawaharlal Nehru. So when Indians today meet to deliberate over them, they single out one man above all for approbation or denunciation. Questions that can be posed in the plural tend to be posed in the singular—instead of asking why the Indian state chose to be secular rather than theocratic, we ask why Nehru did so.

To illustrate how anachronistic these judgements are, consider only the claim that Nehru 'imposed' a socialist economic model on India. In fact, there was a widespread belief that a poor, ex-colonial country needed massive state intervention in the economic sphere. In 1944, the leading industrialists issued a 'Bombay Plan' that called for the state to invest in infrastructure and protect them from foreign competition. This plan, signed by J.R.D. Tata and G.D. Birla, among others, approvingly quoted the claim of the Cambridge economist A.C. Pigou that socialism and capitalism were 'converging' and that a dynamic economy needed to mix the best features of both. When, ten years later, the draft of the Second Five-Year Plan—the manifesto, so to say, of the heavy industry strategy finally adopted—was shown to a panel of twenty-four top Indian economists, twenty-three supported it. Behind the mixed economy model, therefore, was a massive consensus, one shared by economists, technocrats, politicians and, not least, industrialists.

It is less than fifty years since Nehru died. Since Indians still live with the consequences of decisions taken by him and his colleagues, some of them presume that they could have taken better decisions. And so they pass judgements on Nehru the like of which they would never pass on other Indian rulers, on (say) Akbar or even Lord Curzon. Of course, the judgements are anachronistic, made on the basis of what we know in 2010 rather than what Nehru knew in 1950. That does not stop them being made. Far from it. Over the years, I have spoken often about Nehru to audiences in different parts of India, to audiences composed variously of businessmen, students, scholars and activists. Everywhere, I have met people who know that they could have done Nehru's job better than he did it himself; that is, they know that they could have 'saved' Kashmir for India, taken the country onto a 10 per cent growth path from the 1950s itself, solved the Hindu–Muslim problem, eliminated corruption in government, and brought peace with our neighbours. How foolish of us not to have elected them all as prime minister!

A third reason for the fading of the Nehruvian sheen is political, namely, the decline of Congress hegemony. The debunking of Nehru began with the coming to power of the Janata Party in 1977. Since then, the Congress has steadily lost ground in both the Centre and the states. There have now been as many as eight non-Congress governments at the Centre; and more than fifty such in the states. The composition of these governments has been non-Congress; their beliefs and practices, often anti-Congress. In the realms of politics, economics, culture and the law, these groupings have promoted ideas often sharply opposed to those that Nehru stood for. While the opponents of the Congress were out of power, their ideas had little salience or popularity; but now that they are in power, the ideas themselves have power—as well as influence.

A fourth reason for the fall of Nehru's reputation lies in the misdeeds of his family. What we have here, as the sociologist André Béteille has pointed out, is the reversal of a famous biblical injunction. Instead of the sins of the father being visited on his children, for seven successive generations, in Nehru's case the sins of the daughter and grandson (and now granddaughter-in-law and great-grandson) have been visited upon him.

Perhaps the greatest paradox of modern Indian history is that every act of Nehru that nurtured a liberal democratic ethos was undone by his own daughter. He promoted a political opposition, she squelched it. He respected the press, she muzzled it. He allowed autonomy to the executive, she preferred to rely on 'committed' civil servants and judges. His Congress was a decentralized, democratic organization, her Congress was a one-woman show. He kept religion out of public life, she brought it in.

Like his mother, Rajiv Gandhi was a politician of limited mental ability but with an unrivalled capacity for cronyism and manipulation. His regime further undermined the institutions and procedures of liberal democracy. In recent years, Sonia Gandhi has likewise perverted public institutions by appointing friends and cronies to head them. In this she, like her husband and mother-in-law before her, has violated Nehru's own practice of respecting the autonomy and dignity of state institutions.

As an earlier essay in this book documents, Nehru had nothing to do with the 'dynasty'. After his death in May 1964, the Congress chose Lal Bahadur Shastri to become prime minister, a post on which he quickly stamped his authority. Mrs Gandhi herself may never have become prime minister had not Shastri died unexpectedly. She was chosen by the Congress bosses as a compromise candidate who—they thought—would do their bidding. But once in office,

Mrs Gandhi converted the Indian National Congress into a family business. She first brought in her son Sanjay and, after his death, his brother Rajiv. In each case, it was made clear that the son would succeed Mrs Gandhi as head of Congress and head of government. Thus, the 'Nehru–Gandhi dynasty' should properly be known as the '(Indira) Gandhi' dynasty. But blood runs thicker than evidence; and when political commentators persist in speaking knowingly of the 'Nehru–Gandhi dynasty', why will the public think any different?

A fifth reason we Indians tend to give Nehru less credit than his due is that he appears to have lived too long. Lord Mountbatten once claimed that if Nehru had died in 1958, he would have been remembered as the greatest statesman of the twentieth century. Writing in 1957, Escott Reid remarked that Nehru's 'tragedy may be the tragedy of [Franklin Delano] Roosevelt: to remain leader of his country for a year or two after he has lost his grip and thus damage his own reputation and his country's interests'.

This was astonishingly prescient. For, it was after 1957 that the clouds began to descend on Nehru. In 1958, there was the Mundhra scandal, the first signs of serious corruption in government; in 1959, the unfortunate dismissal of the Communist government in Kerala; in 1960, rising tension on the China border; in 1961, the conquest of Goa (which marred both Nehru's non-alignment policy and his professions of non-violence); in 1962, the disastrous war with China. These setbacks emboldened the critics to speak of the other failures of Nehru's regime: such as the continuing conflicts in Kashmir and Nagaland, the lack of attention to primary education, the hostility to business, the failure to effect land reforms.

Finally, Nehru's posthumous reputation has also suffered from the neglect of scholars and scholarship. There is an intriguing contrast here with Mahatma Gandhi. In his lifetime, Gandhi was looked down upon by intellectuals who, even when they admired his ability to move the masses, thought little of his ideas, which were so completely alien to, and often at odds with, the progressive currents of the day. But after his death the intellectuals have rediscovered Gandhi with a vengeance. In Nehru's case the trajectory has been exactly the reverse; while he lived, the cream of the world's intelligentsia crowded around him, whereas after his death they have left him alone.

This contrast is starkly manifest in the continuing production of books about the two men. Thus, the best Indian minds have thought deeply about Gandhi—consider here the fine recent studies on the Mahatma by Ashis Nandy, Bhikhu Parekh, Rajmohan Gandhi, and others. So have some able foreign minds—as for instance, Denis Dalton, David Hardiman, J.T.F. Jordens and Mark Juergensmeyer, all authors of insightful works on Gandhi and Gandhian thought. By contrast, a cast of rather ordinary Indians have written somewhat superficially about Nehru. And we can say the same about the foreigners. For, none of the works on Nehru that now pour off the presses remotely match, in empirical depth or analytical insight, the far older works of Sarvepalli Gopal and Walter Crocker.

I do not mean here to overestimate the power of the printed word. Popular ideas about Nehru will continue to be shaped by propaganda and political prejudice rather than by solid scholarship. Still, had there been a slew of sensitive, empathetic, elegantly written books on Nehru—comparable to those on Gandhi—this might have promoted a more nuanced understanding of the colossal range of problems Nehru had to confront—a range unprecedented in the political history of the modern world—and allowed for a more healthy appreciation of Nehru's achievements.

V

This essay is about the rise and fall of Jawaharlal Nehru's historical *reputation*, but I cannot resist the temptation to pass at least a provisional judgement on Nehru's historical *role*. For, as it happens, I have spent much of the past decade studying the India of the 1950s and '60s. I have been reading private papers and government reports, memoirs and contemporary journals, accounts by anthropologists and political scientists. One man, Jawaharlal Nehru, laid his definitive stamp on those years. How, then, does a historical analysis of what he actually did compare with the criticisms and revisions of the present day? What follows is one historian's answer.

First, Nehru was without question the chief architect of our democracy. It was he, more than any other nationalist, who promoted universal franchise and the multi-party system. He respected other Congressmen and Opposition leaders, and honoured the freedom of the press and the independence of the judiciary.

Second, Nehru had the unique idea of staying non-aligned in a Cold War that was forever threatening to turn Hot. His policy allowed a newly independent, desperately poor, and still vulnerable country room to manoeuvre, and to take economic aid from both sides. This independence also allowed India, and Nehru, to play an important mediating role in critical international conflicts such as Korea and Vietnam.

Third, while it is now fashionable to attack Nehruvian economics from the free-market point of view, his views in this respect were not singular, but representative of a wide spectrum of intellectual and scientific opinion. There was a solid consensus behind the idea of the mixed economy. In any case, Nehru's economic policies have not been altogether unsuccessful. They have built a decent industrial base, helped assure self-sufficiency in food, and have created a pool of technically skilled manpower that has fuelled the recent software boom.

Fourth, Nehru built on the inclusive idea of India framed by Tagore and Gandhi before him. He worked hard to bring women and low castes into public life. He worked overtime to integrate and respect the minorities. It is a striking (if now little-noticed) fact that his period as prime minister was largely free of communal riots.

Set against these manifest contributions, of course, are some notable failures. In the realm of domestic politics, Nehru need not have let his fellow Congressmen persuade him to dismiss the Kerala Communist government in 1959, an act which was wrong in itself and set an unpleasant (and since much-abused) precedent. In foreign policy, he should have been more alert to Chinese adventurism and more critical of the Soviet invasion of Hungary in 1956. As for his economics, he could have listened more to socialists who advocated rapid land reforms and to Gandhians who preached environmental sustainability.

Nehru's critics often focus on failures that were more imaginary than real. The emphasis on planning that free-marketeers now decry was favoured, as we have seen, even by the industrialists of the time—they thought the state should invest in infrastructure, and protect them from foreign competition. Patriots and jingoists blame Nehru for the clash with China—but, as we shall see in the next essay, this conflict was structural rather than personal, with two great civilizations coming out of colonial rule, seeking to find their way in the world, and rubbing against one another in the process.

The one failure of Nehru's that one cannot contextualize, historicize, or euphemize was with regards to primary education. That is something Mahatma Gandhi would have emphasized, as the first and fundamental duty of a newly independent nation. In the 1940s and 1950s, India had a large reservoir of social capital, in the form of an idealistic middle class groomed by the independence movement. If we'd put them to work on schooling everyone, as was done in nineteenth-century Europe or other ex-colonial countries like Cuba or Vietnam, we'd have been in a different position today.

Still, all things considered, Nehru was, in more senses than one, the builder of Indian democracy. Crucially, he respected social diversity as much as democratic procedure; thus his refusal to reduce India or 'Indianness' to a dominant religious or linguistic ethos. Nowhere is this more poignantly illustrated than in an exchange of letters between Nehru and Vallabhbhai Patel immediately after Independence. The refugees pouring in from west Punjab were calling for retribution against the Muslims who remained in India. Their voice was loud, and for many, compelling. But Nehru told his home minister and close co-worker that it must be quelled: for, India, if it was anything at all, was emphatically *not* Pakistan. Over there, they might ill-treat or persecute their minorities; over here, we would protect and respect ours. There was, wrote Nehru to

Patel, 'a constant cry for retaliation and vicarious punishment of the Muslims of India, because the Pakistanis punish Hindus. That argument does not appeal to me in the slightest.' For, India was not a mirror image of Pakistan, a Hindu state to its Islamic state. 'Our secular ideals,' insisted Nehru to Patel, 'impose a responsibility to our Muslim citizens in India.'

But Nehru was catholic with respect to more than matters of faith. Altogether, he was the least chauvinistic of political leaders. Like the Mahatma, he transcended the divisions of race and religion, caste and class, gender and geography. He was a Hindu who was befriended by Muslims, but also a Brahmin who did not observe the rules of caste, a north Indian who would not impose Hindi on the south, a man who could be trusted and respected by women.

It is true that Nehru could appear superior, not least to his colleagues in party and government. They did not share his cosmopolitan outlook, nor his interest in art, music, literature or science. But no one did more than Nehru to nurture the values and institutions of democracy in India. Vincent Sheean once pointed to 'one overwhelming difference between Mahatma Gandhi and Mr. Nehru: the Mahatma would rather retire, fast, pray, take care of lepers and educate children, than go along with a majority opinion in which he could not concur'. Nehru, on the other hand, had in many instances 'yielded to the majority of his party and of the country . . .' Thus Congress chief ministers were always elected by the legislators of the state concerned, regardless of Nehru's opinion on the matter. And once he saw that both party and country wanted it, Nehru yielded to the formation of linguistic states—a policy he was personally opposed to.

VI

Nehru's contribution to the building of modern India is immense. He made mistakes, to be sure, but other people in his place would most likely have made bigger ones. As a historian, I am quite clear that India was very fortunate to have him as prime minister for that crucial first decade after Independence. His record was unquestionably better than that of those who succeeded him. It was better than that of those who came to rule the other ex-colonial countries of Asia and Africa. And, so far as one can judge these matters, it was probably better than what might have been if some other Indian, say Patel or Bose, had happened to become prime minister in 1947.

As I have suggested, Indians are not always well placed to appreciate Nehru's achievements. Indeed, arguably the best single-volume work on Nehru was written by the Australian diplomat, Walter Crocker. His *Nehru: A Contemporary's Estimate*, is a wise, thoughtful and detached book, its objectivity deepened by the fact that the author came from a relatively obscure country without high stakes in the Cold War.

Nehru, writes Crocker, 'was that rare man who is both clever and good'. In his lifetime it was Nehru's intelligence that was exaggerated; whereas after his death it has been his decency that has been depreciated. For, he was indeed a profoundly good man. As Crocker put it, 'Nehru had less of the common and less of the mean than all but a few men. And he is to be numbered amongst the small band of rulers in history whose power has been matched with pity and mercy'—pity and mercy for the weak, the unfortunate, the forgotten and the persecuted among humankind. His selflessness was widely recognized: thus 'the great bulk of the people of India sensed, and they never lost the sense, that Nehru wanted only to help them and wanted nothing for himself . . .'

Nehru's non-communal, non-parochial orientation was a product of his personal beliefs. It also constituted pragmatic politics. For, as Walter Crocker points out, against the backdrop of civil war, partition, angry refugees and recalcitrant princes, Nehru's 'first concern was to see that India did not fall apart. To this end he encouraged a nationalism that would make Indians feel that they were Indians instead of feeling that they were Tamils or Punjabis or Dogras or Assamese or Brahmans or Kshatriyas or this or that caste, as they are apt. He gave special consideration to the Muslims so as to induce them to feel Indian. For the same reason Christians and other minorities could always be sure of Nehru's unflinching protection. The "Secular State", that is to say a non-Hindu and all-Indian State, was fundamental to this concern.'

Crocker shrewdly notes that in promoting adult suffrage, Nehru was acting against the interests of upper-class Brahmins like himself. Writing shortly after his subject's death, he said that it was 'unlikely that there will be a place in India again for a ruler like Nehru—the aristocratic liberal humanist'. Crocker predicted that in time, India would 'be run by politicians, more and more drawn from, or conditioned by, the outcastes and the low castes. For this is the majority, and, thanks to the ballot-box, it will be the votes of the majority which will set up and pull down governments; votes won through promising more and more to the needy and the many.'

Sixty years after universal adult franchise was introduced in India, we can see Crocker's prediction being fulfilled in good measure. Westernized Brahmins like Jawaharlal Nehru, once so dominant in Indian politics, are now on the margins. The main players are drawn from the lower orders, representing—in varying degrees—the backward castes which constitute the majority of the electorate. And so, as Crocker wrote, 'in abolishing the British *raj*, and in propagating ideas of equality . . . Nehru and the upper-class Indian nationalists of English education abolished themselves. Nehru destroyed the Nehrus.'

Walter Crocker's diaries, which are at the University of Adelaide, contain more revealing insights still. For instance, there remains a keen interest in the relationship between Jawaharlal Nehru and Edwina Mountbatten. That they were intimates is not to be doubted—but did the bonds ever move from the merely emotional to the tellingly physical? That one was the prime minister of India and the other the wife of the governor-general of India we know—but was Nehru ever influenced in his policies by the desires and preferences of his friend Edwina?

Despite the column inches devoted to these matters in the press, and the interrogations and speculations on radio and television, we still don't really know. I do not propose here to provide definitive answers to those questions. But I do wish to supply an interesting and possibly telling sidelight on the Nehru–Edwina friendship, drawing on material from Crocker's unpublished diaries.

On the 21st of February 1960, Edwina Mountbatten died in her sleep while on a visit to Borneo. Shortly after midday, the news was communicated to Walter Crocker by his friend Rajkumari Amrit Kaur, the veteran Gandhian and high-ranking minister in the Union government. That evening the Australian diplomat was due to attend a dinner at Hyderabad House in honour of the historian Arnold Toynbee. Toynbee had already published several volumes of his best-selling survey of the rise and fall of civilizations. He was in Delhi at the invitation of the Indian Council for Cultural Relations, who had asked him to deliver the first of what was to become an annual lecture in memory of Maulana Abul Kalam Azad. As Crocker wrote in his diary that night, by the time he reached Hyderabad House,

> Nehru was there. He must have had strong feelings about the utterly sudden death of Lady Mountbatten but he showed no sign of it. He sat next to Toynbee at dinner and for a while was silent, but for the rest of the meal was plunged into a lively conversation with him. As usual everyone around looked by comparison, strained, inhibited, dim. There was not a hint of self-consciousness or fear or hesitation about him. His physical handsomeness in itself was dominating—the eyes, the golden-light brown and healthy skin, the healthy hair . . . What a man, whatever his policies.

As a first-hand account of how Jawaharlal Nehru felt and acted the day Edwina Mountbatten died, this is striking indeed. With an almost magisterial self-will, Nehru appears to have kept his thoughts (and we may presume, his grief) hidden within himself. An honoured guest had come to town, and the prime minister's duty was to entertain and amuse him. At the time, Toynbee had a colossal popular following. Never since (and rarely before) has a mere historian been treated with such deference around the globe or so readily acknowledged as an oracle. That evening at Hyderabad House, the others around the table, whether Indian or western, were inhibited, even tongue-tied. It was only the prime minister who could engage Toynbee in a conversation of intellectual equals. His dearest friend had just died: but his office, and his country, demanded of Nehru that he set aside his personal grief and act as was expected of him.

Indian xenophobes and Pakistani nationalists both charge Nehru with having acted in political matters under the influence of Edwina Mountbatten. Their accusations have not yet been backed by concrete evidence. On the other hand, reading Walter Crocker's account of Nehru's conduct in public on 21st February 1960, it is hard to believe that while Edwina was alive, Nehru would have abandoned principle and patriotism in deference to her whims and charms.

VII

In middle age, as in youth, a photograph of Nehru occupies a prominent place in my house. The photo I grew up with was generic, part of a print run of many thousands (if not millions); this is a one-off, almost certainly the only copy now in existence or display.

The photograph was taken in 1949, while the prime minister was visiting the Forest Research Institute in Dehradun, where my grandfather and father both worked. The great man is signing an autograph book. The right hand carries a pen; the left hand contains a cigarette holder. Also visible is a handkerchief with the monogrammed initials, 'JN'.

I acquired the photograph from my grandmother. She gave it to me shortly before she died in 2001, saying, 'No one else in the family will want it.' My grandmother knew English, although her reading was confined to books and magazines in Tamil. From them, and from the world around, she seemed to know about the fall in Nehru's reputation, and to sense that her grandson was, in his eccentrically obsessive way, seeking to reverse it.

My mother put up her hero's photograph in her bedroom, to be seen only by the family. My Nehru is on the mantelpiece in our drawing room, visible to all visitors. This is not to say that my admiration is as deep or as unforgiving as hers. I do admit that Nehru made mistakes, sometimes serious ones. I do think that there were other modern Indians who were as great as him—Ambedkar, Patel, Rajagopalachari, and Kamaladevi Chattopadhyay come to mind—and others who were even greater (notably, Gandhi and Tagore). That I choose still to have his photograph on public display is in part an act of defiance, a desire to mock the conventional wisdom. For, in the judgement of this historian, Nehru was a true maker of modern India. Besides, it is a charming photograph.

APPENDIX
DEBATING NEHRU WITH A FRIEND

In 2001, when Nehru's historical reputation was at an all-time low (in part, but only in part, because the BJP was in power in New Delhi), I wrote an essay in *The Hindu* on how the debunking of India's first prime minister was mostly misplaced. This prompted a long letter from a friend in Bangalore, a brilliant and public-spirited businessman who both cared deeply about India (he has given away vast sums of money to rural education) and was (rightly) disgusted with the culture of sycophancy in the Congress party. The exchange between my friend (referred to below by the initials 'PP', for 'Patriotic Philanthropist') and myself is reproduced below:

PP: Nehru was a liberal no doubt and a towering figure, but he quietly decimated the political leadership in the Congress. While Gandhi created leaders, Nehru destroyed them. So people asked the question, 'After Nehru Who?' The local leadership at the state level crumbled and no new leaders of good calibre came up.

RG: I think this is to some extent a fair and just criticism . . . [H]e could have more actively sought out and nurtured second-rung leaders. His own preference was for non-political types like Homi

Bhabha and T.T. Krishnamachari—people who shared his liberal
and cosmopolitan world view. However, he did actively try to get
brilliant young socialists like Jayaprakash Narayan back to the
Congress. I think it a real pity that the best, that is, the most
intelligent and idealistic of the young Indians, who were then in the
socialist and Communist parties, set themselves up in opposition to
Nehru. Had they worked with him and within the Congress in the
1950s and 1960s, as he asked them to do, they might collectively
have ended illiteracy and brought about effective land reforms,
which were crucial if India was to progress economically. On that
socialist or social democratic base we could have, from the 1970s,
more effectively built capitalism and private enterprise. That was a
real lost chance.

PP: Nehru stayed non-aligned, but India lost. India today is a third-
rate power, given to pontification on the world stage, obsessed with
Pakistan. Nehru took the Kashmir issue to the UN listening to
Mountbatten, and the British took us to the cleaners. While the
Marshall Plan made Japan and Europe, India got peanuts. His
policies led to India's closing shop which we had never done in our
long history because we are a trading nation. So we became like the
galli ka kutta, nobody wanted us.

RG: Here I am not with you. In fact, the entire Cabinet, including
Patel, was with the decision to go to the UN. We had to, if only
because in Junagadh (which had a Muslim Nawab and a [majority]
Hindu population), Patel helped organize a plebiscite when the
Nawab voted [to join] Pakistan. We could scarcely not agree to a
plebiscite for Kashmir, which was the same situation—in reverse.
Also, I think non-alignment was necessary in the 1950s—though we
could have been more consistent in its application.

PP: It was Nehru's arrogance that turned China against us despite
India supporting China.

RG: Yes, on the China front he made serious mistakes, of his own,
and by trusting Krishna Menon, but given the suspicions and

ambitions of the Chinese after their Revolution, and the ambiguities about the border, conflict was more or less inevitable.

PP: Yes, Nehru created the educated elite and the elite got on to the gravy train. He also created the largest pool of poor people in the world, deprived of education. Look at China for education. The poor paid for the rich and the rich left India ... He warped the thinking of the educated class who depended on the state even for education.

RG: Yes, this was indeed his greatest failure, the failure to abolish illiteracy. Part of this was because of his fascination with high-tech (hence his vigorous promotion of the IITs). But if the socialists had been with him, and Communists like EMS [Namboodiripad] too, who knows?

PP: Yes, he integrated socially. He truly believed in a free society without discrimination, but he forgot what India was, a deeply religious society with religion permeating throughout. He worked on the western concepts which were alien in their approach. Gandhi was a true Indian who believed in an Indian society but sought to achieve it through what existed, our belief in Dharma, our tolerance for others, our acceptance of others and our indifference to others. We are a multi-religious society and not what Nehru defined as a secular society. It is better to accept what we are and then change than build an edifice on top only to see it crumble. Caste was and is a reality and to deny [it] is to live in a make-believe world. Caste could only be eradicated by education and urbanization and by social action as in Kerala. Nehru tried a top–down approach and created the base of a disaster.

RG: I think there might be a real disagreement here. I agree that change must come from above and from below, but insist that religion has no place in public or political life. The Nehru way of secularism remains the only alternative, unless we want to replicate Gujarat everywhere. More on this below.

PP: Nehru had contempt for an Indian, the real Indian in a dhoti, speaking his language, following his rituals and leading his life, howsoever bad. He believed that an Indian was a brown-skinned Englishman, a caricature in his own country. He created all of us who speak English at home, forget our roots, despise our own people and do not know our own country and have forgotten our own culture. His idea of India was not India's idea of itself.

RG: There is no one 'authentic' Indian or even an 'authentic' Hindu as you seem to believe. We are riven apart by our particularities—of caste, language, religion, province. Rajmohan Gandhi (in a chapter of his book *The Good Boatman*) argues that the reason Gandhi chose Nehru as his successor was that he was a genuinely Indian or all-India figure—where Patel was a Gujarati, Rajaji a Tamil, Azad a Muslim, etc. The fact that he was not at all provincial, that non-Hindi speakers, non-Brahmins, women and non-Hindus could all trust him was crucial in his helping build and nurture a unifying and inclusive idea of India. Moreover, he gave Indians hope—that we could build a more prosperous and peaceful society—whereas the politicians nowadays who claim to be authentically Hindu or Indian only stoke our fears—that we will be swamped by Muslims or upper castes or whatever. I think that a modern society needs a liberal cosmopolitan worldview—glorification of what is 'authentic', 'real' or 'indigenous' is a recipe for sectarian violence and, in the worst case, for fascism.

PP: I like Nehru but he is not the God you make him out to me. I would give him 50 per cent in marking.

RG: Fifty per cent is quite good—what would you give Vajpayee or Deve Gowda? Much less I am sure. Nehru had a more difficult task, I believe, than any other politician in history—unifying a desperately divided and very poor country, and doing so democratically. On the whole, he did this very well. We should ask ourselves before we bash him—how would we have done in his position? We might simply have fled or capitulated.

chapter eight

AN ASIAN CLASH OF
CIVILIZATIONS?
THE SINO-INDIAN
CONFLICT REVISITED

~

I

In the late autumn of 1962, there was a short, intense border war between India and China. It resulted in the rout of an underprepared and poorly led Indian Army. The battle was seen in national, civilizational, and ideological terms. India became free of British rule in 1947; and China was united under Communist auspices in 1949. These two nations were, or at least saw themselves as, carriers of ancient civilizations that had produced great literature, philosophy, architecture, science and much else, but whose further evolution had been rudely interrupted by western imperialists. The recovery of their national independence was seen as the prelude to the re-emergence of China and India as major forces in the modern world.

The defeat of 1962 was thus at once a defeat of the Indian Army at the hands of its Chinese counterpart, a defeat of democracy by Communism, a defeat of one large new nation by another, a defeat of one ancient civilization at the hands of another. In India, the defeat was also interpreted in personal terms, as that of Jawaharlal Nehru, who had held the offices of prime minister and foreign minister continuously since Independence in 1947.

That debacle at the hands of China still hangs as a huge cloud over Nehru's reputation. There is an intriguing comparison to be made here with the historical reputation of his fellow Harrovian, Winston Churchill. Robert Rhodes James once wrote a book called *Churchill: A Study in Failure*, whose narrative stopped at 1940. It excavated, perhaps in excessive detail, its subject's erratic and undistinguished career before that date. But of course, all Churchill's failures were redeemed by his heroic leadership during the Second World War. It is tempting to see Nehru's career as being Churchill's in reverse, insofar as it was marked for many decades by achievement and success, these nullified by the massive, humiliating failure, with regard to China, which broke his nation's morale and broke his own spirit and body. The war was fought in October–November 1962; a year and a half later, Nehru was dead.

II

The four towering figures of twentieth-century India were Rabindranath Tagore, Mohandas K. Gandhi, Jawaharlal Nehru and B.R. Ambedkar. All four had a close connection with England, a country they each spent extended periods in, and by whose literature and politics they were deeply influenced. But all also had a long engagement with a second foreign country. In the case of Tagore, this was Japan, which he visited on four separate occasions, and whose culture and art he greatly admired. In the case of Gandhi, this second country was South Africa, where he spent two decades working as a lawyer, community organizer and activist. In the case of Ambedkar it was the United States, where he studied, and by whose democratic traditions he was influenced.

As for Nehru, other than India and England, the country that interested him most was China. His first major book, *Glimpses of*

World History, published in 1935, has as many as 134 index
references to China. These refer to, among other things, different
dynasties (the Tang, Han, Ch'in, etc.), corruption, Communism,
civil war, agriculture, and banditry. Already, the pairing of China
and India was strongly imprinted in Nehru's framework. Thus,
China is referred to as 'the other great country of Asia' and as
'India's old-time friend'. There was a manifest sympathy with its
troubles at the hands of foreigners. The British were savaged for
forcing both humiliating treaties and opium down the throats of the
Chinese, this being an illustration of the 'growing arrogance and
interference by the western Powers'.

More notable, perhaps, was Nehru's chastisement of Japan, which
'not only followed Europe in industrial methods', but, at least with
regard to China, 'also in imperialist aggression'. Speaking of the
wars between the two nations in the 1890s, Nehru writes that 'no
scruple had ever troubled Japan in the pursuit of her imperial policy.
She grabbed openly, not caring even to cover her designs with a
veil.' He also judged Japan harshly with regard to the war with
China that took place at the time of the book's writing. Thus, when
the aggressor met with resistance from Chinese nationalists, it 'tried
to break it by vast and horrible massacres from the air and other
methods of unbelievable barbarity'. But, continued Nehru, 'in this
fiery ordeal a new nation was forged in China, and the old lethargy
of the Chinese people dropped away from them ... The sympathy
of the people of India was naturally with the Chinese people, as it
also was with the Spanish Republic, and in India and America and
elsewhere great movements for the boycott of Japanese goods grew.'

The sympathy of this particular Indian manifested itself in a trip
he made to China in August 1939. The visit was cut short by the
outbreak of hostilities in Europe, which forced Nehru to come
home to discuss with his nationalist colleagues the impact of the
War on their movement. Even so, the two weeks he spent in China
were, wrote Nehru, 'memorable ones both personally for me and
for the future relations of India and China. I found, to my joy, that
my desire that China and India should draw ever closer to each

other was fully reciprocated by China's leaders . . . I returned to India an even greater admirer of China and the Chinese people than I had been previously, and I could not imagine that any adverse fate could break the spirit of these ancient people, who had grown so young again.'

Shortly after writing these words, Nehru was jailed by the British. While in prison for the next three years, he composed *The Discovery of India*, a brilliant and idiosyncratic work that mixes autobiography with history, and cultural analysis with political prophecy. One important strand in the book relates to relations between the two great Asiatic civilizations. Nehru speaks of the exchange of ideas and artefacts carried on down the centuries by pilgrims, mystics, scholars, travellers and diplomats. 'During the thousand years and more of intercourse between India and China,' he writes, 'each country learnt something from the other, not only in the regions of thought and philosophy, but also in the arts and sciences of life. Probably China was more influenced by India than India by China, which is a pity, for India could well have received, with profit to herself, some of the sound commonsense of the Chinese, and with aid checked her own extravagant fancies.'

In *The Discovery of India*, Nehru again compares China favourably with Japan. China's struggle for national dignity attracted 'much sympathy' in India, in contrast to 'a certain antipathy' for Japan. The Chinese leader Chiang Kai-shek had visited India during the War; he, and his attractive and forceful wife, met Nehru and were impressed by him. The viceroy, Lord Linlithgow, commented cattily that Madame Chiang had 'a kittenish weakness for Nehru's eyelashes'. The Indian returned the affection, albeit in political rather than personal terms. The presence of the Generalissimo and his wife, thought Nehru, 'and their manifest sympathy for India's freedom, helped to bring India out of her national shell and increased her awareness of the international issues at stake. The bonds that tied India and China grew stronger, and so did the desire to line up with China and other nations against the common adversary' (namely, fascism and imperialism).

Writing at the conclusion of the Second World War, Nehru could clearly see the decline of Great Britain, and the emergence of the United States and Soviet Russia as the two major powers. This bipolar world would, in time, become a multipolar world. Nehru thought that 'China and India are potentially capable of joining that group. Each of them is compact and homogeneous and full of natural wealth, man-power and human skill and capacity . . . No other country, taken singly, apart from these four, is actually or potentially in such a position . . . It is possible of course,' wrote Nehru presciently, 'that large federations of groups of nations may emerge in Europe or elsewhere and form huge multinational States.'

In his pre-1947 writings, Nehru saw China through the lens of a progressive anti-imperialist, from which perspective India and China were akin and alike, simultaneously fighting western control as well as feudal remnants in their own society. Chiang and company, like Nehru and company, were at once freedom fighters, national unifiers and social modernizers. It stood to reason that, when finally free of foreign domination, the two neighbours would be friends and partners.

III

I turn now to Jawaharlal Nehru's attitude to China during the years (1947 to 1964) he served as India's prime minister and foreign minister. The bridge between these two periods, pre-and-post Indian Independence, is provided by the Asian Relations Conference, held in New Delhi in March–April 1947. In his speech to the conference, Nehru called China 'that great country to which Asia owes so much and from which so much is expected'. The conference itself he characterized as 'an expression of that deeper urge of the mind and spirit of Asia which has persisted in spite of the isolationism which grew up during the years of European domination. As that domination goes, the walls that surrounded us fall down and we look at one another again and meet as old friends long parted.'

The Chinese delegation to this conference represented Chiang Kai-shek's Guomindang party; there was also a separate delegation from Tibet. Two years later the Communists came to power in Beijing. The Indian ambassador, K.M. Panikkar, was greatly impressed by the new rulers of China. He compared Mao Zedong to his own boss, Nehru, writing that 'both are men of action with dreamy, idealistic temperaments', both 'humanists in the broadest sense of the term'.

One does not know what Nehru made of this comparison. But an Indian who had a more realistic view of Mao and his comrades was the home minister, Vallabhbhai Patel. When China invaded Tibet in October 1950, Patel wrote to Nehru that 'communism is no shield against imperialism and . . . the Communists are as good or as bad imperialists as any other. Chinese ambitions in this respect not only cover the Himalayan slopes on our side but also include important parts of Assam . . . Chinese irredentism and Communist imperialism are different from the expansionism or imperialism of the Western Powers. The former has a cloak of ideology which makes it ten times more dangerous. In the guise of ideological expansion lies concealed racial, national or historical claims.'

The prime minister, however, continued to give the Chinese the benefit of doubt. Speaking in the Indian Parliament in December 1950, he said: 'Some Hon. Members seem to think that I should issue an ultimatum to China, that I should warn them not to do this or that or that I should send them a letter saying that it is foolish to follow the doctrine of communism. I do not see how it is going to help anybody if I act in this way.'

Through the first half of the 1950s, Nehru continued to see China as a kindred soul. Like India, it had embarked on an ambitious and autonomous programme of economic and social development, albeit under Communist auspices. Once more these civilizations could interact with and learn from each other. As Nehru wrote to his chief ministers in June 1952: '[A] variety of circumstances pull India and China towards each other, in spite of differences of forms of government. This is the long pull of geography and history and, if I may add, of the future.' Later the same year, after a visit to India's north-east, Nehru insisted that there was not 'the slightest reason to expect any aggression on our north-eastern frontier. A little clear thinking will show that it is a frightfully difficult task for any army to cross Tibet and the Himalayas and invade India. Tibet is one of the most difficult and inhospitable of countries. An army may possibly cross it, but the problem of logistics and feeding it becomes increasingly difficult. The climate is itself an enemy of any large-scale movement. Apart from this, there was no particular reason why China should think of aggression in this direction.' Nehru even thought 'there is a definite feeling of friendliness towards India in China'.

In June 1954, Zhou Enlai visited New Delhi. In a letter to his chief ministers written immediately afterwards, Nehru reported that the Chinese prime minister 'was particularly anxious, of course, for the friendship and co-operation of India . . . His talk was wholly different from the normal approach of the average Communist, which is full of certain slogans and cliches. He hardly mentioned communism or the Soviet Union or European politics.' Nehru then reported his own talk: 'I spoke to him at some length about our peaceful struggle for independence under Gandhiji's leadership and how this had conditioned us. Our policies had developed from that struggle and we proposed to follow them.'

Nehru made a return visit to China in October 1954. His reception there is described in a diary maintained by his security officer, K.F. Rustamji. In Beijing, a million people lined the roads to greet and cheer Nehru and Zhou as they drove in an open car from the airport to the city. 'All along the route,' observed Rustamji, 'not a single police in uniform was visible.' Then Nehru visited Canton, Dairen, Nanking, and 'at each place the cheers became louder, the clapping more vigorous. At each place we felt that nothing could be better than the reception given there. Then we moved on and found that there was something better— Shanghai. There the airport was a mass of people waving gladioli flowers—there were so many flowers that they seemed to change the colour of the airport.'

This reception must certainly have flattered Nehru. But it seems also to have convinced him of the depth of popular support for the regime (with not a policeman in sight), and of the desire for friendship with India. As he wrote to his closest friend, Edwina Mountbatten, 'I had a welcome in China, such as I have in the big cities of India, and that is saying something . . . The welcome given to me was official and popular . . . One million took part on the day of arrival in Peking. It was not the numbers but their obvious enthusiasm. There appeared to be something emotional to it.'

In a letter to his chief ministers, Nehru likewise insisted that 'this welcome represented something more than political exigency. It was almost an emotional upheaval representing the basic urges of the people for friendship with India.' He had 'no doubt at all that the Government and people of China desire peace and want to concentrate on building up their country during the next decade or so'.

IV

Towards the end of 1956, Zhou Enlai visited India again. The Dalai Lama was also in his party. The Tibetan leader briefly escaped his Chinese minders, and told Nehru that conditions were so harsh in his country that he wished to flee to India. Nehru advised him to return. In 1958, the Indian prime minister asked to visit Tibet, but was refused permission. Now the first seeds of doubt, or at least confusion, were planted in his mind. Perhaps the Chinese were not as straightforward, or indeed as progressive, as he had supposed.

In July 1958, a map was printed in Beijing which showed large parts of India as Chinese territory. It was also revealed that the Chinese had built a road linking Xinjiang to Tibet, which passed through an uninhabited, and scarcely visited, stretch of the Indian district of Ladakh. There were protests from New Delhi, whereupon Zhou Enlai wrote back saying that the McMahon Line, marking the border between India and China, was a legacy of British imperialism and hence not 'legal'. The Chinese leader suggested that both sides retain control of the territory they currently occupied, pending a final settlement.

Meanwhile, a revolt broke out in Tibet. It was put down, and in March 1959 the Dalai Lama fled into India. That he was given refuge, and that Indian political parties rushed to his defence, enraged the Chinese. The war of words escalated. That autumn there were sporadic clashes between Indian and Chinese troops on the border. In October 1959, Nehru wrote to his chief ministers that 'this tension that has arisen between India and China is, of course, of great concern to us. That does not mean that we should get alarmed in the present or fear any serious consequences. I do not think any such development is likely in the foreseeable future. But the basic fact remains that India and China have fallen out and, even though relative peace may continue at the frontier, it is some kind of an armed peace, and the future appears to be one of continuing tension.'

'Behind all this frontier trouble,' Nehru continued,

There appears to me to be a basic problem of a strong and united Chinese State, expansive and pushing out in various directions and full of pride in its growing strength. In Chinese history, this kind of thing has happened on several occasions. Communism as such is only an added element; the real reason should be found to lie deeper in history and in national characteristic[s]. But it is true that never before have these two great countries, India and China, come face to face in some kind of a conflict. By virtue of their very size and their actual or potential strength, there is danger in this situation, not danger in the present, but rather in the future. That danger may be minimized by other developments and by the world moving gradually towards peace. But the danger will still remain, partly because of the tremendous rate of increase of the population of the Chinese State. Apart from population, there has been and is a certain homogeneity among the Chinese people which probably we lack. I have no doubt, however, that in the face of danger there will be much greater cohesion in India than we have at present. Perhaps, that may be one of the good effects of this new and unfortunate development.

By now, Nehru appeared to have come around, at least in part, to the point of view articulated by Vallabhbhai Patel in 1950. The Chinese state was more nationalist than Communist. Still, he felt that there was no chance of a full-fledged war between the two countries. To protect India's interests, Nehru now sanctioned a policy of 'forward posts', whereby detachments were camped in areas along the border claimed by both sides. This was a pre-emptive measure, designed to deter the Chinese from advancing beyond the McMahon Line.

In 1960, Zhou Enlai came to New Delhi in an attempt to find a settlement. India's case was stronger in the western sector, where Chinese interests were greater. Here lay the access road linking the two troublesome provinces of Tibet and Xinjiang, a road that passed through territory claimed by India. On the other hand, in the eastern sector, where Chinese claims were more robust, their strategic interests were minimal.

Zhou offered a quid pro quo. The Chinese would not challenge Indian control of the eastern sector, so long as the Indians in turn winked at their incursions in the west. It was a practical, and in terms of realpolitik, a reasonable proposal. Nehru himself was open to considering it favourably. But by this time knowledge of the road in Ladakh had become public, and there was an outcry in Parliament and the press. The border clashes and the flight of the Dalai Lama had further inflamed public opinion. Opposition politicians accused Nehru of betraying the national interest by talking to the Chinese. Not an inch of Indian territory, they said, could or should be ceded to the Chinese. In the prevailing climate, Nehru chose not to pursue the idea of a settlement.

V

In July 1962, there were clashes between Indian and Chinese troops in the western sector, followed, in September, by clashes in the east. In the third week of October, the Chinese launched a major military strike. In the west, the Indians resisted stoutly, but in the east they were overwhelmed. The Chinese swept through the Brahmaputra Valley, coming as far as the Assam town of Tezpur. The great city of Calcutta was in their sights. However, on the

22nd of November, the Chinese announced a unilateral ceasefire, and withdrew from the areas they had occupied.

Why did the Chinese act when they did? One school of historians argues that they were reacting to Nehru's provocative 'forward posts' policy. Another school argues that the military adventure was to distract the attention of the Chinese people from domestic events, such as the failure of the Great Leap Forward. This had led to increasing criticism of Mao within the Chinese Communist Party, to deflect and answer which the plan to invade India was sanctioned.

This dispute, between those who see India as the instigator and those who see China as the aggressor, dominates the literature to this day. A third explanation for the war was offered by Jawaharlal Nehru himself, in a fascinating, forgotten letter written to his chief ministers on 22nd December 1962. Here, Nehru admitted the army was not prepared for a full-fledged war. The political leadership had erred in not building roads up to the border to carry supplies and ammunitions. On the other side, the invasion of Tibet and the Korean War had primed the Chinese for battle. Then he asked the question—why did the Chinese attack when and in the manner they did? The answer, he argued, had to do not so much with the border dispute as with their larger desire to keep the Cold War going.

Between Russia and the United States, said Nehru, lay a large number of countries which, though weak in conventional military terms, had become symbols 'of peaceful co-existence and their policy of non-alignment to military blocs has gradually been appreciated more and more even by the big blocs. Both the United States of America and the Soviet Union have appreciated this policy of non-alignment and peaceful co-existence, even though they cannot adopt it for themselves because of their fear of each other . . . While some individuals in either group of countries may think and behave like war-mongers, the fact is that most countries or nearly all, including the leaders of the two blocs, do not want a war and would welcome some peaceful arrangement. The hunger for disarmament is itself witness of this urge.'

In Nehru's view, to this 'desire for peace and co-existence there is one major exception, and that is China ... It believes in the inevitability of war and, therefore, does not want the tensions in the world to lessen. It dislikes non-alignment and it would much rather have a clear polarization of the different countries in the world. It is not afraid even of a nuclear war because as it is often said, they can afford to lose a few hundred million people and yet have enough numbers left.'

China, claimed Nehru, was upset with 'Russia's softening down, in its opinion, in revolutionary ardour and its thinking of peace and peaceful co-existence ...' In recent years, this difference in opinion had led Russia to withdraw economic support to China. To make matters worse, Russia had even offered technical aid to India. Nehru wrote that

It was possible for China to fall into line with Russian thinking and present policy, and thus perhaps get more aid. But they are too proud to do this and trained too much in the old revolutionary tradition to accept defeat in this matter. What else then could they do? The other course was to heighten tensions in the world and to make non-alignment and peaceful co-existence more and more difficult to maintain ... India was said to be the chief non-aligned country in the world, and a country which constantly preached the virtues of peaceful co-existence. If India could be humiliated and defeated and perhaps even driven into the other camp of the Western Powers, that would be the end of non-alignment for other countries also, and Russia's policy would have been broken down. The cold war would be at its fiercest and Russia would be compelled then to help China to a much greater degree and to withdraw help from the nations that did not side with it completely in the cold war.

If this reasoning is correct [continued Nehru], then India became the stumbling block to China in the furtherance of its wider policy. The removal of India as a power which has become an obstacle in the way of China becoming a great power, became the primary objective of Chinese policy, and the elimination of non-alignment became particularly important from China's viewpoint. China wanted to show that Soviet policy was wrong. If this could be demonstrated then the Communist countries and those that followed them would veer round to the Chinese point of view and a hegemony of that bloc would be created. At the same time, the Asian and African countries would have to choose one way or the other. Many of them would be frightened of China. In this state of affairs, China would get much more help from the Soviet and allied countries and her industrialization would proceed more rapidly. If war comes, well and good. If it does not come, the strength of the Communist and allied bloc would grow and there would be interdependence of [the] Soviet Union and China.

This then was Nehru's explanation for the war—that China hoped by its actions to thrust India into the American camp, and thus restore the clear, sharp boundaries that once separated the Russian bloc of nations from the American one, boundaries that however had become blurred and porous owing to the success of the Indian, or more specifically, Nehruvian, idea of non-alignment.

VI

I now move on to an analysis of how Indians, then and now, have written or spoken of Jawaharlal Nehru's policies vis-à-vis the Chinese. There have been three distinct views on the subject. The first is empathetic. Affirmed by Nehruvians, supporters of the Congress party, and a large swathe of the middle-aged middle class, this holds Nehru to be a good and decent man betrayed by perfidious communists.

This point of view finds literary illustration in a novel by Rukun Advani called *Beethoven among the Cows*. A chapter entitled 'Nehru's Children' is set in 1962, 'the year the Chinese invaded India, a little before Nehru died of a broken heart'. The action, set in the northern Indian town of Lucknow (a town Nehru knew well, and visited often) takes place just before the war, when much sabre-rattling was going on. The people in Lucknow were spouting couplets 'shot through with Nehru's Shellyean idealism on the socialist Brotherhood of Man' (a brotherhood now being violated by the perfidious Chinese). Drawing on his childhood memories, the novelist composed four couplets that reflect the mood of the times. Here they are, in Hindi:

Jaisé dood aur malai, Hindi–Chini bhai bhai
Hosh mé ao, hosh mé ao, Chou, Mao, hosh mé ao.

Jaisé noodle, vaisé pulao, Nehru saath chowmein khao
Chou, Mao, hosh mé ao, hosh mé ao aur chowmein khao.

Haath milao, gaal milao, Nehru saath haath milao
Chou, Mao, hosh mé ao, hosh mé ao aur haath milao.

Dono bhai Chou, Mao, Nehru saath baith jao
Baith jao aur chowmein khao, Chou, Mao, hosh mé ao.

I will not attempt here a literal translation of the couplets, but content myself with the one-line summary of the novelist, which is that these verses 'asked the Chinese leaders to shake hands with Nehru, eat chowmein with him, and generally come to their senses'.

The second view, opposed to the first, is contemptuous of Nehru. It sees him as a foolish and vain man who betrayed the nation by encouraging China in its aggressive designs on the sacred soil of India. This viewpoint is associated with ideologues of the Hindu right, speaking for organizations such as the Rashtriya Swayamsevak Sangh and the Jana Sangh, forerunner of the Bharatiya Janata Party. In the 1960s, the RSS chief M.S. Golwalkar wrote witheringly that 'the slogans and paper compromise like "peaceful co-existence" and "Panchsheel" that our leaders are indulging in only serve as a camouflage for the self-seeking predatory countries of the world to pursue their own ulterior motives against our country. China, as we know, was most vociferous in its expression of faith in Panchsheel. China was extolled as our great neighbour and friend for the last two thousand years or more from the day it accepted Buddhism. Our leaders declared that they were determined to stick to China's friendship "at all costs" . . . How much it has cost us in terms of our national integrity and honour is all too well known.'

Writing in 1998, the journalist M.V. Kamath named names. Saluting the nuclear tests overseen by the BJP, he recalled the 'time, under Jawaharlal Nehru and V.K. Krishna Menon when a decision must have been taken not to engage in a "debilitating and criminally wasteful arms race"; it was very noble of the two gentlemen who taught us to sing Hindi–Chini-bhai–bhai in chorus. For our efforts China kicked us in the teeth.'

Kamath was writing decades after the conflict, but a contemporary expression of this point of view can be found in the writings of Deen Dayal Upadhyaya, the leading ideologue of the BJP's mother party, the Jana Sangh. When the first clashes broke out on the border in September 1959, Upadhyaya argued that 'the present situation is the result of complacency on the part of the Prime Minister. It seems that he was reluctant to take any action till the situation became really grave.' The Jana Sangh leader complained that Nehru had 'more faith in his Panch Sheel perorations than in preparation and performance'. The prime minister was compared to the notoriously incompetent nineteenth-century ruler of Awadh, Wajid Ali Shah. 'Only he [Nehru] knows when a crisis is not a crisis,' wrote Upadhyaya sarcastically; only Nehru knew 'how to emit smoke without fire and how to arrest a conflagration in a Niagara of verbiage!'

Week after week, Upadhyaya excoriated Nehru's China policy in the pages of the RSS journal, *Organiser*. 'As usual the Prime Minister has exhibited his temperamental weakness in dealing with the issue of Chinese aggression,' he remarked. 'Why can't he [the Prime Minister]—with equal justification, and more justice—accept Tibet's case [over China's], which is also in our national interest? What native impotence makes him willing to strike but afraid to wound? What confuses him into subverting all three aims of his Northern policy by his single misunderstanding of the position of Tibet? Is it plain ignorance? Is it simple cowardice? Or is it a simple national policy induced by military weakness, ideological ambiguities and weakening of nationalism?'

Upadhyaya accused Nehru of showing little serious intent in acting upon border transgressions by the Chinese. 'While on the one hand, he [Nehru] had been declaring that India was firm in her stand, on the other he counselled forbearance in the Lok Sabha, saying that there were limits to firmness also. Of course there are

limits to everything, but unfortunately the Prime Minister's limits
are set to startling points.'

The prime minister's attitude to China, concluded Upadhyaya,
was 'characteristic of his weak and timid nature'.

The argument that India's first prime minister was pusillanimous
with regard to China was also articulated by that obsessive critic of
all that Nehru stood for, the brilliant socialist thinker Ram Manohar
Lohia. In a speech in Hyderabad in October 1959, Lohia asked
Nehru and his government 'to take back the territory the Chinese
have captured by whatever means it thinks fit . . . Increase the
country's strength and might,' he thundered; 'then alone China's
challenge can be met.' Then, when Zhou Enlai visited Delhi in
April 1960 and was met with a hostile demonstration organized by
the Jana Sangh, Lohia said that 'if any one deserves a black flag
demonstration, it is no one else but Mr. Nehru for extending an
invitation to an outright aggressor'.

The third view of Nehru's attitude to Chinese claims was perhaps
the most interesting. Exuding pity rather than contempt, this held
Nehru to be a naïve man misled by malign advisers and by his own
idealism. Responding to the border clashes in the second half of
1959, C. Rajagopalachari wrote several essays urging Nehru to
abandon his long held and deeply cherished policy of non-alignment.
'Rajaji' had once been a colleague of Nehru in party and government.
Now, however, he was a political rival, as the founder of the
Swatantra Party.

In the realm of domestic policy, Rajaji and the Swatantra Party
which he headed criticized Nehru for his hostility to the market. In
the realm of foreign policy, they deplored his reluctance to identify
more closely with the western bloc of nations, led by the United
States. The growing tension between India and China provided, in
Rajaji's view, one more reason to abandon non-alignment. The
change in creed, he said, was made necessary by the fact that 'one
of the nations engaged in the cold war makes aggression on an
uninvolved nation . . .' 'The path of peace,' wrote this other and
equally remarkable disciple of Gandhi in the first week of December

1959, is 'not always smooth. China has incontinently betrayed India and Nehru. He dare not resist Indian public resentment over China's aggression and her attempt to sabotage India's position in the Himalayan frontier. Whatever be China's objective, this aggression and show of power have put an end to any meaning in non-alignment.'

Rajaji sympathized with Nehru's desire to avoid full-scale war, which lay behind his reconciling attitude to the Chinese. Nor had he any illusions about the western powers, whose policies reflected a general unwillingness to accommodate the aspirations of the post-colonial world. Still, the border conflict had, wrote Rajaji in the last week of December 1959, called for 'a complete revision of our attitude and activities in respect of foreign policy'. With China backed by the Soviet Union, India had no alternative but to seek support from the western powers. Rajaji found justification for this tilt in a verse of the ancient Tamil classic, the Kural of Tiruvalluvar, which, in his translation, read: 'You have no allies. You are faced with two enemies. Make it up with one of them and make of him a good ally.'

In May 1960, after Zhou Enlai had come and gone, and Nehru himself had begun making noises about standing firm, Rajaji warned that it would be a mistake to seek to unilaterally evacuate the Chinese forces from the thousands of square miles of territory it controlled which were claimed by India. 'Our armed forces can be used against this trespass,' he wrote, 'but no one can guarantee the localisation of conflict. It would be foolish to start an operation knowing fully well that it would be a leap in the dark. The only legitimate and wise course is to drop the isolationist policy which we have been hugging to our bosom, and get into closer bonds of alliance with the World Powers that are ranged against Communism.' There was, he said, 'no other way, and so it must be followed, for the rehabilitation of India's prestige and gathering of moral power against the aggressor.'

There were, of course, points of overlap between the positions articulated by Rajaji, Deen Dayal Upadhyaya and Lohia. This is not surprising, since all were opponents of Jawaharlal Nehru and the ruling Congress party. However, there were also points of divergence. Rajaji more clearly recognized that India did not have the military might to combat, still less overcome, the Chinese. Hindu ideologues like Upadhyaya suggested that India's deficiencies in this regard could be made up by a mobilization of militantly spiritual energy; while socialists like Lohia thought that the gap could be filled by collective social action. Rajaji could see, however, that it was not merely a failure of nerve, but of capacity, which could be remedied only through the forging of a new strategic alliance, with the West.

VII

First articulated in the late 1950s, the three views outlined above found powerful expression in the immediate aftermath of the war. A debate in Parliament in November 1962 saw many members express solidarity with the prime minister. India's leader had been betrayed, and it was time to close ranks and stand behind him. The debate ended with a resolution affirming 'the firm resolve of the Indian people to drive off the aggressor from the sacred soil of India however long and hard this struggle may be'.

Ordinary citizens also rallied around Nehru, with young men lining up outside army recruitment centres and young women donating their jewels to the National Defence Fund. 'Letters to the editor' urged Opposition leaders to forget past differences and work in cooperation with the prime minister.

In the first weeks of the war, when it became clear that the Chinese advance had not and could not be stopped, there was much criticism of the defence minister, V.K. Krishna Menon. Menon was not new to controversy; in April 1961, in a polemic described at the time as 'perhaps the greatest speech that has been made on the floor of [the Indian Parliament] since Independence', J.B. Kripalani had attacked Krishna Menon for having 'created cliques [and] lowered the morale of our [armed] forces', by promoting incompetent officers congenial to 'his political and ideological purpose'. Now, with the Indian defences disintegrating, there were loud calls for Menon to resign.

These criticisms usually stopped short of attacking Nehru himself. The respected editor of the *Indian Express*, Frank Moraes, wrote that it was 'the Defence Minister who is most culpable for the deficiency of arms'. The lack of preparedness of the army under his leadership now made Menon look 'like Cardinal Wolsey, left naked to his friends and enemies'. The readers of the newspaper agreed. The defence minister, said one G.R. Subbu, 'should make room for another man. All our Defence losses spring from the policies of Mr Krishna Menon.' When the prime minister at first resisted the calls for Menon's head, Frank Moraes offered a very muted criticism of Nehru himself, remarking that 'the Prime Minister's loyalty to his colleagues is commendable provided it is not pushed to a point where it endangers the safety and unity of the country'.

A rare personal attack on Nehru came from N.G. Ranga of the Swatantra Party. Speaking in Parliament in the third week of November 1962, he noted that 'the Prime Minister has also been good enough to make a number of admissions in regard to the failure of his dreams [as regards Asian solidarity]. We all dream, true. And our dreams do not come true. That is also true. But, at the same time it is very dangerous to go on dreaming and dreaming for years and years and over such a terrific crisis and problem as this with the result that not only our people but also people abroad have had to wonder how this country's leadership has been guiding our people with all this atmosphere of dreaming.'

The three views of Nehru and China analysed above first became visible in the period 1959–62, as the border dispute was revealed to be serious, and as it resulted in war. These views have each been held and articulated these past fifty years, by politicians and by ordinary citizens alike. The first, empathetic, view, was probably dominant in the aftermath of the 1962 war. The second, contemptuous, view, has become more widespread in recent years, with the rise to political salience of the BJP and its ideology of Hindutva. The third, pitying, view, was energetically articulated in the 1950s and 1960s by Rajaji and some other associates of Nehru in the freedom movement (such as Acharya Kripalani, Jayaprakash Narayan and Minoo Masani). It may be now enjoying a sort of after-life, in the form of the argument, now quite common in the press and in policy circles in New Delhi, that India must actively pursue closer military and economic ties with the United States to thwart and combat an assertive China.

VIII

In retrospect, it is evident that in the years between the invasion of Tibet in 1950 and the war of 1962, Jawaharlal Nehru made a series of miscalculations in his dealings with China. These errors were of two kinds. The first were personal—his faith in officials who gave him wrong or foolish advice, or who executed the jobs assigned to them with carelessness or lack of foresight. Two men in particular appear to have been unworthy of his trust: the intelligence officer, B.N. Mullick, who advised Nehru to sanction the provocative forward posts; and Krishna Menon, who as defence minister refused to properly arm the military, and who promoted incompetent generals and otherwise damaged the morale of the armed forces.

A second set of miscalculations were political, namely, his ignorance or underestimation of the ideological dimensions of Chinese politics. Nehru did not, or could not, see beyond the professions of internationalism and Asian solidarity; had he done so, he would have more properly understood the reservations the Chinese had about the McMahon Line, and their irritation, and then anger, that India stood by an 'imperialist' demarcation that silently legitimized the case for Tibetan independence from China.

Nehru's mistakes were considerable; however, beyond the merely personal, there were important structural and conjunctural reasons behind the clash of armies and national egos between India and China. If Jawaharlal Nehru had not been prime minister, there would still have been a border dispute between India and China. Indeed, all other things remaining constant, India and China may still have gone to war had Jawaharlal Nehru never lived.

The most consequential question that divided the two countries concerned the status and future of Tibet. The Tibet factor in India–China relations had three dimensions—which we may gloss as the long-term dimension, the medium-term dimension and the short-term dimension respectively.

The long-term dimension had its origins in a conference held in 1913 in the British imperial summer capital, Simla. This was convened by the Government of India, and attended also by Chinese and Tibetan representatives (Tibet was then enjoying a period of substantial, indeed near-complete political autonomy from Chinese overlordship). A product of this conference was the McMahon Line, which sought to demarcate the frontiers of British India.

When India became independent in 1947 it recognized the McMahon Line, and adopted it as its own. The Chinese however had serious reservations about this Line, which intensified after the Communists came to power in 1950. The Chinese government said the border had been imposed by the British at a time when they were powerless; besides, they did not recognize that Tibet had a right to send a separate delegation of its own. All through the 1950s, while India insisted on the sanctity of the McMahon Line, the Chinese said that since it was a legacy of imperialism, the border question had to be negotiated afresh and a new boundary decided upon.

The medium-term dimension related to the Chinese invasion and occupation of Tibet in 1950. So long as it was semi-independent, Tibet served as a buffer state for India. Besides, there were close and continuing connections between India and Tibet, as in an active cross-border trade, and regular visits of Hindu pilgrims to the holy mountain of Kailas. There were thus strategic as well as sentimental reasons for India to be concerned about what, from their point of view, was an excessive Chinese presence in Tibet after 1950.

The short-term dimension was the flight of the Dalai Lama into India in the spring of 1959. That he was given refuge the Chinese government could perhaps accept; that he was treated as an honoured visitor, and that a steady stream of influential Indians queued up to meet him, they could not abide. What upset them most was the mobilization of anti-Chinese and pro-Tibetan sentiment by the Opposition parties in India.

Nehru could have perhaps been less trusting of the Chinese in the early 1950s. But he could scarcely have gone to war on the Tibetans' behalf. India was newly independent; it was a poor and divided country. There were a clutch of domestic problems to attend to, among them the cultivation of a spirit of national unity, the promotion of economic development, and the nurturing of democratic institutions. War would have set back these efforts by decades. It would have led to political instability, and economic privation.

After the Dalai Lama fled into India, the balancing act became more delicate still. Nehru could scarcely hand him back to the Chinese. Nor could be keep him imprisoned and isolated. The exiled leader had to be provided refuge, consistent with his dignity and stature. In a democracy that encouraged debate, and in a culture that venerated spiritual leaders, the Dalai Lama would attract visitors, who would make public their admiration for him and their distaste for his persecutors. Nehru could hardly put a stop to this; nor, on the other hand, could he use the situation of the Dalai Lama to wag a threatening finger at the Chinese.

The open manifestation of support for the Tibetans and their leader brings us to the second structural reason behind the failure to solve the border dispute—the fact that China was a one-party state and India a multiparty democracy. When, on his visit to New Delhi in 1960, Zhou Enlai complained about the protection afforded to the Dalai Lama, the senior Cabinet Minister Morarji Desai compared the status of the Tibetan leader to that of Karl Marx, who was given sanctuary by the British after he was exiled from his native Germany.

This, perhaps, was a debating point—and Morarji Desai was a skilled debater—but the fact that the two political regimes differed so radically had a powerful bearing on the dispute. Thus, when a group of anti-Communist protesters raised Free Tibet slogans and defaced a portrait of Mao outside the Chinese consulate in Mumbai,

Beijing wrote to New Delhi that this was 'a huge insult to the head of state of the People's Republic of China and the respected and beloved leader of the Chinese people', an insult which 'the masses of the six hundred and fifty million Chinese people absolutely cannot tolerate'. If the matter was 'not reasonably settled', the complaint continued, the 'Chinese side will never come to a stop without a satisfactory settlement of the matter, that is to say, never stop even for one hundred years'.

In its reply, the Indian government accepted that the incident was 'deplorable'. But it pointed out that 'under the law in India processions cannot be banned so long as they are peaceful ... Not unoften they are held even near the Parliament House and the processionists indulge in all manner of slogans against high personages in India. Incidents have occurred in the past when portraits of Mahatma Gandhi and the Prime Minister were taken out by irresponsible persons and treated in an insulting manner. Under the law and Constitution of India a great deal of latitude is allowed to the people so long as they do not indulge in actual violence.'

That one state was totalitarian and the other democratic had a critical impact on how the debate was framed, on why it escalated, and why it could not be resolved. After the border clashes of 1959, Opposition MPs asked that the official correspondence between the two countries be placed in the public domain. The demand was conceded, whereupon the evidence of Chinese claims further inflamed and angered public opinion. Now Zhou arrived in Delhi, with his offer of a quid pro quo. You overlook our transgressions in the west, said the Chinese leader, and we shall overlook your transgressions in the east.

In a dictatorship, such as China, a policy once decided upon by its top leaders did not require the endorsement of anyone else. In India, however, treaties with other nations had to be discussed and debated by Parliament. In purely instrumental terms, Zhou's proposal was both pragmatic and practicable. However, Nehru could not implement the agreement on its own; he had to discuss it with his colleagues in party and government, and, pending their acceptance, place it on the floor of the House, with the ensuing debates reported and widely discussed in the newspapers.

Cabinet, Parliament, and public opinion were three facets of social and political life in India, that were wholly absent in China. Mao and Zhou did not have to contend with these facets or forces, whereas Nehru was confined and circumscribed by them. Thus, knowledge of Chinese maps that made claims that clashed with India's, knowledge of a Chinese road on land claimed by India, knowledge of Indian soldiers killed by Chinese soldiers, knowledge of the persecution of supporters of the Dalai Lama—all this led to a rising tide of nationalist outrage inside and outside Parliament. And with members of his own Cabinet firmly opposed to a settlement, Nehru had no chance of seeing it through.

IX

Behind the border dispute lay the respective national and civilizational aspirations of the two countries. Now, in 2012, with surging growth rates and sixty years of independent development behind them, China and India seek great power status. In the 1950s, however, they sought something apparently less ambitious but which, in the context of their recent colonial history, was as important, namely a respect in the eyes of the world comparable with their size, the antiquity of their civilization, and the distinctiveness of their national revolution.

Towards the end of 1959, after the first clashes on the border, and the arrival into India of the Dalai Lama, Jawaharlal Nehru was interviewed by the American journalist Edgar Snow. In Snow's recollection, Nehru told him that 'the basic reason for the Sino-Indian dispute was that they were both "new nations", in that both were newly independent and under dynamic nationalistic leaderships, and in a sense were meeting at their "frontiers" for the first time in history; hence it was natural that a certain degree of conflict should be generated before they could stabilize their frontiers.' Nehru added that in the past there were 'buffer zones' between the two countries/civilizations, but now India and China were 'filling out, and meeting [for the first time] as modern nations on the borders'.

Nehru was speaking here not as a politician—whether pragmatic or idealist—but as a student of history. In this, more detached, role, he could see that a clash of arms, and of ideologies and aspirations behind it, was written into the logic of the respective and collective histories of India and China.

X

In 1961, when relations between the two countries had more or less broken down, India withdrew its ambassador to Beijing. China did likewise. For the next fifteen years, the two countries ran skeletal offices in each other's capital. Finally, in 1976, full diplomatic relations were resumed. In the same year Mao Zedong died.

Deng Xiaoping, who emerged as the most important leader in China soon after Mao's death, wished to overcome the baggage of 1962, and set relations between the two countries on a new footing. In the early 1980s, he invited Prime Minister Indira Gandhi to visit Beijing. Serving diplomats were sympathetic, but Mrs Gandhi's foreign policy advisor—who had been the last ambassador in Beijing before the war—rejected the proposal, saying that the Chinese could never be trusted. 'They killed her father', were the words he used, when the gist of Deng's invitation was conveyed to him.

After Nehru's grandson, Rajiv Gandhi, took over as prime minister of India, the invitation was renewed. In December 1988, Rajiv Gandhi visited China, the first Indian leader of any substance to do so for more than thirty years. He had a ninety-minute meeting with Deng, who is said to have told him, 'You are the young. You are the future.'

In a public speech in Beijing, Rajiv Gandhi remarked that 'it is now time to look beyond the past; it is now time to look forward to the future. It is now time to restore the relationship between our countries to a level commensurate with the contribution which

our civilizations made to the world, to a level commensurate with
the centuries of friendship between our two countries, to a level
commensurate with the contribution which today we must take
together to the building of a new world order. Between us, we
represent a third of humanity. There is much we can do together.'

The sentiments were Nehruvian, and indeed, the speech was most
likely drafted by two scholars who had watched Nehru work
firsthand. However, Rajiv Gandhi's hopefulness was called into
question by some Indian commentators. A columnist in the *Statesman*
noted that the territorial disputes between the two countries
remained unresolved. These were, he said, 'the strongest and
certainly the most important element in the connection between the
two countries'. He chastised 'the myth-makers, the political pundits,
the fashionable fellow-travellers, [and] the fervent promoters of
Pan-Asianism' for 'working overtime to build up the case for
friendship in disregard to the border . . .'

This scepticism was also expressed in a letter to *The Hindu* from
K. Vedamurthy, who had been a close associate of Nehru's
colleague-turned-critic, Rajaji. He recalled the debacle of 1962, and
noted also that China had seamlessly moved from being pro-Soviet
to being pro-American when it suited them. 'We in India,' wrote
Vedamurthy, 'should not be once again caught in any euphoria of
the kind in which we were when Pandit Nehru returned to Delhi
from his apparent triumph in the Bandung Conference [of non-
aligned nations] of the '50s. By all means let us repair our relations
. . . but let us also remember that what governs international
relations is the enlightened self-interest of the countries concerned
and not any ideology . . . Eternal vigilance, as always, remains the
price of liberty.'

Three years after Rajiv Gandhi visited Beijing, the Indian economy
opened itself out to the world. At first, the growing international
trade was chiefly with the West and the Middle East. Slowly,
Chinese goods began to enter the Indian market, and vice versa.

In 2003, another Indian prime minister visited Beijing. This was
Atal Bihari Vajpayee, who, as a young, right-wing, pro-American

member of Parliament in the late 1950s, had regularly attacked Jawaharlal Nehru for being too trusting of the Chinese. Now, Vajpayee signed a document accepting that Tibet was an integral part of China.

Two years later, the Chinese prime minister, Wen Jiabao, came to India. He chose first to come to Bangalore, the centre of the software industry, going later to the political capital, New Delhi. Seconding (or perhaps explaining) the sequence, the Chinese ambassador in New Delhi said in a press conference that 'the "B" of business is more important than the "B" of boundary'.

The most recent figures estimate the annual trade between China and India at $60 billion, up from roughly zero in the 1990s. India exports iron ore and cotton to China, and imports heavy machinery and electronics in return. Indian software and pharmaceutical firms seek a share of the Chinese market; Chinese companies think that they are best placed to build the highways, bridges and ports that India so urgently requires.

Still, despite the steady increase in trade, and the rhetoric that sometimes accompanies it, the 'B' of boundary disputes has not entirely gone away. Every now and then, Chinese newspapers claim the eastern state of Arunachal Pradesh to be their territory. In 2009, when the Dalai Lama sought to visit the ancient Buddhist monastery in Tawang—which lies deep inside Arunachal—Beijing demanded that the Government of India stop him. New Delhi declined to interfere—the Dalai Lama, they said, was a spiritual leader who was going on a spiritual pilgrimage. Pressing their case, the Chinese have since refused to issue visas to residents of Arunachal Pradesh, as to do so would be to recognize it as being part of India.

On the Indian side, suspicions linger about Chinese intentions. Among the Hindu right-wing and some sections of the military, there is talk of Chinese attempts to throw a 'string of pearls' to encircle India, by building and then controlling ports in Gwadar in Pakistan, Hambantota in Sri Lanka, Chittagong in Bangladesh, and Kyaukphyu in Myanmar. China's consistent support to Pakistan (long a haven for terrorists who have regularly attacked India) is also a sore point in the relationship.

China and India are not the deadly enemies they were between 1959 and 1962; nor are they the close and intimate friends that, back in the 1940s and early 1950s, Jawaharlal Nehru had hoped they would be. The border dispute remains unresolved; and so it will be for some time. After denouncing the McMahon Line for so long, the Chinese cannot suddenly turn around and accept it; while any significant concessions from the Indian side will have to be discussed in Parliament, to be subjected to, and very likely rejected by, an always contentious Opposition. Meanwhile, the presence of a large and vocal Tibetan community in India still irks the Chinese; as does the steady popularity the Dalai Lama enjoys within India and across the world.

XI

There is a noticeable asymmetry in the ways in which the war of 1962 is viewed in the two countries that fought it. The Indian sense of humiliation, so visible in some circles even five decades later, is not matched by a comparable triumphalism in China. This may be because the Chinese fought far bloodier wars against Japan, and among themselves. At any rate, while histories of modern India devote pages and pages to the conflict (my own *India after Gandhi* has two chapters on the subject), histories of modern China (such as those written by Jonathan Fenby, Jonathan Spence, and others) devote at most a few paragraphs to it. Likewise, the conflict with India merits barely a passing reference in biographies of Mao or Zhou, whereas the conflict with China occupies a dominant place in biographies of Nehru.

This asymmetry is also in part a product of the fact that while Nehru wrote a great deal about how he saw China, his counterparts in Beijing did not leave behind books or essays that speak about India. Meeting Mao Zedong in the 1930s, Edgar Snow told him about Gandhi and his non-violent movement for freedom, without evoking much interest. Mao's collected works hardly refer to India at all. From Zhou Enlai's statements on the border dispute we get a sense of the great stress he laid on the antiquity of the Chinese civilization. But of his impressions and opinions of the other great Asian civilization we get no hint.

In the popular imagination, Nehru's place in history is assessed principally across three axes—his role in the independence movement; his economic policy; and his foreign policy in general but with particular reference to China. With regard to the first he is generally judged a hero. With regard to the second the judgement has varied across time—once celebrated for forging an autonomous path of economic development, Nehru has more recently been demonized for shackling the forces of individual enterprise and innovation. (However, with the global financial crisis and the growth of crony capitalism within India, Nehru's economic record may yet be regarded in less dark terms.) With regard to the third, the verdicts are less ambiguous. Most Indians now believe that Nehru betrayed the country's interests in his dealings with China.

This essay has sought to qualify and nuance that judgement. For, Nehru was not as much in control of these events as commonly supposed. The border conflict had deep structural roots, and was made more intractable by contingent factors such as the Tibet question and the different, and in a sense rival, political regimes in the two countries. At the same time, the massive emotional investment of Indians in the defeat of 1962 is also not commensurate with the event itself. A mere 3,000 soldiers died on the battlefield, far fewer than Indian casualties in the two World Wars, and a trivial number compared with the loss of life that accompanied the Partition of India. It was really a skirmish rather than a war. Nor did it really change the facts on the ground, since the Chinese withdrew to where they were before the battle began.

The border dispute, the question of Tibet, and the difference between the two countries' political systems—these remain, to influence and determine India–China relations in 2012, as they did in 1952 or 1962. Such is the argument of the historian, based (he thinks) on a dispassionate analysis of both evidence and context. But while the historian may document, and contextualize, the conventional wisdom will most likely remain impervious to his

work. Citizens and ideologues shall continue to personalize a
political conflict, seeing it principally through the lens of what
Jawaharlal Nehru did or did not do, or is believed to have done and
not done, with regard to China. Neglecting the deeper structural
forces that underlay the conflict, neglecting also the lack of foresight
or preparedness of other arms of government—the bureaucracy and
army among them—Indian public opinion has made the military
defeat of 1962 Nehru's failure alone. Thus the image, so popular
then and now, of an old and broken man taking his defeat to the
cremation ground, an image that may be emotionally satisfying but
which altogether lacks historical plausibility.

I shall end this essay with a verdict on Nehru's China policies that
combines the empathetic, the pitying, and the contemptuous. It was
offered by H.V. Kamath, a former civil servant turned freedom
fighter, who served several terms in Parliament and was jailed both
by the British and during Indira Gandhi's Emergency. In a book
entitled *Last Days of Jawaharlal Nehru*, published in 1977, Kamath
took his readers back to a Parliament session in September 1963,
when he saw 'an old man, looking frail and fatigued, with a marked
stoop in his gait, coming down the gangway opposite with slow,
faltering steps, and clutching the backrests of benches for support as
he descended'. The man was Jawaharlal Nehru, prime minister of
India at this time for the past sixteen years.

As H.V. Kamath watched 'the bent, retreating figure', a cluster of
memories came to his mind. Was this the same man who, while
Kamath was studying at the Presidency College in Madras, he had
seen 'sprightly, slim and erect', speaking at the Congress session of
1927 in that city? The same man who, when he visited him in
Allahabad ten years later, had 'jumped two steps at a time, with me
emulating him, as I followed him upstairs from his office room on
the ground floor to his study and library above?' The same man
who, when they were both members of the Constituent Assembly
of India, during one session 'impulsively ran from his front seat and
literally dragged a recalcitrant member from the podium rebuking
him audibly *yeh Jhansi ki public meeting nahin hai*'? [This is not a public

meeting in Jhansi.] The same man on whom the nationalist poetess, Sarojini Naidu, had 'affectionately conferred the sobriquet "Jack-in-the-box"—a compliment to his restless agility of body and mind'?

Kamath was clear that it was the war with China that was responsible for this deterioration and degradation. As he wrote, 'India's defeat, nay, military debacle in that one-month war not only shattered [Nehru] physically and weakened him mentally but, what was more galling to him, eroded his prestige in Asia and the world, dealt a crippling blow to his visions of leadership of the newly emancipated nations, and cast a shadow on his place in history.'

It was, the affectionate yet critical observer insisted, a debacle that could have been avoided, had Nehru not 'stubbornly turned a deaf ear to all friendly warnings', offered, for example, by his own deputy prime minister, Vallabhbhai Patel, who, as far back as 1950, had alerted him to 'China's intentions and objectives in invading Tibet, and its dangerous implications for India's future security', and more recently by his old comrades Jayaprakash Narayan and Acharya Kripalani, who had 'cautioned against appeasement and adulation of China'. Kamath himself, after a tour of the India–Tibet border in the summer of 1959, had said publicly that 'Nehru will have to adopt a firmer attitude towards China and her colonisation in Tibet must be exposed and condemned, just as he had criticised European imperialism in the past'. Alas, recalled Kamath twenty years later, Nehru 'pooh-pooh[ed] all criticisms of his China policy but even dubbed the critics as war mongers who were spreading fear and panic in the country'. Thus it was that in 1962, as a consequence of Jawaharlal Nehru's 'supine policy', 'our Jawans, ill-clad, ill-shod, ill-equipped were sent like sheep to their slaughter'.*

---

*Apart from Nehru's major books, cited in the text, the essay draws upon his letters to chief ministers, his interventions in Parliament, and his correspondence with the Chinese government. The quotes from Rajagopalachari come from his articles in the journal *Swarajya*; those from Deen Dayal Upadhyaya from the journal *Organiser*; those from Lohia from collections of his speeches and articles. The account of Zhou Enlai's visit to India draws on contemporary newspapers and on a file in the P.N. Haksar Papers in the Nehru Memorial Museum and Library. The account of Rajiv Gandhi's trip to China draws on reports in the Indian press.

chapter nine

THE BEAUTY OF COMPROMISE

~

The fundamental principle that governs—or ought to govern—human affairs, if we wish to avoid misunderstandings, conflicts, or pointless utopias, is negotiation.

—Umberto Eco

I

Over the past few decades, the nation states of South Asia have been home to some of the most bitter conflicts of the modern world. Women have opposed the domination of men; subaltern classes have resisted the hegemony of the elite; regions on the periphery have protested exploitation by the centre. To class and gender and geography have been added the fault lines of language, caste, religion and ethnicity.

No region of the world—not even the fabled Balkans—has had a greater variety of conflicts within it. South Asians are an expressive people, who have expressed their myriad resentments in a diversity of ways—through electing legislators of their choosing; through court petitions and other legal mechanisms at their command; through marches, *gheraos*, *dharnas*, hunger strikes and other forms of non-violent protest; through the burning of government buildings; and through outright armed rebellion.

The record of our nation states in dealing with these conflicts is decidedly mixed. Some conflicts, which once threatened to tear a nation apart, have, in the end, been resolved. Other conflicts have persisted for decades, with the animosities between the contending parties deepening further with every passing year.

From this vast repertoire of experience within South Asia, this essay will foreground some of the more intractable of these conflicts. I will analyse, among others, the Kashmir dispute and the Naga insurgency in India, and the rebellion of the Tamils in Sri Lanka. I will argue that these conflicts persisted for so long because of the inflexibility and, dare I say, dogmatism of the contending parties. The question I pose here is this: Could a middle path of accommodation and reconciliation, adopted by either party to a conflict or both, have helped in reducing or mitigating the suffering and the violence?

II

In search of an answer to this question, let me first turn to some forgotten episodes in the career of a man who might be considered a paradigmatic South Asian, Jayaprakash Narayan (JP). Narayan was an Indian patriot, but he retained close links with the republican struggle in Nepal as well as the socialist movement in Sri Lanka. He worked actively for conciliation between India and Pakistan. And he was an early supporter of the rights of the Tibetan people.

Within India, JP is celebrated for his role in two major movements: the Quit India struggle of 1942, and the 'Indira Hatao' movement of 1974–75. During Quit India, JP achieved countrywide renown for his daring escape from Hazaribagh jail, after which he spent more than a year underground, eluding the colonial police. The movement of 1974–75 was, of course, led and directed by him. Starting in his native Bihar, it soon became an all-India struggle against the corrupt and tyrannical regime of Prime Minister Indira Gandhi.

Both those struggles saw Jayaprakash Narayan in, as it were, an uncompromising mode. In 1942, he was a charismatic young leftist, who sought to throw out the British and help rebuild India on socialist lines. In 1974–75 he was a charismatic old radical, who sought to throw out Indira Gandhi and bring about a 'Total Revolution' in India.

Thirty years after his death, JP is still remembered for his part in the upheavals of 1942 and 1974–75. What is now forgotten is his equally interesting and, in my view, even more noble work in the decade of the 1960s, when he tried heroically—if, in the end, unavailingly—to resolve the two civil conflicts that have plagued the Indian nation state since its inception. These conflicts were at either end of the Indian Himalaya—namely, Kashmir and Nagaland.

Among the politicians and social workers of mainland India, Narayan spoke out longest and loudest against the illegalities of the Union government in Kashmir. He was a close friend of the popular Kashmiri leader Sheikh Abdullah, who was jailed by the Indian government in 1953. JP called repeatedly for the release of Sheikh Abdullah, and when the Sheikh was finally set free in April 1964, encouraged the idea of sending him over to Pakistan as an emissary for peace. That idea, originally, was that of Prime Minister Jawaharlal Nehru. However, it was opposed across the political spectrum, by the Jana Sangh on the right as well as by the Communists on the left. Even the majority of Nehru's own Congress party thought that the Sheikh should have remained in confinement.

Bucking the jingoist trend, two men of conspicuous independence supported Jawaharlal Nehru's initiative despite being, on other matters, fierce critics of the prime minister's policies. One was C. Rajagopalachari; the other, Jayaprakash Narayan. When some Cabinet ministers threatened to put the Sheikh back in jail, JP wrote that 'it is remarkable how the freedom fighters of yesterday begin so easily to imitate the language of the imperialists'.

Nehru died in May 1964; the peace initiative died with him. The next year Sheikh Abdullah was placed under arrest once more. In June 1966, Narayan wrote an extraordinary letter to Prime Minister

Indira Gandhi asking that the Sheikh be freed in time for the next elections, due at the beginning of 1967. To 'hold a general election in Kashmir with Sheikh Abdullah in prison', remarked Narayan, 'is like the British ordering an election in India while Jawaharlal Nehru was in prison. No fair-minded person would call it a fair election.' If 'we miss the chance of using the next general election to win the consent of the [Kashmiri] people to their place within the Union', continued JP, 'I cannot see what other device will be left to India to settle the problem. To think that we will eventually wear down the people and force them to accept at least passively the Union is to delude ourselves. That might conceivably have happened had Kashmir not been geographically located where it is. In its present location, and with seething discontent among the people, it would never be left in peace by Pakistan.'

This letter got a brief, non-committal reply in return. It took another eight years for Mrs Gandhi to allow the Sheikh to re-enter politics. When Abdullah was made chief minister of Jammu and Kashmir in February 1975, Narayan welcomed the move (despite being, by now, a bitter opponent of the prime minister). But the concession itself was perhaps eight years too late. For, by then the Sheikh had become reconciled to subservience to New Delhi; and in time was to place the interests of his own family above the interests of the Kashmiri people as a whole. What might have been the fate of Kashmir and the Kashmiris had Mrs Gandhi listened to JP in June 1966, released Sheikh Abdullah, allowed him to contest a free and fair election that he would certainly have won, and then allowed him to run the administration in the best interests of the people themselves?

III

Let me now move away from India, and JP, to a civil conflict in another South Asian nation. In 1967, the rulers in New Delhi were too nervous to allow Sheikh Abdullah to contest a provincial election in Kashmir. Three years later, the rulers in Islamabad permitted a radical Bengali politician to contest a national election. To their great surprise, and shock, his party won a majority. What were they to do now?

Before answering that question, let us briefly rehearse the history of the nation of Pakistan. Created in 1947, it had two wings, these separated by several hundred miles of Indian territory. On his first visit to Dhaka, the governor-general of Pakistan, Mohammed Ali Jinnah, told his Bengali audience that they would have to take to Urdu sooner rather than later. 'Let me make it very clear to you,' said Jinnah, 'that the State Language of Pakistan is going to be Urdu and no other language. Anyone who tries to mislead you is really the enemy of Pakistan. *Without one State language, no nation can remain tied up solidly together and function.*' (emphasis mine)

In 1952, bloody riots broke out in Dhaka after the police fired on a demonstration of students demanding equal status for the Bengali language. (Ever since, the Bengalis have observed the day of the firing—21st February, or Ekushey February—as 'mother language day'.) In 1954, Bangla was recognized as one of the state languages of Pakistan, but the feelings of being discriminated against persisted. The eastern part of the nation provided jute, coal and other valuable commodities, yet government revenues were mostly spent in and on the west. The West Pakistanis, and the Punjabis in particular, dominated the army and the civil services. Bengalis were under-represented in the upper echelons of the diplomatic corps and the judiciary. This being South Asia, there were even complaints of talented East Pakistanis being left out of the national cricket team.

Between 1958 and 1970 Pakistan was under military rule. Towards the end of 1970 General Yahya Khan called for elections. Apparently, the general hoped that the ambitious West Pakistani politician Zulfiqar Ali Bhutto would become prime minister, and allow him to continue as President. But these calculations went awry. The Awami League, led by Sheikh Mujibur Rahman, won 167 out of the 169 seats in the more populous eastern part of the country. The Awami leader had skilfully played on Bengali sentiments of being excluded and discriminated against over the years.

After the elections, Mujib's party had a majority in the new Parliament. Its platform included a federal constitution, in which each wing would manage its social, political and economic affairs, with only defence and foreign relations in the hands of the Centre. (A key feature was that each wing would get to spend the foreign exchange it earned—previously, the gleanings from jute exports had been in the discretionary control of the generals in the west.) The proposals to reform the Constitution were deemed unacceptable by the generals as well as the politicians of West Pakistan. In any case, the self-proclaimed martial Punjabi could not abide the thought of conceding power to the allegedly effete Bengali. Another reason for spurning Mujib was the large presence of Hindus in the professional classes of East Pakistan. As one general put it, if the Awami League came to power, 'the constitution adopted by them will have Hindu iron hand in it'.

Rather than honour the democratic mandate and invite Mujib to take office, Yahya Khan postponed the convening of the National Assembly. (In this he was encouraged and abetted by Bhutto.) The response was a general strike in all of East Pakistan. Now, the Pakistani Army decided to settle the matter by force of arms. But with the Indians choosing to ally with the Bengali dissidents, the task was made much harder than they had anticipated. Eight months of episodic fighting culminated in a full-fledged war in December 1971, which led to the defeat and dismemberment of the nation of Pakistan. But would this still have been a single nation if Yahya and Bhutto had permitted Mujib to take over as prime minister?

In asking this question, I do not mean to turn the clock back, to suggest that the creation of Bangladesh was a mistake. I mean only to highlight how the techniques of suppression, so often used by a state to settle a political conflict, may seek only to intensify and deepen it. The ruling elite of Pakistan was both obdurate and deaf; obdurate in hanging on to its privileges, deaf to the justice of the demands of those who asked merely for their rights as citizens. In this respect, the break-up of Pakistan holds lessons for the other nations of South Asia—not least Bangladesh itself—which seek, not always successfully, to deal judiciously with social and political divisions within their boundaries.

As it happens, the language problem is one issue the Republic of India has successfully resolved. Back in the 1920s, Mahatma Gandhi and the Congress party had promised that when India became independent each major linguistic group would have its own province. However, after 1947 the Congress leaders went back on their promise. India had just been divided on the basis of religion—would not conceding the linguistic demand lead to a further Balkanization? Then, in 1952, a protest fast by a former Congressman named Potti Sriramulu forced New Delhi to agree to the creation of a Telugu-speaking state of Andhra. Other linguistic groups now intensified their claims for states of their own. A States Reorganization Commission was constituted, which in 1956 recommended that the map of India be redrawn to accommodate these demands.

Now, five and a half decades later, it is possible to deem the creation of linguistic states as a success. Once the fear of one's language being suppressed has been removed or allayed, the different linguistic groups have been content to live as part of the larger nation called India. There have been periodic manifestations of chauvinism, as in calls for preferential employment for speakers of the local language, but these protests have not in any way threatened the unity of the country.

In 1956, the year the states of India were reorganized on the basis of language, the Parliament of Sri Lanka (then Ceylon) introduced an Act recognizing Sinhala as the sole official language of the country. This made Sinhala the medium of instruction in all state schools and colleges, in public examinations, and in the courts. The new Act was opposed by the Tamil-speaking minority who lived in the north of the island. 'When you deny me my language,' said one Tamil MP, 'you deny me everything.' 'You are hoping for a divided Ceylon,' warned another, adding: 'Do not fear, I assure you [that you] will have a divided Ceylon.' An Opposition member, himself Sinhala-speaking, predicted that if the government did not change its mind and insisted on the Act being passed, 'two torn little bleeding states might yet arise out of one little state'.

The protests were disregarded. The insecurity of the Tamils was intensified by riots against them in the capital city, Colombo, in 1958. Then, in 1972, Sinhala was confirmed as the official language of the state, and Buddhism added on as the official religion (most Tamils were Hindus or Christians). Now, the Tamil youths became disenchanted by the incremental, parliamentary methods of their elders. In the decade of the 1970s several paramilitary groups were formed, these known by their abbreviations or acronyms, to wit, EROS, PLOTE, ERPLF and, not least, LTTE.

Some Tamils still kept their faith in compromise. However, two events in the early 1980s decidedly put paid to hopes of a peaceful, democratic reconciliation of the linguistic question. The first was the burning, by the Sri Lankan Army, of the great Tamil library in Jaffna in 1981; the second, the anti-Tamil pogrom in Colombo in 1983, this directed by Sinhala politicians. Now the Tamils increasingly took to armed struggle to meet their ends. And so unfolded a quarter-century of civil war that cost tens of thousands of lives and deeply undermined the economic and social development of Sri Lanka.

IV

Having illustrated my thesis with examples from Pakistan and Sri Lanka, let me now return to my own country, and to the compatriot with whom I began my essay. In the decade of the 1960s, Jayaprakash Narayan was concerned not just with an honourable solution in Kashmir, but with the restoration of peace in Nagaland, likewise a most troubled part of the Indian Union. In 1946, a Naga National Council (NNC) had been formed; this was undecided as to whether to join the soon-to-be free India. Then, in the early 1950s, one faction decided to make a compact with New Delhi. The other faction, led by A.Z. Phizo, held out for an independent Naga state. This was not acceptable to India; as a consequence, an armed conflict broke out in the Naga hills, with the Indian Army on one side, and Phizo's guerrillas on the other. The main casualties in this conflict were the villagers caught in between.

Finally, in 1964, after a decade of civil war, a ceasefire was declared between the NNC and the Indian government. A three-member 'peace mission' was formed, consisting of the Anglican missionary Michael Scott, the Gandhian nationalist B.P. Chaliha, and Jayaprakash Narayan. Tragically, the mission collapsed within a year, and the rebels returned to the jungle. It was at this stage that JP wrote an extraordinary if still little-known booklet in Hindi, based on a speech he delivered in Patna on Martyrs Day, 30th January 1965. The booklet is called *Nagaland mein Shanti ka Prayas* (The Attempts to Forge Peace in Nagaland). While ostensibly about a dispute within a single small state of the Union, it is actually a meditation on the meanings of democracy everywhere.

'In the history of every nation,' began JP, 'there have been disagreements among the servants and leaders of the nation. Where democracy prevails, these disagreements are discussed and resolved by democratic means; but where democracy is absent, they are resolved by the use of violence.' However, history teaches us that violence begets counter-violence and, eventually, violence on one's own comrades. Thus 'when disputes arise, past alliances and friendships are forgotten, and allegations of betrayal, traitorous behaviour, etc. are levied on one's opponents'.

JP proceeded to recount the history of the civil war in Nagaland, the recourse to the gun by one side, then by the other, and the brutalities committed by both. Then, in the spirit of his master, Gandhi, he asked each party to recognize and respect the finest traditions of the other. First, he told the Nagas that, among the nations of Asia, India was unusual in having a democratic and federal Constitution. Were the rebels to abandon the dream of independence and settle for autonomy within the Union, all they had to give up control over was the army, foreign affairs, and currency. In every other respect, they would be free to mould their destinies as they pleased.

Narayan recognized the distinctiveness of Naga cultural traditions. While both East and West Pakistan bore the impress of the Indic civilization, 'what we call Indian culture has not made an entry into

Nagaland'. That said, JP thought that the Nagas could not sustain an independent country, what with China, Pakistan and Burma all close by and casting covetous eyes on their territory. Why not join up therefore with a democratic and federal India? When New Delhi could not dominate Bihar or Bengal, how could it dominate Nagaland? Were the rebels to come overground and contest elections, said Narayan, they could give their people the best schools, hospitals, roads and so on.

Towards the end of his lecture, JP turned to educating his Patna audience about the virtues of the Nagas. He was particularly impressed by the vigour of their village councils. Anywhere else in India, he said, to construct an airport the 'government can uproot village upon village', whereas in Nagaland it could not do so without the consent of the local people. He was even more struck by the dignity of labour, and the absence of caste feeling. In matters of cooperative behaviour, said JP, the Nagas could teach a thing or two to the people of India. He gave the example of a magnificent church recently constructed in a village near Mokokchung—with a seating capacity of five thousand, it had been built entirely with local materials and local labour, much of it contributed voluntarily by men with BAs and MAs. Narayan contrasted this with the contempt for manual work among the educated, upper-caste elite of the Indian heartland.

V

The conflicts I have dealt with had their origins in an inflexible state, but were often exacerbated by recalcitrant rebels. If such conflicts are to be successfully resolved, then they require both the state to be flexible, as well as the rebels to be more accommodating. That, certainly, is the lesson to be learnt from the most successful peace negotiations of contemporary times, which led to the demise of apartheid and the birth of a democratic South Africa. Had President de Klerk and his National Party not begun a dialogue with the African National Congress, and had Nelson Mandela and his comrades not turned their backs on the gun, there might yet be a civil conflict raging in that beautiful land.

One notable aspect of the transition in South Africa was that the reconciliation was racial as well as political. The whites handed over power, but did not relinquish their rights as citizens or professionals. The need for black economic advancement was recognized, but it was not pursued in wanton haste. The comparison with neighbouring Zimbabwe is striking. There, the end of settler colonialism was followed by savage retribution, where the whites were forcibly dispossessed of their lands and encouraged—one should rather say coerced—to leave the country. As a result, what was once the bread basket of Africa has become a basket case where scarcity and famine stalk the land.

Looking further west, South Asians may also take heart from the political transition that took place after the fall of the Berlin Wall. Once run with an iron hand from Moscow, countries such as Poland and the Czech Republic have emerged as vigorous democracies. After the hold of the Soviets was loosened—through a process initiated by the visionary Mikhail Gorbachev—the different sections of Polish and Czech society eschewed the politics of revenge and retribution. Instead of turning on one another, Communists and anti-Communists formed political parties of their own and fought elections based on universal adult franchise. Autocrats became democrats, while rebels became governors (most famously, Lech Walesa and Vaclav Havel). Who, in 1960 or even in 1980, would have imagined a transition as painless and productive as this?

South Asians might also profit from a look at the recent history of Ireland. After the Good Friday Agreement, the previously militant Sinn Fein put away their guns and entered the democratic process. The two parts of the island remain under separate sovereignties; however, the ceasefire has permitted a deeper engagement with the democratic process within the Republic of Ireland as well as within Ulster, a free movement of people across the borders, and a sharp diminution of sectarian violence. These changes led to a surge in economic growth, with investments pouring into an island always legendary for its natural beauty, but now known also for being a rule-bound and largely peaceful society. In forging their compromise, the two sides to the Irish conflict gave up pride and prestige, to gain, in exchange, prosperity and peace.

VI

I return now to South Asia, and move on from political conflicts to a celebrated environmental dispute. Consider the controversy over the Sardar Sarovar dam in central India. The benefits of this project flow wholly to one state, Gujarat; whereas the costs are borne disproportionately by another state, Madhya Pradesh. When it is built to its full height, the dam will displace close to 200,000 people, a majority of whom are tribal. From 1989 the oustees have been organized under the banner of the Narmada Bachao Andolan (NBA), whose leader is the remarkable Medha Patkar.

Between 1989 and 1995, the NBA organized a series of *satyagrahas* to stop the construction of the dam. Their struggle won wide appreciation, both for its principled commitment to non-violence and for its ability to mobilize peasants and tribals. By now, several scientific studies had been published calling into question the viability of large dams. These studies adduced environmental arguments—the submergence of scarce forests and wildlife; economic arguments—the fact that high sedimentation rates and soil salinity had greatly diminished the financial returns from such projects; and social arguments—namely, the utter despair and demoralization of the communities whom the dams had rendered homeless.

The struggle and the science notwithstanding, the construction of the Sardar Sarovar dam proceeded. Now, K.J. Joy and Suhas Paranjape, two engineers based in Pune, worked out an innovative compromise. Given that the dam had already come up to a height of about 260 feet, clearly work on it could not be stopped. But its negative effects could be minimized. The Pune engineers advocated a dam smaller than that originally envisaged, but with 'overflow' canals to take water directly to the drought-prone regions of Kutch and Saurashtra. The redesign of the dam would greatly reduce the area to be submerged, yet retain many of the benefits that were to accrue from the dam. The districts in Gujarat most desperately in need of water would get it. At the same time, many fewer families in Madhya Pradesh would be displaced.

Unfortunately, the compromise was rejected both by the Gujarat government and by the NBA. The former insisted that the dam had to be built to its originally sanctioned height of 456 feet. The latter insisted that the dam must be brought down. As the Andolan's slogan went, '*Koi Nahi Hatega! Baandh Nahin Banega!*' (No one will leave their homes, for the dam will not be built.) However, a good chunk of the dam had already been built. Hundreds of tons of concrete had already been poured into its foundations. And thousands of families had already been displaced.

At a meeting in Bangalore in November 2000, I heard the writer Arundhati Roy lead a group of college students in shouting: '*Baandh Nahin Banega, Koi Nahin Hatega!*' This was an act that, to put it politely, was irresponsible. It was also in character, for shortly before this meeting, Ms Roy had written that the half-built dam should be made a museum for failed technologies. However, even as Ms Roy spoke the dam was eighty metres high. Some people were at work building it further upwards, as a consequence of which other people were being displaced. Not however, the college students or their cheerleader, who would move on to make lives of their own while the Sardar Sarovar dam continued to rise.

In retrospect, it must be considered a pity that the NBA did not adopt the dam of lower height proposed by the Pune engineers. They could have asked the Supreme Court to order a moratorium on future large dams, while seeking to find the most feasible solution to this dam, which lay not in demolishing it or in completing it in full, but in the Joy–Paranjape 'compromise'. Meanwhile, the Chipko leader Chandi Prasad Bhatt had suggested that the Narmada Andolan ask for irrigated land in Gujarat for those made to surrender their homes and lands in Madhya Pradesh. This proposal was likewise met with a resounding silence.

The call to demolish the dam only made Gujarat and the Gujaratis more intransigent. They saw it as symptomatic of a lack of concern for their predicament. If the Narmada Andolan said 'Bring down the Dam!', they answered: 'Build it to its Full Height, not an Inch Less!' Both sides were adamantly opposed to any compromise. But, I still think, if the petition to the Supreme Court had placed the Joy–Paranjape alternative in the foreground, it might yet have been favoured. Faced with the alternatives of continuing with the dam's construction or putting an end to the project, the court would always be inclined to the former course—if only because many thousands of crores of public money had already been spent on the project. But if the court had been adequately alerted to the compromise solution, which would still bring water to the most deprived parts of Gujarat, while minimizing the suffering of the displaced, they may have been persuaded towards reducing the height of the dam.

VII

The case of Sardar Sarovar forcefully brings home the need for social movements to be flexible in their strategies. What seems feasible and plausible in Year 0 may no longer be so in Year 5 or Year 10. (As John Maynard Keynes liked to say, 'When the facts change, I change my mind.') Unfortunately, the leaders of the major oppositional movements in South Asia have found it hard, if not impossible, to change their approach and strategy. In Kashmir, in Nagaland, and in northern Sri Lanka, the rebels have refused to abandon their dream of a sovereign homeland in exchange for greater autonomy within an existing nation state.

Kashmir is in part a conflict between two South Asian nations. On the other hand, the Naga and the Tamil insurgencies are manifestations of conflicts *within* a single nation, and, as such, perhaps more amenable to dialogue and reconciliation. Now the Nagas in India and the Tamils in Sri Lanka share certain attributes. They are both hard-working peoples. They have a better-than-average acquaintance with English, the language of professional advancement in the global economy. As compared to other South Asian cultures, they practise less gender discrimination—here, there are many women who assume leadership roles, women who are teachers, doctors, entrepreneurs, and guerrilla fighters. And if one is able to make the last of these professions redundant, there will be much greater scope for the others.

Among the things that have stood in the way of a successful resolution of the Naga and the Tamil issues is the burden of history. Both sides to these conflicts have much to complain about. The Jaffna Tamils cannot forget the burning of the great library or the pogrom of 1983; the Sinhalese remember only the assassinations of their leaders and the bombs that exploded in markets, killing innocent civilians. The Nagas recall the burning of villages and the killings of civilians by the paramilitary and the army; the Indian state remembers only the seeking by the Naga rebels of Chinese help and the killings of Naga moderates. If one looks at the past, then one only sees crimes committed by the other party—crimes real as well as imagined. How can one then get the contending parties to look to the future instead, to think of the fate of the generations that are yet to come? Or do they want them too to live a life of uncertainty and instability, plagued by the shadow of the gun?

History is a burden in another way too. In the thick of the rebellion, rebels are prone to rhetorical excess, to make commitments and promises that make compromise at a later stage difficult. Thus, the LTTE often said that it will hold out for nothing less than an independent nation, a Tamil Eelam. The NSCN has likewise stood for an independent Nagalim—this to consist of the Naga-speaking areas of the Indian states of Manipur, Arunachal Pradesh and Assam as well as Nagaland. When the rebels come to the negotiating table, these past promises come back to haunt them. If they are not reminded of these claims by their own cadres, then surely rivals within the movement will make certain to draw the public's attention to them. (In the same manner, Medha Patkar was constrained by the stirring slogan that captivated her followers when the Narmada movement was at its height: '*Baandh Nahin Banega! Koi Nahin Hatega!*'.)

Then there is the issue of pride: having fought for so long for a certain goal, it cannot be let go of easily, or at all. There is the issue of sacrifice—having lost so many lives in the cause, would it be fair to the memory of the martyrs to settle for less than what they gave their lives for? Sentiments such as these have been widespread among the leadership of the Naga National Socialist Council (I-M), the leading insurgent group in Nagaland, and among the Liberation Tigers of Tamil Eelam, which was for many years the main, indeed, unchallenged, representative of the Sri Lankan Tamil cause.

In both the Naga and the Tamil cases, compromise has also been made more difficult by the desires of the diasporic community. Nagas and Tamils in exile have been even more emphatic that no solution short of complete independence is acceptable or desirable. Since they often paid for the guns, their voice carried much weight. This is a depressingly familiar story, the story of the expatriate who is even more unyielding than those who live on the ground. Palestine might be a less violent place were it not for the Jews of the East Coast of the United States. The Good Friday Agreement might have come earlier had it not been for Americans of Irish–Catholic extraction. Many fewer lives would have been lost in the Indian Punjab in the 1980s had Sikhs in the United Kingdom, Canada and the United States not decided to support and encourage the struggle for an independent Khalistan.

One last parallel between the Naga and the Tamil struggles lies in the character of their main leaders. Like the pre-eminent Naga separatist, T. Muivah, the Tamil Tiger supremo, Velupillai Prabhakaran, possessed an extraordinary energy and drive. Like Muivah, he nurtured, by personal example, the strengths and talents of countless cadres and followers. The Naga struggle was inconceivable without Muivah; so too the Tamil struggle without Prabhakaran. Their charisma and determination played a crucial part in the making and deepening of the struggle. But once the struggle had acquired a certain credibility, could not that same charisma and determination have played their part in forging a compromise? For, if anyone could have persuaded the Tamils to give up the gun, it was Prabhakaran. If anyone can charm the Nagas now into accepting the Indian Constitution, it is Muivah.

In a prescient essay published in 2007, that long-time student of the Sri Lankan conflict, D.B.S. Jeyaraj, speculated on the future of Tamil separatism when its leader died or disappeared. 'Will the LTTE be as effective without Prabhakaran at the helm?' asks Jeyaraj. He continued: 'The answer clearly is "no". If Prabhakaran is no more, it will not be an immediate end of the LTTE. It will however be the beginning of the end and the decline and fall could be quite rapid.'

Prabhakaran had a legitimacy and popular appeal denied to his colleagues, and possibly also to his successors. While he was alive and in command, the state may have considered giving up more than it wished to. However, now that he is dead, the Sri Lankan state may be tempted to withhold these concessions, in the hope that in their leader's absence the rebel movement shall splinter into factions and thus lose its energy and legitimacy.

That is indeed what seems to be happening now in Sri Lanka, where the end of the civil war has led to an upsurge of Sinhala triumphalism. Writing in the *Economic and Political Weekly*, the political scientist Neil DeVotta quotes a government minister in Colombo as saying: 'The Sinhalese are the only organic race of Sri Lanka. Other communities are all visitors to the country, whose arrival was never challenged out of the compassion of the Buddhists. But they must not take this compassion for granted. The Muslims are here because our kings let them trade here and the Tamils because they were allowed to take refuge when the Moguls were invading them in India. What is happening today is pure ingratitude on the part of these visitors.'

Such statements, says DeVotta, form part of a 'nationalist narrative that combines jeremiad with chauvinism'. In this narrative, 'the Sinhalese only have Sri Lanka while the island's other minorities have homelands elsewhere; Sri Lanka is surrounded by envious enemies who loathe the Sinhalese; those living across the Palk Straits in Tamil Nadu especially those who want to overtake the island; and NGOs, Christian missionaries, human rights groups, and various western powers and their organizations conspire to tarnish the image of the Sinhalese Buddhists and thereby assist the LTTE. Those who subscribe to this narrative are patriots; the rest are traitors.*

In truth, far from being 'the only organic race' of their island, the Sinhala almost certainly migrated there from eastern India. In any case, in later centuries the culture of the island has been influenced and enriched by many races and peoples, among them Tamils, Arabs, the Dutch, the Portuguese and the British, who in religious terms were variously Hindu, Christian, Muslim, and atheist as well as Buddhist. The LTTE were a terrorist organization—it is impossible to defend them. However, if their defeat at the hands of the Sri Lankan army leads to the triumph of Sinhala chauvinism, it will be impossible to defend that, too.

There may be a lesson here for the Nagas, namely, that it is likely that they will get a better—perhaps even a far better—bargain now, when their leader is alive, than might be possible ten or twenty years down the line. It is quite likely that a post-Muivah NSCN will be far less influential and credible than it is now. All the more reason, perhaps, for a deal to be struck and implemented while the leader is still living.

Back in 1966, when the state was strong and the rebels weak, the Indian government refused to rehabilitate Sheikh Abdullah. The break-up of Pakistan in 1971 was likewise the fault mainly of an arrogant and overbearing state. Have the roles been reversed now? Was it that the window of opportunity in Sri Lanka was shut principally because of the dogmatism and insecurity of the rebels? And that the same might now happen in Nagaland? In the several

*Substitute 'Hindu' for 'Buddhist' and 'India' for 'Sri Lanka', and this could be the narrative of Hindutva. Make it 'Jews' and 'Israel', or 'Christians' and the 'United States', or 'the Khalsa' and 'Khalistan', or 'Shias' and 'Iran', and you get other variants of faith-based nationalism, which despite their claims to exceptionalism and singularity are all so strikingly alike in their chauvinism and paranoia.

decades since these struggles commenced, tens of thousands of lives have been lost, tens of thousands of families broken. But the dream of an independent homeland seems as distant as ever.

Were this generation of Nagas to put down their weapons, the next generation would reap untold benefits. They would be part of a larger economy in which they would enjoy advantages that other Indians do not. Apart from their facility with English and the advanced status of their women, the Nagas have another great asset, namely, that the landscapes they inhabit are utterly gorgeous. Aside from taking some of the best jobs in the national economy, the Nagas might also attract a healthy stream of tourists to their own homelands.

For more than a decade now, an uneasy truce has prevailed in Nagaland. The NSCN (I-M) and the Government of India have had many rounds of talks, but no agreement has been reached. How can one get Muivah and company to drop the demand for national sovereignty and ask instead for an honourable place within the Indian Union? If, as Jayaprakash Narayan told the Nagas long ago, they can run their own economy and promote their own culture, then why does it matter that they do not have their own sovereign nation? A deeper federalism can also handily serve the aspirations of the Sri Lankan Tamils. With the attributes that the Nagas and the Tamils share, they stand to gain enormously from the forging of an agreement that gives them an honourable place within the constitutional framework of their respective countries.

However, to get the rebels to even drop the sovereignty demand might require a handsome gesture or two from the central Governments of India and Sri Lanka. As some mediators suggested, perhaps the people of Nagaland could have some recognition of their distinctive status on their passport itself—which might say, in their case, not 'Indian', but 'Naga Indian'. Likewise, if it is to convince the Tamils that they are something other than second-class citizens, Colombo should explicitly disavow the earlier enactment making Buddhism 'the state religion' of Sri Lanka, while at the same time placing the Tamil language on par with Sinhalese. Other measures will also be necessary—among them, the framing of new laws to allow greater autonomy for the regions concerned, special grants to rehabilitate victims and former combatants, and even— why not?—a public recognition of and apology for the sufferings caused by armed personnel.

VIII

The proposals I have put forward here might meet with scorn and derision, not just from the Nagas and the Tamils, but from my fellow writers and scholars as well. For, as the American critic Lionel Trilling noted long ago, intellectuals have tended to embrace an 'adversary culture': standing against the state, against the market, against the Establishment, against anything and everything but themselves. Conciliation and compromise do not come naturally to them.

However, conciliation and compromise were an integral part of the vocabulary and political repertoire of a man to whom I owe the title of this essay, the man whom I can, I think, uncontroversially refer to as the greatest South Asian of them all, Mohandas K. Gandhi. Gandhi knew when to begin a movement, but also when to call it off; when to challenge an opponent, but also when to talk to and seek to understand him. The only thing he was uncompromising about was the use of non-violence.

In many ways, Gandhi was the arch reconciler, the builder of bridges—bridges between Hindus and Muslims, between India and Pakistan, between high castes and low castes, between men and women, between the colonizer and the colonized. Independent India has had many failures, but also some successes. The most conspicuous of these successes are owed to Gandhi's political followers having honoured his spirit of compromise. India is not— or not yet—a 'Hindu Pakistan' because its first prime minister followed Gandhi in promoting religious pluralism. The Indian Constitution provided special privileges for low castes and tribals under the inspiration of Gandhi. Remarkably, the man who piloted this Constitution through the Assembly was himself a lifelong opponent of Mahatma Gandhi and the Congress party. How and why B.R. Ambedkar was chosen as the first law minister of the government of independent India remains a mystery. It has been speculated that Gandhi instructed Nehru and Patel to include Ambedkar in the Cabinet, on the grounds that freedom had come to all of India, not merely to Congressmen. This seems in keeping with Gandhi's extraordinary combination of personal generosity and political sagacity, whereby he was willing to overlook Ambedkar's savage denunciations of himself in view of the younger man's acknowledged abilities as a scholar and administrator.

Among the less adequately recognized of Gandhi's compromises was the forging of a stable, harmonious, and even affectionate relationship between the United Kingdom and independent India. Certainly, nowhere else have Empire and Colony maintained such a friendship after the sundering of the imperial (and essentially inequitable) tie that once bound them. Consider the bitter relations that have existed—and indeed still exist—between the French and the Algerians, the Dutch and the Indonesians, the Belgians and the residents of the Congo, the Russians and the Poles, the Japanese and the Koreans.

That most Indians do not hate the English is owed largely—one might even say entirely—to Gandhi. In the latter half of 1931, Gandhi visited England to participate in the Round Table Conference. While the conference was in recess, Gandhi spent two weekends at Oxford. He stayed with A.D. Lindsay, the Master of Balliol College, a distinguished political theorist, a socialist, a member of the Labour Party, and a supporter of the Indian independence movement. While at Oxford the Mahatma met with the Indian Majlis and also with the Raleigh Club. His session with the Raleigh Club included this fascinating exchange:

Q. How far would you cut India off from the Empire?

A. From the Empire entirely; from the British nation not at all, if I want India to gain and not to grieve. The British Empire is an Empire only because of

India. The Emperorship must go and I should love to be [an] equal partner with Britain, sharing her joys and sorrows . . . But it must be a partnership on equal terms.

Q. To what extent would India be prepared to share the sorrows of England?

A. To the fullest extent.

Q. Do you think India would unite her fortunes inextricably with England?

A. Yes, so long as she remains a partner. But if she discovers that the partnership is like one between a giant and a dwarf, or if it is utilized for exploitation of the other races of the earth, she would dissolve it. The aim is the common good of all nations of the earth and, if it cannot be achieved, I have patience enough to wait for ages rather than patch up an unreal partnership.

Gandhi's closest friend was an Englishman, Charles Freer Andrews. While his admirers called him 'Mahatma', 'Gandhiji', or 'Bapu', and his critics addressed him as 'M.K. Gandhi' or 'Mr Gandhi', among the few people to address Gandhi by his first name, 'Mohan', was this English priest. When Andrews died, in 1940, Gandhi wrote that while the numerous misdeeds of the English would be forgotten, 'not one of the heroic deeds of Andrews will be forgotten as long as England and India live. If we really love Andrews' memory, we may not have hate in us for Englishmen, of whom Andrews was among the best and noblest. It is possible, quite possible, for the best Englishmen and the best Indians to meet together and never to separate till they have evolved a formula acceptable to both.'

In the six decades since the Raj ended, the 'best Englishmen and the best Indians' have met regularly and amicably—to their mutual advantage. Theirs has been, as Gandhi hoped and worked for, an enduring partnership of equals. Can there be a time when the same can or will be said of Nagas and Punjabis, or Jaffna Tamils and Kandyan monks? It would take a great deal of give and take on both sides, an honest acknowledgement of error, a willingness to compromise, and, perhaps above all, the ability to think of a hopefully harmonious future rather than a bitter and bloody past.

The Naga and Tamil struggles are founded on the principle of *identity*. These two peoples have a strong sense of who they are and what unites them, this defined by a shared territory, religion, culture and language. It is the denial, perceived and real, of this identity by the nation state and its policies that explain the origin and persistence of the secessionist movement. The key to a solution lies in converting the currency of identity into the currency of *interest*. The groups that are currently protesting about threats to their identity must be provided with a stake in power and decision-making. That is how, for example, the Solidarity generation in Poland, or the leaders and cadres of the African National Congress in South Africa, were encouraged to move from being rebels and freedom fighters to becoming administrators and governors. But for inspiration, one does not necessarily have to look so far afield. The Dravidian movement in Tamil Nadu, and the Mizo National Front, once stood out for independence as solidly as the LTTE and the NSCN. In the end, however, they dropped the demand for sovereignty, in exchange for a secure place within the federal system.

One may take heart from the history of Tamil Nadu and Mizoram or, indeed, from contemporary Nepal. It is too early yet to say whether this particular South Asian story will have a happy ending. But it has certainly had a salutary beginning. For Comrade Prachanda to embrace multiparty democracy was, in ideological terms, just as difficult as Prabhakaran or Muivah giving up on 'national self-determination'. Credit must also be given to the parliamentary parties, and perhaps to the elder statesman Girija Prasad Koirala in particular, that they set aside their old animosities and suspicions and welcomed the Maoists into the democratic process.

These examples suggest that for there to have been an honourable peace in Sri Lanka, Velupillai Prabhakaran did not have to become a Mahatma Gandhi. He—or his advisers and well-wishers—could have taken their cues instead from leaders and struggles closer to them in history and geography. Mandela's ANC was once just as devoted to the cult of the gun. C.N. Annadurai was once just as committed to an independent Tamil homeland—this to be carved out of the Republic of India, rather than the Republic of Sri Lanka. And that other rebel in the jungle, Prachanda, also fought on for years in the hope—and belief—that the struggle would ultimately end in a one-party state dominated by his men. The compromises made by Mandela, Annadurai and Prachanda might now compel the attention of T. Muivah, although he has an exemplar even closer at hand, in Laldenga and the Mizo National Front.

Jayaprakash Narayan liked to say that compromise was impossible only when one side to the dispute was 100 per cent in the wrong. Following this argument, one could not ask the Jews of Germany to compromise with the Nazis. However, in the South Asian conflicts described here, rights and wrongs are distributed more evenly. Sheikh Abdullah once compared Kashmir to a beautiful damsel coveted by two avaricious and amoral men (namely, India and Pakistan). By this he meant that both countries disregarded and at times abused the rights of the Kashmiri people. Meanwhile, since Abdullah's death, the dispute has been further complicated by the violence and intolerance expressed by Kashmiri jehadis, as in their expulsion of the Pandits in 1989–90. In Sri Lanka and Nagaland too, mistakes and crimes have been committed by all sides. The fact that vice is not the monopoly of a single party alone makes the case for reconciliation and compromise all the more compelling.

In a fine essay on the history of political moderation in the western world, Robert M. Calhoon suggests that 'moderates are made not born'. They are 'creatures of the moment, and of circumstance, who move away from antagonistic stances and toward [the] middle ground to achieve a goal or serve a purpose through a wider political advocacy and association'. This definition works well in explaining the moves away from extremism of those great rebels, Nelson Mandela and Mahatma Gandhi, or indeed of the ending of repression by their respective rivals, the apartheid regime and the British Raj.

Calhoon also writes that 'in our own time, moderation rebukes the corrosive partisanship from the Right or the Left'. In our own region, however, Right and Left may be better represented as Rebel and State. It is the task of the moderate, and of moderation, to find common ground between these two actors, thus to replace a regime of suspicion and violence with one based on trust and cooperation.

That said, those who advocate moderation—including the present writer—live more in hope than expectation. Calhoon quotes a passage from Aristotle's *Nicomachean Ethics*, where the Greek sage notes that 'it is no easy task to find the middle'. Closer home, this sentiment was echoed by C. Rajagopalachari, a close follower and associate of Gandhi, when he wrote to a Quaker friend that 'those who are born to reconcile seem to have an unending task in this world'. If not in the whole world, at least in South Asia, this region that has been so deeply marked by conflict and antagonism between high caste and low caste, between Hindus and Muslims, between Sinhala speakers and Tamil speakers, between the massed armies of its nation states . . .

It is precisely because our region is such a cauldron of conflict that a special responsibility devolves on the writer and intellectual. The writer and intellectual has an obligation to the truth; the modern writer and intellectual an additional obligation to democracy and pluralism. For the signal lesson of the twentieth century was that dictatorships of both left and right are equally inimical to human dignity and well-being. Thus, as part of their calling, writers must stand consistently for the right to freely elect one's leaders, the right to seek a place of residence and company of one's choosing, the right to speak the language of one's choice and the right to practise the faith of one's belief (which may be no faith at all).

These responsibilities are onerous enough, but for the South Asian writer and intellectual there are other obligations still. Because our recent history has been so bloody and divisive, here the writer and intellectual must always be in search of paths that might make our future less bloody, and less divisive. She, and he, should seek, wherever possible, to moderate social and political conflicts rather than to intensify or accelerate them. The extreme positions are well represented and passionately articulated in any case. Rather than take sides on behalf of one caste against another, one religion against another, one nation against another, or to throw oneself in alignment with the state or to be always against the state, the writer and intellectual needs to keep away from an identification with one party to a dispute. Rather, he and she must try to interpret and reconcile opposing positions, to make each side see the truth in the other, thus to urge each party to move beyond dogmatism and self-justification towards acknowledging and embracing the beauty of compromise.

PART II

THE WORD AND THE WORLD

chapter ten

THE RISE AND FALL OF THE BILINGUAL INTELLECTUAL

~

I

This essay is inspired by an argument between the scholar–librarian B.S. Kesavan and his son Mukul that I was once privy to. I forget what they were fighting about. But I recall that the father, then past ninety years of age, was giving as good as he got. At periodic intervals he would turn to me, otherwise a silent spectator, and pointing to his son, say: 'Makku!' 'Paithyam!' Those were words that Mukul, born in Delhi of a Hindi-speaking mother, did not himself understand. But I did. They meant, roughly and respectively, 'imbecile' and 'lunatic'.

B.S. Kesavan knew that I lived in Bangalore, that both my parents were Tamil, and that one of my great-uncles had been a Tamil scholar. Thus, when his son's stupidity (real or alleged) could not be adequately conveyed in their shared language, namely, English, he took recourse to his mother tongue, which was also theoretically mine. The emphasis must be on 'theoretically'. My great-uncle the Tamil scholar used to write postcards asking me to learn Tamil and lead a simple life'. I failed him wholly in the second respect, but have down the years managed to pick up a few dozen words of Tamil, among them *makku* and *paithyam*.

B.S. Kesavan was formidably multilingual. He was fluent in Tamil, Kannada and English, spoke Bengali adequately and Hindi passably, and had a good grasp of Sanskrit. No doubt his multilingualism came in handy in his work as the first Indian director of the National Library, his nurturing of a national information system, and his pioneering histories of publishing and printing. His taste for languages was shared by many other Indians of his generation who did not necessarily require those skills in their jobs or careers. My own father, for instance, who was a paper technologist by profession, speaks English and Tamil well, and Kannada and Hindi passably. He also has a reading knowledge of French and German. On the other hand, Mukul Kesavan and I are essentially comfortable in English alone. We can speak Hindi conversationally, and use documents written in Hindi for research purposes. But we cannot write scholarly books or essays in Hindi. And neither of us can pretend to a third language at all.

II

Let me move now from the personal to the historical, to an argument on the question of language between two great modern Indians. In the month of April 1921, Mahatma Gandhi launched a broadside against English education. First, in a speech in Orissa, he described it as an 'unmitigated evil'. Bal Gangadhar Tilak and Rammohan Roy would, said Gandhi, have 'been far greater men had they not the contagion of English learning'. In Gandhi's opinion, these two influential and admired Indians 'were so many pigmies who had no hold upon the people compared with Chaitanya, Sanker, Kabir, and Nanak'. Warming to the theme, Gandhi insisted that 'what Sanker alone was able to do, the whole army of English-knowing men can't do. I can multiply instances. Was Guru Govind a product of English education? Is there a single English-knowing Indian who is a match for Nanak, the founder of a sect second to none in point of valour and sacrifice? . . . If the race has even to be revived it is to be revived not by English education.'

A friend, reading the press reports of this talk in Orissa, asked Gandhi to explain his views further. Writing in his own newspaper, the Mahatma clarified that 'it is my considered opinion that English education in the manner it has been given has emasculated the English-educated Indian, it has put a severe strain on the Indian students' nervous energy, and has made of us imitators. The process of displacing the vernaculars has been one of the saddest chapters in the British connection . . .' 'Rammohan Roy would have been a greater reformer,' claimed the Mahatma, 'and Lokmanya Tilak would have been a greater scholar, if they had not to start with the handicap of having to think in English and transmit their thoughts chiefly in English.' Gandhi argued that 'of all the superstitions that affect India, none is so great as that a knowledge of the English language is necessary for imbibing ideas of liberty, and developing accuracy of thought'. As a result of the system of education introduced by the English, 'the tendency has been to dwarf the Indian body, mind and soul'.

One does not know whether the Mahatma's anonymous friend was content with this clarification. But someone who was less than satisfied with Gandhi's views was the poet Rabindranath Tagore. He was then travelling in Europe, where he received, by post, copies of Gandhi's articles. Tagore was dismayed by their general tenor, and by the chastisement of Rammohan Roy in particular. On the 10th of May 1921, he wrote to their common friend C.F. Andrews, saying, 'I strongly protest against Mahatma Gandhi's depreciation of such great personalities of Modern India as Rammohan Roy in his zeal for declaiming against our modern education.' Gandhi had celebrated the example of Nanak and Kabir, but, as Tagore suggested, those saints 'were great because in their life and teaching they made organic union of the Hindu and Muhammadan cultures—and such realization of the spiritual unity through all differences of appearance is truly Indian'.

In learning and appreciating English, argued Tagore, Rammohan Roy had merely carried on the good work of Nanak and Kabir.

Thus, 'in the modern age Rammohan Roy had that comprehensiveness of mind to be able to realize the fundamental unity of spirit in the Hindu, Muhammadan and Christian cultures. Therefore, he represented India in the fulness of truth, and this truth is based, not upon rejection, but on perfect comprehension.' Tagore pointed out that 'Rammohan Roy could be perfectly natural in his acceptance of the West, not only because his education had been perfectly Eastern—he had the full inheritance of the Indian wisdom. He was never a school boy of the West, and therefore he had the dignity to be the friend of the West. If he is not understood by modern India, this only shows the pure light of her own truth has been obscured for the moment by the storm-clouds of passion.'

Tagore's letter to Andrews was released to the press, and read by Gandhi. His answer was to say that he did 'not object to English learning as such', but merely to its being made a fetish, and to its being preferred as a medium of education to the mother tongue. 'Mine is not a religion of the prison-house,' he insisted: 'it has room even for the least among God's creation.' Refuting the charge that he or his non-cooperation movement were a manifestation of xenophobia, he said: 'I hope I am as great a believer in free air as the great Poet. I do not want my house to be walled in on all sides and my windows to be stuffed. I want the cultures of all the lands to be blown about my house as freely as possible. But I refuse to be blown off by any.'

These words are emblazoned in halls and auditoria across India, but always without the crucial first line: 'I hope I am as great a believer in free air as the great Poet.' In truth, despite this argument in theory, in practice Gandhi and Tagore were more or less on the same side. Gandhi wrote his books in Gujarati, but made certain that they were translated into English so as to reach a wider audience. And when required he could use the conqueror's language rather well himself. His first published articles, that appeared in the journal of the Vegetarian Society of London in 1891, were written in the direct and unadorned prose that was the hallmark of all his work in English, whether petitions to the colonial government, editorials in his journals *Indian Opinion*, *Young India* and *Harijan*, or numerous letters to friends.

In writing in more than one language, Gandhi was in fact merely following in the footsteps of those he had criticized. For, Bal Gangadhar Tilak's mother tongue was Marathi, a language in which he did certainly publish essays. On his part, Rammohan Roy had published books in Persian and essays in Bengali before he came to write in English (he was also fluent in Sanskrit and Arabic). As for Tagore, this man who shaped and reshaped the Bengali language through his novels and poems, made sure that his most important works of non-fiction were available in English. His major political testament, *Nationalism*, was based on lectures he wrote and delivered in English. His important and still relevant essays on relations between the East and the West were either written in English or translated by a colleague under his supervision. Tagore understood that while love and humiliation at the personal or familial level were best expressed in the mother tongue, impersonal questions of reason and justice had sometimes to be communicated in a language read by more people and over a greater geographical space than Bengali.

By writing in English as well as their mother tongue, Gandhi and Tagore were serving society as well as themselves. They reached out to varied audiences—and, by listening to other people's views, broadened the bases of their own thought. This open-mindedness was also reflected in their reading. Thus Gandhi read (and was influenced by) thinkers who were not necessarily Gujarati. The debt he owed to Ruskin and Tolstoy was scarcely less than that owed to Raychandbhai or Narsing Mehta. Gandhi was also enriched by the time he spent outside Gujarat—the several years in England, the several decades in South Africa, the millions of miles travelling through the Indian countryside.

On his part, Tagore was widely read in European literature. When he visited Germany in the 1920s at the invitation of his publisher, Kurt Wolff, his host remembered the 'universal breadth of Tagore's learning', their conversations revealing 'without doubt that he knew far more of the West than most of the Europeans he encountered knew of the East'. Tagore had spoken, among other things, of the works of T.S. Eliot. 'It is quite remarkable,' said Wolff, 'that someone born in India in 1861 should display such an interest in and grasp of an Anglo-American poet thirty years his junior.'

III

For Gandhi, and for Tagore, the foreign language was a window into another culture, another civilization, another way (or ways) of living in the world. For them, the command of a language other than their own was a way of simultaneously making themselves less parochial and their work more universal. Their readings and travels fed back into their own writing, thus bringing the world to Bengal and Gujarat, and (when they chose to write in the foreign language) Bengal and Gujarat to the world. Bilingualism was here a vehicle or something larger and more enduring—namely, multiculturalism.

In these respects, Gandhi and Tagore were representative. Before them there was Sir Syed Ahmad Khan, who moved between Urdu and English as he strove simultaneously to make the British more sensitive to Muslim interests and the Muslims more willing to engage with modernity. After them there was B.R. Ambedkar, who wrote in Marathi for a local constituency; and in English for the rest of India and for the world. Ambedkar knew his Tukaram, but also his John Stuart Mill. To take another example, C. Rajagopalachari is still admired for his English style; but few now know that he was a pioneering essayist and short-story writer in Tamil. He knew his Kural, but—as he once reminded an interviewer—he had also read the works of Henry David Thoreau well before he met Mahatma Gandhi. Rajaji's contemporary V.D. Savarkar also wrote books in English, as well as plays and polemical tracts in Marathi. From the other end of the political spectrum, consider the Communist E.M.S. Namboodiripad, who was a prolific writer and polemicist in both Malayalam and English.

(Possible exceptions to this trend are M.A. Jinnah, Jawaharlal Nehru and Subhas Bose, who were also all thinker–politicians, albeit of a monolingual variety. Jinnah, as is well known, was not exactly fluent in Urdu. Nehru could give a public lecture in Hindustani, and Bose in Bengali; however, their major writings, like Jinnah's, are all in English.)

A thinker–politician who, at first glance, may seem to have been an aberration is Ram Manohar Lohia. To be sure, Lohia called for the abolition of English from educational institutions and in public life, and, at the same time, for the countrywide promotion of Hindi. However, Lohia advocated not monolingualism but multilingualism. He asked for school instruction to be provided in the mother tongue, but insisted that children must, in addition, learn two other languages—Hindi, and either a foreign language or another Indian language. He saw the need for an international language, to be used in communications between nations, but was not convinced that this had necessarily and for all time to be English. The role had been played by French in the past; and would, he thought, perhaps be played by Russian or Chinese in the future. Lohia himself knew excellent German (he had taken his PhD at the University of Berlin), while some of his finest polemical essays against the use of English were written in that language itself.

So in fact, Lohia was not an exception after all. Bilingualism and multiculturalism came naturally to him, as it did to the other leaders of his generation. It also came naturally to the social scientists who were their contemporaries. Of those active in the 1940s and 1950s, the anthropologists Nirmal Kumar Bose and Irawati Karve, the economist D.R. Gadgil, and the sociologist D.P. Mukerji—all made a name for themselves for their work in English as well as for their writings in their mother tongue. They tended to publish academic papers in English, and more popular or literary essays in Bengali or Marathi. Sometimes their work in the mother tongue was translated into English, and made a considerable impact (as, for example, with Karve's re-rendition of the Mahabharata, *Yuganta*.) As with Gandhi and Tagore, the process of enrichment was two-sided—they themselves became less parochial, while through their writings they allowed their parish to feel palpably part of a wider world.

The bilingualism of the politicians and scholars was matched by the writers and critics. It was, I think, Harish Trivedi who first noted that many of the finest creative writers of the middle decades of the twentieth century were professors of English, yet wrote their poems and stories in other languages. His essay is not at hand as I write, but among the names Professor Trivedi may have mentioned were the poet Gopalkrishna Adiga and the novelist U.R. Anantha Murthy in Kannada; the poet Harivanshrai Bachchan and the short-story writer Nirmal Verma in Hindi; and the poet Firaq Gorakhpuri in Urdu. All taught English literature; some even had PhDs in the subject from the best British universities. Literary historians could doubtless add many other names to the list—of established writers in Assamese, Oriya, Bengali, Tamil, Telugu, etc. who made their living teaching English yet wrote in the mother tongue in order to live.

Here, too, facility with more than one tongue was a matter not just of skill but also of sensibility. The writer, his work, and his audience, all benefited from the fact that the person in question was in command of more than one linguistic or cultural universe. Surely, Bachchan's Hindi verse must have at some level been influenced by, or been a response to, his doctoral work at Cambridge on W.B. Yeats. By the same token, his classroom teaching and the occasional essays he wrote in English must certainly have been enriched by his immersion in the world of Hindi letters.

(Perhaps the most striking instance of this bilingualism concerns the crafting of Premchand's *Godan*. This work, published in 1936, is considered the very archetype of the modern Hindi novel, yet the author first outlined the plot in English!)

In the inter-war period, no Indian town better expressed this multilinguality than the town where B.S. Kesavan spent some of his best years: Mysore. Among the town's residents in the 1930s and 1940s were the Kannada poet K.V. Puttappa (Kuvempu), who wrote political essays in English; the English novelist R.K. Narayan, who was equally fluent in Tamil and Kannada; and the journalist H.Y. Sharada Prasad, who thought and wrote in Kannada, but whose command of English was later put to good effect in the very many speeches he ghosted for successive prime ministers of India. A somewhat younger resident was A.K. Ramanujan, who later recalled that, growing up in Mysore, he was equally familiar with the language of the street (Kannada), the language of the kitchen (Tamil, spoken by his mother), and the language of the study upstairs (occupied by his father, who liked to converse in English). Ramanujan was an accomplished poet in both Kannada and English, and achieved undying fame for his translations into English of Kannada and Tamil folklore and folk poetry—work that was enabled, in the first instance, by his growing up in the multilingual intellectual universe of Mysore.

Mysore was here representative of other towns in colonial India. The intellectual culture of Dharwad, Cochin, Allahabad, etc., was likewise bilingual, with writers and professors operating both in English and in the language of the locality or province. There was a cultural continuum that ran between *qasba* and *mahanagar*, between the smaller urban centres and the great cities of the Presidencies.

The bilingualism I have described was a product of a particular historical conjuncture—namely, the advent first of colonialism, and later, of nationalism. The British required some Indians to learn English, to interpret between them and their subjects, and to assist in governance and administration (as well as in commerce and trade). However, over time the language of the rulers also became a vehicle to demand equal rights from them. Thus, from being an accessory in the process of conquest and control, English became an ally in the process of protest and profanation. It was the language in which Indian nationalists chastised the British for not living up to their own best traditions. Simultaneously, it also became the language in which intellectually or politically minded Indians could communicate across the different linguistic zones of the Empire. Notably, even as they acquired a working knowledge of English (or better), these reform-minded Indians continued to operate in their mother tongue. The latter served best for creative literary expression and when focusing on the abolition of reactionary social practices; the former was necessary for nurturing or deepening cross-provincial networks of political action.

It is worth noting, however, that unlike in the case of social scientists and political activists, the bilingualism of the creative writer did not necessarily mean 'English and another'. It was once not uncommon to find a novelist who wrote stories in both Konkani and Marathi, or a poet who composed his verses in Bengali as well as in Maithili.

IV

Between (roughly) the 1920s and 1970s, the intellectual universe in India was—to coin a word—'linguidextrous'. With few exceptions, the major political thinkers, scholars and creative writers—and many of the minor ones too—thought and acted and wrote with equal facility in at least two languages, one of which was the mother tongue, another usually (but not always) English. It appears that this is no longer the case. The intellectual and creative world in India is increasingly becoming polarized—between those who think and act and write in English alone, and those who think and write and act in their mother tongue alone.

The state of West Bengal appears to have held out longest against this separation of literary and intellectual discourses. At least in Kolkata, there are still very many intellectuals who are properly linguidextrous. In 2009, Ranajit Guha was awarded the prestigious Ananda Puraskar for a book on Tagore in Bengali. Coincidentally, his collected essays in English were published in the same week. Ranajit Guha is of course a *prabasi*, but of those still resident in Kolkata, Supriya Chaudhuri, Sukanta Chaudhuri, Partha Chatterjee and Swapan Chakravarty are all world-renowned scholars for their writings in English—and they have written first-rate essays and books in Bengali as well. These scholars are all on the wrong side of fifty, but there are, I am reliably told, some Bengali men and women now in their thirties and forties who likewise move effortlessly between the language of the world and the language of the locality.

In a life lived in between the interstices of the academy and the press, I have had the privilege of knowing many linguidextrous intellectuals. Some are Bengalis, such as those remarkable prabasi couples Tanika and Sumit Sarkar, Kalpana and Pranab Bardhan, and Meenakshi and Sujit Mukherjee. Others have come from more subaltern linguistic zones, for example, Kumar Ketkar, Madhav Gadgil, Dilip Chitre and Rajendra Vora (Marathi), Shahid Amin and Krishna Kumar (Hindi), Girish Karnad and D.R. Nagaraj (Kannada), C.V. Subba Rao (Telugu), Jatin Kumar Nayak (Oriya) and N.S. Jagannathan (Tamil). Like me, all these writers have written a great deal in English; but unlike me, they have published important work in their other language too. In countless conversations down the decades, I have been to them what the readers of Gandhi and Tagore were to those great Indians—namely, a grateful recipient of knowledge and understanding derived from languages that I do not myself speak or read.

Notably, the individuals mentioned in the preceding paragraph were all born more than fifty years ago. Speaking of the younger generation, linguidextrous intellectuals run more thinly on the ground— at least outside of Bengal. Of scholars in their forties, I can think easily of only three who would qualify—A.R. Venkatachalapathy, Tridip Suhrud and Yogendra Yadav. All have considerable, and independently won, reputations for their writings in their own language (Tamil, Gujarati, and Hindi respectively) as well as in English. A fourth name might be that of the young historian Arupjyoti Saikia, who writes in both Assamese and English.

In general, though, the gap between the generations is telling. Consider thus the career of Sadanand More, whose major works include a reception history of the poet-saint Tukaram and a study of the transition from Tilak to Gandhi in the politics of western India. As I have discovered on several visits to Puné, he is something of a cult figure in Maharashtra, because of his books and his columns in newspapers. Had he written in English, he might have been considered the Partha Chatterjee of Maharashtra—he is comparable in the range of his interests and the quality of his mind.

A distinction must be made here between reading a language and knowing it through and through. There are those who are *functionally* bilingual; and yet others who are *intellectually* and *emotionally* bilingual. I use letters and news reports written in Hindi for my research, raiding them for facts and opinions. But I do not read Hindi for pleasure, nor could I think of writing an essay in Hindi in a quality journal. In this I believe I speak for many other social scientists of my age or younger. These too may be able to use an Indian language as source material, but—unlike their predecessors N.K. Bose and Irawati Karve—cannot see themselves as contributing to literary or academic debate in that language. They, and I, are admittedly cosmopolitan, but in a somewhat shallow sense, knowing the world well without knowing the locality much—or at all.

At the same time, at the other end of the linguistic spectrum, many—perhaps most—of the best poets and novelists in Tamil, Kannada, Hindi, Oriya, Gujarati, etc. are likewise completely comfortable in one language only. They may occasionally read a novel or tract in English, but most of their reading—and all their writing—is confined to a single language. No Kannada novelist of the younger generation has anything like the acquaintance with western literature and social theory once commanded by U.R. Anantha Murthy. The Hindi writers I meet are all deeply rooted in their environment, yet few follow Nirmal Verma in his curiosity about, or knowledge of, the wider world.

My evidence is somewhat anecdotal, but I believe most observers will agree with the thrust of my conclusions—namely, that there has been a decline in the number and visibility of scholars and writers who are properly linguidextrous. The third class of bilingual thinkers, the politicians, is wholly depopulated now. In my view, the last active politician to have any serious claims to intellectual originality was Jayaprakash Narayan, who, of course, wrote and thought and argued in both Hindi and English. (Critics with more lax standards may offer the names of Mani Shankar Aiyar and Arun Shourie. In any case, whether intellectual or not, original or not, they operate in English alone.)

One sphere of life which has somewhat retained its linguidextrousness is the theatre. Playwrights and stage directors such as (among others) Arundhati Nag, K.V. Akshara and Sudhanva Deshpande move easily between the worlds of Kannada or Marathi or Hindi theatre on the one hand and English theatre on the other. All across the subcontinent, plays written in one language are regularly performed in another. Among stage actors who are multilingual, Naseeruddin Shah is perhaps the best known and most widely admired; but there are many others, among them even some in their twenties and thirties.

The robust linguidextrousness of Indian theatre may be illustrated by the following anecdote. I was once travelling on a flight with the playwright Girish Karnad. All through, I was reading a book in English; while he, a few rows ahead, was busy correcting a set of proofs. When the plane reached its cruising altitude I walked over to take a closer look. I knew that Karnad writes his plays in Kannada; and then translates them himself into English. What he was reading this day was a Marathi translation of one of his plays. That language he knows almost as well as Kannada and English; and yet, he insists that he is most comfortable speaking Konkani, the language in which he was reared.

V

There is still a certain amount of functional bi-linguality among India's intellectual class; but emotional or intellectual bi-linguality, once ubiquitous, is now present only in pockets, these too of chiefly older women and men. What are the reasons for this? A key reason, in retrospect, was the creation and consolidation of linguistic states after 1956. When viewed from a historical and comparative perspective, there is little question that linguistic states helped save the unity of India. Had we not allowed states to be constituted around language, and had we instead imposed Hindi on the whole country, we might have gone the way of a now-divided Pakistan and a war-torn Sri Lanka.

I believe that on balance, linguistic states were indeed a good thing. Even in the particular context of intellectual work, they have had good as well as bad effects. The expansion of the school network, and the entry into the political system of previously excluded groups, has greatly deepened the social bases of the intellectual class. Literature and scholarship across India was once dominated by Brahmins, Banias, Kayasths and well-born Muslims. But from the 1950s, very many Dalits and OBCs began entering schools and colleges. Some went on to become professors and writers, taking to jobs and careers that would have been closed to men and women of their background half a century previously.

In most states, however, instruction in government schools was conducted in the official language of the state alone. There was little room for English—sometimes, no room at all. English was removed from Gujarati schools in the 1950s and from schools in West Bengal in the 1970s—each time, at the insistence of men (Morarji Desai in the first case, Jyoti Basu and Ashok Mitra in the second case) who were themselves superbly fluent in English. It has been claimed— not altogether implausibly—that the parochialism and xenophobia that underlies the rise of a certain Gujarati politician is not unrelated to the banning of the one language which, to quote that other and more broad-minded Gujarati politician, would have best allowed the cultures of other lands to be blown freely around and about the west coast of India. Similarly, the decline of West Bengal as a centre of science and scholarship is not unconnected to the equally misguided decision to ban English-teaching in the state-run schools of the province.

In the 1960s and 1970s, at the same time as the subaltern classes were producing their first major crop of scholars and writers, the elites were choosing to patronize English-language schools alone. In the north Indian public school I studied in, Hindi was verboten— the boy most badly ragged in my time spoke ungrammatical English with a Hindi accent. The experience was representative—in other towns and cities across India, upper-caste children whose fathers may have, in colonial times, studied in government schools where both Sanskrit and the local language had an important place, were sent to 'convent' or public schools where English was the preferred language of communication, with Hindi (or its equivalent) allotted a minor, residual and contemptible place in the curriculum.

English in post-colonial India was the language of status and prestige. With the opening of the economy after 1991 it also became the language of economic and material advancement. The spread of English was further helped along by the growing number of inter-caste and inter-community marriages in urban India. If, for example, a Tamil-speaking girl met a Bengali-speaking boy in an office which functioned in English, and the two fell in love and later married, the chances were, and are, that the home language would, by default, be English, this becoming, in time, the first, preferred and perhaps also the sole language of the children of the union. Cases like these must, by now, number in the hundreds of thousands. And it is from professional unions such as these that some of India's most prominent scholars and writers have been and will be born.

The separation of discourses is reflected in the growing distance— cultural as much as geographical—that now exists between the qasba and the mahanagar. Smaller towns tend to produce thinkers and writers who operate in the local language alone, whereas professors and students in the elite colleges of the metropolis are often comfortable only in English. In a cultural and linguistic sense, Karnatak College, Dharwad, is worlds removed from Christ College, Bangalore; D.A.V. College, Dehradun, from St. Stephen's College, Delhi.

The Kannada writer U.R. Anantha Murthy uses the term 'vernacular anxiety' to describe the condition of many writers in Indian languages. There may perhaps be a comparable 'cosmopolitan anxiety' among those who write in English alone. Sometimes, this anxiety masquerades as arrogance (as in the case of Salman Rushdie, who once claimed that all the best writing about India appeared in English); at other times, as defensiveness.

Notably, the decline of intellectual bilingualism has been accompanied by a rise of functional bilingualism among the population at large. Many more Indians now speak more than one language than they ever did in the past. The universe of the farm and village is classically monolingual, whereas the universe of the office and factory emphatically is not. Thus, industrialization and urbanization have brought together millions of people who speak different languages at home. Migrants to cities and towns find that the lingua franca of their workplace is, as often as not, something other than their mother tongue. Bihari labourers in the informal sector in Kolkata have perforce to speak Bengali, while Malayali workers in public sector units in Bangalore have necessarily to learn some Kannada.

Meanwhile, Hindi and English have emerged as pan-Indian languages of communication and conversation. Where official attempts to promote Hindi in southern and eastern India conspicuously failed, the language has nonetheless spread through the more informal, and hence more acceptable, medium of television and film. In cities like Bangalore and Hyderabad, in Mumbai, and now even in Kolkata, Hindi is widely used as the default language of conversation between two Indians reared to speak other tongues. The spread of English owes itself to more instrumental factors—the fact that it is the language of the international marketplace, and of the larger companies and firms that operate in it. Since the best-paying and often most prestigious jobs demand a knowledge of English, there is a huge incentive to acquire it.

And so, while intellectuals tend increasingly to operate in a single linguistic sphere, millions of Indians in other jobs, trades and professions are acquiring proficiency in tongues other than their own.

VI

In the essays opposing English that so distressed Tagore, Gandhi had hedged his opposition with a series of caveats. 'I am opposed to make a fetish of English education, I don't hate English education,' he said. 'I know what treasures I have lost not knowing Hindustani and Sanskrit,' he continued. We may endorse these sentiments while recognizing, sixty and more years after Gandhi's death, that an equal danger lies in making a fetish of the opposition to English. Those who banned English in West Bengal deprived millions of schoolchildren of a wider education. Now, to those Kannada writers who ask for instruction in the mother tongue alone, the Dalits answer—first you did not allow us to learn Sanskrit, now you want to deny us access to English.

The decline of the bilingual intellectual in contemporary India is thus a product of a combination of many factors: public policy—which emphasized the mother tongue alone; elite preference—which denied or diminished the mother tongue altogether; social change—as in new patterns of marriage; and economic change—as in the material gains to be had from a command of English.

The temporal sphere of my arguments is restricted to the twentieth century; the spatial sphere, to my country alone. Those who know the history of precolonial India may have interesting and important things to say about the multilingual nature of intellectual discourse in past times. Meanwhile, as someone who has a casual acquaintance with contemporary Europe, let me suggest that the intellectuals in that continent have gone in exactly the reverse direction to ours. Once, they operated mainly or even exclusively in the language that defined their nation—the French in French, the Spanish in Spanish, etc. Now, with the emergence of the European Union and the growth of English as a global language, these French and Spanish and German thinkers have abandoned their opposition to the foreign tongue without disavowing their own. The best (or at any rate most successful) French thinkers now are linguidextrous, writing essays and books in their own language as well as in English. Scholars in other European nations have gone even further. Thus the distinguished ecological thinker J. Martinez-Alier writes in English for a global audience, in Spanish for his compatriots, and in Catalan for the people of his own province.

I shall end this essay with two stories that illustrate the sometimes unanticipated glories of the best kind of linguidextrousness. When H.Y. Sharada Prasad died in 2009, a correspondent in *Outlook* magazine complained that in all of Sharada Prasad's years in New Delhi, working for prime ministers and earning their trust and respect, he had never lifted a finger for a single Kannadiga. The

letter-writer's parochialism was characteristic of our times. For, what
he did not recognize is that by translating the novels of Shivaram
Karanth into English, Sharada Prasad had done a far greater service
to the Kannada language, and to Kannadigas, than had he got some
of them ten minutes with Indira Gandhi or an out-of-turn
gas connection.

Sharada Prasad spoke Kannada, Tamil, Telugu and English very
well—and knew some Sanskrit and Hindi too. The other Indian of
my acquaintance who comes closest to this multilingual dextrousness
is the writer and public servant Gopalkrishna Gandhi. Literary critics
know Gopal Gandhi as the translator into Hindi of Vikram Seth's
novel, *A Suitable Boy*. He has also written his own books, in
English. However, these are only two of the languages he can
fluently read, write and speak. I recently discovered that his first
literary production was undertaken as a boy of seventeen, when he
translated the memoirs of Manu Gandhi from Gujarati into English.
He speaks Tamil, which was the language of his mother, quite
beautifully. More recently, he has acquired an adequate knowledge
of Bengali.

For all his achievements, among Indian intellectuals at any rate
Gopal Gandhi can only be known as the younger brother of the
philosopher Ramchandra (Ramu) Gandhi. Although he wrote
several important books, Ramu Gandhi was at his best at the
lectern. I have never heard a more brilliant lecturer—a judgement
that would I think be endorsed by most people who heard him
speak in either Hindi or English, among them the very many
students he trained and inspired at the universities of Rajasthan,
Delhi, Hyderabad and Santiniketan. After he quit academic life,
Ramu Gandhi's main theatre of operation was the India International
Centre (IIC), where he would lecture occasionally in the auditorium,
and more informally—if to equal effect—in the lounge or the bar.

Ramu Gandhi was the son of Mahatma Gandhi's youngest son,
whereas his mother was the daughter of C. Rajagopalachari. In the
mid-1950s, when Ramu was entering university, Rajaji took an
extended holiday from politics to write modern renditions of the

Ramayana and the Mahabharata. He wrote them first in his native Tamil, and then translated them into English.

These modern versions of the epics proved so popular that a demand arose for translations into other languages. Rajaji's daughter, Lakshmi Devadas Gandhi, volunteered to do them in Hindi, a language she knew well in part due to her long residence in New Delhi. The Hindi versions sold briskly and continuously—they were still selling in the 1960s, and well into the 1970s. Sometime towards the end of that decade, Mrs Devadas Gandhi decided to make a will. However, as the daughter and daughter-in-law of ascetic and incorruptible politicians, she had no worldly possessions to speak of.

Except, of course, for the royalties from those translations. Who then to will them to? Mrs Gandhi had three sons. The first, Rajmohan was a journalist and author of popular works of biography and history—surely the Fourth Estate and his publishers would take care of him were he ever in distress? The youngest son, Gopal, was a member of the Indian Administrative Service—he would, in time, get a *sarkari* pension linked to the cost-of-living index. That left the middle son, the dreamy philosopher who had left six jobs and declined to accept six others.

So it was to Ramu Gandhi that the royalties were willed, and to him, after his mother's death in 1983, that they came. Every year, without fail, Ramu would get a cheque for several thousand rupees, which would comfortably cover the cumulative bills, for that year, from the IIC bar. And so, in this manner, works originally composed in Sanskrit, then rendered in Tamil and still later translated into Hindi, were to fuel the belly and the mind of the most brilliant man to have walked the lawns or entered the bar or spoken in the auditorium of the India International Centre.

The story may be apocryphal, but it deserves to be true. For, it illustrates like nothing else the beauty and potency of literary bilingualism—practised, in this case, across three successive generations—father, daughter and grandson.

chapter eleven

PLURALISM IN THE INDIAN UNIVERSITY

~

I

In 2007, the National Archives mounted an exhibition on the founding of the first modern universities in India. A Kolkata newspaper gave its report on this exhibition the headline: 'The Other Revolution of 1857'. This was apt, for the founding of these universities was indeed a revolution, and indeed also the 'other' to the better known revolution of 1857. Call it by whatever name, a sepoy mutiny or a war of independence, that uprising was essentially reactionary, looking back to a period before the white man set foot on the subcontinent. On the other hand, the revolution set in motion by the universities was essentially progressive, looking forward to a time when the white man would finally leave the subcontinent.

Founded in 1857, the universities of Calcutta, Bombay and Madras were the crucible of modernity in India. As the sociologist André Béteille has written, these universities 'opened new horizons both intellectually and institutionally in a society that had stood still in a conservative and hierarchical mould for centuries'. These universities were 'among the first open and secular institutions in a society that was governed largely by the rules of kinship, caste and religion'. Thus 'the age-old restrictions of gender and caste did not disappear in the universities, but they came to be questioned there'.

The universities were also a crucible of nationalism. It was there that young men and women learnt to question the logic of colonial rule, to hold up, as a mirror to their rulers, the British ideals of liberty and justice that were haphazardly upheld at home and comprehensively denied in the colonies. Gandhi and Ambedkar had their early education under the auspices of the Bombay University, C.R. Das and Subhas Chandra Bose under the auspices of the Calcutta University, C. Rajagopalachari and C. Subramaniam under the auspices of the Madras University. Tens of thousands of more 'ordinary' freedom fighters were also educated—in all senses of the word—by their time in these universities or in other universities set up in the period of colonial rule—such as those in Allahabad, Punjab, Banaras and Aligarh. These soldiers of non-violence, who defied their family and sacrificed their careers to fill the jails on Gandhi's call, came from all sections of society. They were high caste as well as low caste, men as well as women, Hindu and Sikh and Parsi as well as Muslim and Christian and Jain.

It is not just that the Indian university trained those who led and manned the freedom struggle. It was also that they trained those who led and manned the creation of a modern, democratic nation state. For, no new nation was born in more difficult circumstances—against the backdrop of civil war and privation, with eight million refugees to be resettled, and 500 princely states to be integrated. That a nation was forged out of these fragments, and that it was henceforth governed on the basis of a democratic Constitution, was a miracle—and not a minor one. The miracle was the handiwork of a group of visionary leaders—Nehru, Patel and Ambedkar pre-eminent among them—aided by thousands of now-forgotten civil servants, lawyers, doctors, teachers, social workers and soldiers, a majority of whom were shaped and formed by the Indian university system.

That 'system' was, and is, based on constituent colleges. The nurturers of nationalism and the nation state were educated as much in these colleges as in the universities of which they were part. Places such as Presidency College, Calcutta; Presidency College,

Madras; Elphinstone College, Bombay; St. Stephen's College, Delhi; Government College, Lahore; Patna College, Patna; and Maharaja's College, Mysore, have all contributed in ways large and small to the shaping of modern India.

It behoves us to recognize (and salute) the role played by our universities and colleges in nurturing Indian nationalism and building Indian democracy. But, since we live in the present, we must also admit that the state of our universities (and colleges) is not what it could and might be. I myself live in what is claimed to be the capital of India's 'knowledge economy', yet the university that my city houses is less than distinguished. In this respect, Bangalore University fairly represents the state of universities in the country as a whole.

II

I have long believed that while India is sometimes the most exasperating country in the world, it is at all times the most interesting. Which other land can match India in its mix of different castes, classes, languages, faiths, forms of dress, cuisines, musical styles, et al.?

For the scholar or writer, at his desk or in his ivory tower, the diversity of human forms is perennially interesting. For the citizen living life on the ground, however, it can at times be deeply exasperating. When people of one habit or temperament—or ideology or social custom—are placed close to people of another, they tend sometimes—oftentimes?—to react with prejudice and suspicion, this sometimes—oftentimes?—manifesting itself in conflict and combat, whether intellectual or physical, individual or institutional. Life would be altogether less discordant if everyone around us spoke and thought and dressed and ate just as we did. But altogether less interesting.

Broadly, there have been two responses to the prevalence or persistence of social and cultural diversity. The first has been to flatten it, to try and make citizens as alike as one another in the ways they think and speak and live. Or at least in the *important* ways—

such as in religion or language or political ideology. The second response has been to permit citizens their own individual ways of living, while crafting institutions that allow them to collaborate and coexist.

Fortunately, the men and women who built modern India chose the second path. They did not follow Israel or Pakistan in fusing faith with state by granting special privileges to citizens of one religion. They did not follow Germany or the United States by making it mandatory for all citizens to speak one language. And they did not follow Soviet Russia and Communist China in constructing a single-party state.

At least in theory, the Indian nation state is the most plural on earth. It demands less conformity among its citizens than every other state we know. The practice of pluralism is another matter. At various points in Indian history, vast influence has been exercised by those who would seek to make one religion (Hinduism), one language (Hindi), one party (the Congress), or even one family (the Nehru-Gandhis) dominant over the other religions, languages, parties, and families of India.

The theory and practice of pluralism in (and by) the Indian nation is a fascinating subject. So is the theory and practice of pluralism in the states and cities of India. Take the capital city of the state of Maharashtra, whose social diversity is reflected most immediately in the different names we know it by. There is, of course, a Marathi Mumbai, but also a Goan and East Indian Bombay, as well as a Hindustani Bambai. But this is also in some part a Gujarati city, also a Tamil city and a Kannadiga city. Every linguistic group in India is richly represented here, as is every religious community and political ideology. At the same time, Mumbai is the capital of a state formed to protect the interests of a single linguistic group. What are the tensions this creates in the lives and labours of the citizens of Mumbai/Bombay/Bambai?

The linguistic division of India has worked very well—for India *as a whole*. There has been friction at the edges, conflicts about towns and villages on the border, and about riparian rights, but had these states not been created I believe the conflicts would have been much more serious. Consider the examples of Pakistan and Sri Lanka, the first of which broke up, and the second of which experienced a brutal and bloody civil war. If a single language had been imposed on all of India—as the Hindi zealots wanted—this massive country might have been torn apart into fifteen or twenty states at war with each other.

So, without question, linguistic pluralism has strengthened Indian unity. But how does this diversity of language groups play itself out within a state, rather than in the country as a whole? As residents of Mumbai/Bombay/Bambai know all too well, diversity has sometimes produced sharp conflicts. If Mumbai is the capital of the state of Maharashtra, some ask, why must so many of the best or most lucrative jobs be taken by those whose mother tongue is not Marathi? These 'outsiders' answer that the Constitution of India grants all its citizens the right to live and work anywhere in the Union. For forty-five years now this debate has raged in Mumbai. It is now making itself heard in my native Bangalore, likewise the capital of a state based on language, likewise a city where the wealthy and powerful mostly do not speak the local tongue. Here, too, the conflict has manifested itself in the city's renaming, with 'Bangalore' becoming 'Bengaluru'.

III

Diversity is a *social condition*; it is what India is. Pluralism is a *political programme*; it is a manifestation of what we wish India to be. At the level of the nation, the practice of pluralism poses one set of challenges; at the level of the city or state, yet another. What then, of the university? What are the varieties of pluralism that a university in India must seek to foster? In my view, these are principally of five kinds:

First, the university must foster pluralism in the *student body*. There must be students of all ages; from those in their late teens to those in their early thirties (or even beyond). One way to do this is to have, within a single campus, programmes running all the way from BA or BSc right up to PhD. There must be many women students; in the ideal situation, 50 per cent or more. Students from low caste and working class backgrounds must be adequately represented; so also those from minority religions. Finally, a university is made more Indian if it can attract students from other states of the Union.

Second, the university must foster pluralism in the *teaching staff*. Like the students, these must be both women and men, who come from different classes, castes, and religious groupings. And—this is even more crucial here—from different parts of India. But—unlike in the case of students—it is not enough that the teachers come from different social backgrounds. They must also have diverse intellectual credos. Some must prefer abstract theoretical work; others, research that is more applied in nature. Since scholars are also citizens, university teachers have political beliefs; but these, again, must be of varied kinds. A university where all the teachers were Communists, or all of them Shiv Sainiks, would be a very boring place indeed.

Third, the university must offer a plurality of *disciplines*. It should have at least some—if not all—undergraduate colleges which offer degrees in the sciences as well as the humanities. There must be graduate programmes in the major disciplines—mathematics, economics, history, political science, physics, chemistry, biology, literature, etc; but also professional schools offering degrees in law, medicine, and business as well as, ideally, faculties of fine arts and music. At the same time, the university must have the flexibility—and imagination—to create new departments when scientific progress or social developments oblige it to do so.

Fourth, a university must foster a pluralism of approaches *within a discipline*. Its department of economics must have Friedmanites and Keynesians as well as Marxists. Its department of biology should have space for experimentalists who splice genes, for Darwinians who study speciation, and for fieldworkers who live with animals in the wild. A university department where all of whose members were wedded to one particular theoretical—or experimental—approach would be a very boring place indeed.

As Max Weber pointed out, unlike political parties or religious seminaries, universities are 'not institutions for the inculcation of absolute or ultimate moral values'. Put less politely, universities must not be allowed to become vehicles of indoctrination, promoting a particular political or religious point of view. They teach the student 'facts, their conditions, laws and interrelations', serving in this manner to 'sharpen the student's capacity to understand the actual conditions of his own exertions . . .' However, 'what ideals the [student] should serve—"what gods he must bow before"—these they require him to deal with on his own responsibility, and ultimately in accordance with his own conscience'.

This pluralism of methodological and theoretical approaches must be promoted at various levels: that of the university as a whole, in each of its constituent departments, and by each individual teacher as well. A century ago, in words that seem strikingly contemporary, Max Weber deplored the tendency of some professors 'of educating their students into certain political beliefs and ultimate outlooks'. He was himself clear that the university teacher 'is under the sternest obligation to avoid proposing his own position in the struggle of ideals. He must make his chair into a forum where the understanding of ultimate standpoints—alien to and diverging from his own—is fostered, rather than into an arena where he propagates his own ideals.'

(If I may interject a personal note here: I was myself taught sociology by a committed Marxist, Anjan Ghosh, who in this respect was a first-class Weberian. Within the classroom, he suspended his political beliefs while introducing his students to the works of the great classical sociologists—Durkheim, Marx, Simmel and Weber himself—all of whom he treated with equal seriousness and empathy.)

Fifth, a university must encourage a pluralism of *funding sources*. It must not rely only on state patronage, but raise money from fees, from its alumni, and from private corporations. By diversifying its portfolio, so to speak, the university reduces its dependence on a single source of patronage, while also engaging with (and making itself relevant to) a wider swathe of society.

Stated in this straightforward manner, these ends seem self-evident. Surely any self-respecting university will always be plural in all these ways? Not, perhaps, in India, where one cannot say with confidence that any of our universities have met these ideals wholly or consistently. However, at various points in history, one Indian university or another has been plural in one or other of these ways. As André Béteille has noted, it took six hundred years for Oxford or Cambridge to admit women, whereas Calcutta and Bombay universities admitted them from their inception. They also provided avenues of upward mobility for the lower castes: in the traditional system, an Untouchable like B.R. Ambedkar would have been condemned to a life of illiteracy. Those from minority religions also got, and took, their chances—some of the finest scholars and teachers in the history of Mumbai University have been Parsi and Muslim.

Likewise, there have been splendid examples of Indian universities promoting diversity in the social background of their teachers, and of these teachers in turn promoting a diversity of intellectual approaches. Determined to make Calcutta University more than a home for Bengalis, Sir Ashutosh Mukherjee appointed C.V. Raman and Sarvepalli Radhakrishnan to chairs when they were young and unrecognized—which Sir Ashutosh did not care about—but also talented and hardworking—which he appreciated. Raman and Radhakrishnan eventually moved on to other pastures, but a contemporary of theirs who stayed in Calcutta was the Malayali from Merton, Kuruvilla Zachariah, among whose students at Presidency College were many future leaders of free India.

Third, many Indian universities have been inclusive in a disciplinary sense. The pattern was set by the three founding universities, which all had departments of science and social science, as well as a faculty of law and a school of medicine. Thus in the 1930s and 40s, Bombay University was perhaps best known, on the research side, for its School of Economics and Sociology; while for the past half

century that honour has consistently been held by the university's
Department of Chemical Technology.

Fourth, the best university departments in India have promoted a
variety of intellectual approaches. The long-time head of the
sociology department in Bombay University, G.S. Ghurye, was a
bookish conservative; yet among the students he sent out into the
world were the superb ethnographer M.N. Srinivas and the Marxist
theoretician, A.R. Desai. Srinivas, in turn, bestrode the Delhi
University department of sociology like a colossus; like his teacher,
he did not impose his methodological preferences on those he
taught or guided. Srinivas had little interest in comparative sociology,
or in the industrial working class, or in the Sanskritic tradition;
yet three of his distinguished students were to make these subjects
their own.

It is with the fifth kind of pluralism that the record is most
disappointing. The Indian university has relied too heavily on
subsidies and handouts from the state. Middle-class and even rich
students pay the same fees as the poorer students; in effect, almost
no fees. There has been little attempt to tap the generosity of
alumni—even the most prosperous ones. Few universities cultivate
active links with the private sector or with philanthropic foundations.

Pluralism is one important ideal of the Indian university; it is not,
of course, the only one. A university must also have an institutional
cohesiveness, which allows it to reproduce itself regardless of the
particular individuals who lead or staff it. Again, a university must
have a particular and recognizable character, which encourages its
students, staff, faculty and alumni to identify with it. And it must set
standards of academic excellence consistent with those in the nation
and the world, and it must continually strive to maintain them.

These ends might not always be mutually compatible. Thus, in
one particular case or another—say the recruitment of students from
under-represented social groups or the appointment of a new
dean—pluralism might conflict with institutional efficiency, or
efficiency in turn conflict with academic excellence. Compromises
have to be made, judgement calls taken. It would be foolish not to

recognize that a public university serves multiple ends, and that these may sometimes be in conflict. That said, the varieties of pluralism enumerated above are, I believe, among the most important ends an Indian university should strive to fulfil.

IV

In the history of the Indian university, the forces favouring pluralism have had to contend with the opposing forces of parochialism. These are ever present, often powerful, and sometimes overwhelming.

One form of parochialism is identity politics. Particularly in staff appointments, the claims of caste or region or religion can play as significant a role as academic qualification or distinction. Often, the candidate with the best connections gets the job rather than the best candidate. And so, as André Béteille notes, 'the disputes that now dominate many if not most of our universities are not over the principles and methods of science and scholarship; they are over pay and promotion and the distribution of seats and posts among different castes, communities, and factions.'

A second form of parochialism is ideological. When the NDA government was in power in New Delhi, there was much criticism of the role played by the HRD minister, Murali Manohar Joshi, in placing, in important posts, intellectuals more amenable to his own political ideology. The criticism was just—it would have been more just still if it had acknowledged that in this respect Joshi was merely following the lead of the Communist Party of India (Marxist), which, in both West Bengal and Kerala, has consistently interfered with university appointments. Between 1977 and 2011, for example, no critic of Marxism stood a chance of becoming the vice chancellor of Calcutta University, or even of becoming a head of department in that university.

A third form of parochialism is institutional. There is, in almost every Indian university, a marked tendency to employ one's own graduates to teaching positions. This inbreeding has infected even the best departments in the best universities. Thus the history department in the Jawaharlal Nehru University and the sociology department in the Delhi University are largely staffed by those who have, at some stage or another, passed through the same portals as students.

Whether based on identity or ideology or institution, these varieties of parochialism have had a corrosive effect on university life. They have undermined the quality of teaching, narrowed the range of subjects taught, and polluted the general intellectual ambience. By now, they have collectively impacted millions of Indians, who got a more limited education than they hoped for, or, indeed, deserved.

Provincialism apart, there are other hurdles to the fostering of a plural ethos in the Indian university. One is short-sighted public policy. In the colonial period, the best science in India was done in the universities: by scholars such as C.V. Raman and Satyen Bose in Calcutta; Meghnad Saha and K.S. Krishnan in Allahabad; T.R. Seshadri in Delhi; and K. Venkataraman in Bombay. However, at Independence the decision was taken to set up a series of laboratories under the auspices of the Council for Scientific and Industrial Research (CSIR). It was made clear that these would be the favoured sites for research, and that the universities would focus mostly on teaching. The best talent drifted away to these prestige institutes, impoverishing the universities. On the other side, without the challenge and stimulation of students, laboratory science got steadily more bureaucratic, and did not deliver on its promises either.

In any case, in the Indian context what C.P. Snow called the 'two cultures'—the humanistic and the scientific—always had an uneasy relationship. Almost from the beginnings of modern education, Indian men were brought up to believe that the 'arts' were inferior to the 'sciences'. Even in universities where the two coexisted, science students or professors scarcely came into contact with their counterparts in the humanities. After Independence, apart from the CSIR, the creation of the Indian Institutes of Technology also contributed to the further moving apart of the two cultures. Although the IITs had departments of humanities, their concerns were integrated in a desultory way into the curriculum. The precedent had been set, well before, by the Indian Institute of Science, whose original charter (influenced by its visionary founder, Jamsetji Tata) had room for a department of social science, which, however, remains to be activated a century after the institute's founding. And so the finest young minds in the sciences have been encouraged to cultivate an indifference to (and even contempt for) the social sciences and history.

The plural ambitions of the Indian university have also been severely tested by a now-rampant populism. I have in mind the widespread suspicion of what are termed 'elite' departments and 'elite' universities. There is continuous pressure towards the equalization of resources, so that the public pie is shared equally by institutions good and bad, old and new. Institutions that were intended to be small and select are urged to let in more and more students, regardless of whether they can maintain standards while doing so. Where institutions of excellence should serve as a benchmark towards which others can aspire, they are instead asked to come down to the level of the lowest. In this manner, policies conducted in the name of democracy and egalitarianism serve only to degrade the education system as a whole.

These prejudices sometimes operate within a single university. Thus the Delhi School of Economics has long attracted widespread (and, for the most part, undeserved) opprobrium. Professors in other departments resented its international reputation, actually a product of intellectual excellence and an institutional culture of teamwork, but in the eyes of its critics a consequence of western-oriented 'elitism'. Successive vice chancellors sought to erode its autonomy and bring it on par with, or down to the level of, the other departments of Delhi University. Teaching vacancies were unfilled, sometimes for years upon end. Proposals to reform syllabi were held up. The end result could have been foretold—the Delhi School of Economics no longer has an international reputation.

A final hurdle is constituted by the invisible hand of the market. Universities work best when they have an integrated campus, bringing together undergraduate colleges, postgraduate departments of the arts and sciences, and professional schools, thus allowing the students and teachers of these different units to mingle with and learn from one another. Among the major universities of India, only Delhi University even remotely approximates this ideal. The reason for this is that a large chunk of territory was set aside for it when the new capital of British India was being planned. As the university expanded, the new colleges that sought affiliation had to be located elsewhere, but by then the campus itself had a sufficient density of institutions to have a character of its own. It was also close enough to the city to be connected to it. On the other hand, the universities of our other metros, Bombay, Calcutta, Madras and Bangalore, grew in a random fashion, so that their constituent units were far-flung and in no real contact. Since the price of real estate forbids the consolidation of these units, the undergraduate colleges remain isolated from one another and from the postgraduate departments; even the latter are often fragmented, spread unit by unit across the city. Some universities, for example, Bangalore University, then thought to construct a new campus on land available on the outskirts. The postgraduate departments were relocated here, with the undergraduate colleges staying where they were. This new campus has only served to further separate the university from the city whose name it carries and of which it is presumed to be an integral part.

Rising property prices have inhibited the growth of university pluralism in another respect: by making it very hard for Indians to study or teach in parts of India far from their own. In about 1940, a modest apartment could be rented in Bombay at about 20 per cent of a professor's salary; by about 1970, this figure might have jumped to 50 per cent. Now it must be close to, or even in excess of, 100 per cent. What this means is that the pool of available teachers has steadily shrunk; it now contains only those who have homes in the city itself. The consequences of this for the quality of intellectual life in the university are depressingly obvious.

The market works in mysterious ways. On the one hand, it has discouraged the movement of students and teachers within India; on the other hand, it has encouraged their movement to distant parts of the globe. In the 1960s and 1970s, large numbers of Indian scientists studied and then found employment in western universities; now, they are increasingly joined by social scientists, historians and literary scholars, the trade in whom is especially brisk in the American academy, to meet the demands of the growing Indian diaspora and the new-found fashions of 'postcolonial' studies. Once, names such as Ghosh, Mukherjee, Srinivasan and Reddy were quite common in the payrolls of the universities of Bombay and Puné; now, they are more likely to be found in the faculty web pages of the universities of Minnesota and Chicago.

The influence of parochialism and populism on our universities is, in part, a consequence of the clash or contradiction between two varieties of pluralism. For the survival of the Republic of India it was perhaps necessary to create linguistic states, so as to inhibit the dominance of one language group over the others. However, this enactment of a plural politics at the level of the nation as a whole has sometimes led to a denial of pluralism at the lower levels. This is particularly true in the state sector, where one can manipulate recruitment in a manner that the private sector forbids. Since an overwhelming majority of our universities are managed by state governments, they are particularly prone to local or regional chauvinism.

Ideally, a university would not want to be parochial even at the level of the nation state. The best western universities seek to draw students and faculty from all over the world. Such was also the original intention of Rabindranath Tagore's university, as witness the name 'Viswabharati'. That our universities become more international in their composition may be too much to hope for, but let us at least try and make them adequately Indian.

V

Writing in 1968, the sociologist Edward Shils singled out student unrest as a major threat to the proper functioning of universities in India. Shils observed that Indian students had been restive in the

1930s and 1940s as well, but that this had found a focus and a constructive outlet through the independence movement. In the 1960s, however, student protest was directionless; it was, in fact, a form of 'juvenile delinquency'. Indian student agitation, wrote Shils, was 'demoralizing and degrading the academic profession which is already in a worse situation than one cares to see'. If unchecked, student unrest would disrupt more than the universities—'if they go on, they will demoralize the Indian police services and render them incompetent to maintain public order or they will precipitate harsher repression resulting in many deaths which will in turn place very heavy strains on the Indian political system'.

These predictions were not entirely falsified. A few years later, students across India found a focus in the JP movement, which did in fact 'precipitate harsher repression' as well as the heavy strain on the Indian political system known as the Emergency. Still, it would be unfair to blame the general deterioration of our institutions of higher education solely or even primarily on discontented students. Indian universities have been undermined from above rather than degraded from below, corrupted and corroded by the forces of parochialism and populism itemized in this essay.

This writer is not the first to comment on the dangers of parochialism in the university—nor, to be sure, will he be the last. In September 1962—a month before war broke out between India and China—a group of liberal intellectuals met in Bombay to discuss the prospects for 'a national university'. The convenor of the symposium, the mathematician A.B. Shah, pointed to the 'growing regionalization of the universities under the pressures of a developing multilingual society'. This 'process of regionalization', he continued, 'is accompanied by increasing fragmentation of the intellectual élite and a weakening of the university tradition, which was never very strong in India'. Shah felt that the solution lay in 'the creation of a few national universities that would keep the tradition of the university alive till experience makes men re-examine the wisdom of what they have done'. He identified five likely carriers of this noble ideal—the three 'premier universities' in Bombay, Calcutta and Madras, plus two new universities to be sited in the north and the south respectively. These national universities, he felt, 'could ensure the continuity and development of all-India cultural life so essential in the context of regionalization'. They would 'provide the nation with a window to the world, and also a yard-stick by which the work of the regional universities could be evaluated'.

In the 1970s, the central government did establish one national university in the north (the Jawaharlal Nehru University) and another in the south (the University of Hyderabad). These two institutions, along with the far older Delhi University, have (as Shah hoped) helped in keeping some kind of all-India intellectual discourse alive. On the other hand, the three founding universities of Bombay, Calcutta and Madras have become more parochial rather than national in their orientation.

In his contribution to that symposium in 1962, the economist B.R. Shenoy focused on the declining quality of university and college teachers. This, he felt, was due to three reasons: abysmally low salaries, which meant that alternative professions were more attractive; the reproduction in the university of bureaucratic red-tapism, which meant that administrators were more important and more powerful than professors; and regionalism, which 'on the one hand, repels from the academic profession men from outside the region and, on the other, adds to the pressure for migration out of the profession'. Shenoy also called for the creation of national universities which would be 'wholly autonomous ... free from interference by the government or any political organization'.

This writer is also not the first to sing the praises of university pluralism. In a talk broadcast over the Delhi station of All India Radio on 17th March 1940, Sir Maurice Gwyer outlined what he saw as the future of the university he was then heading. He called, first of all, for 'the transference of all the constituent colleges of the [Delhi] University to a common site where they may stand together as a solid token of that sense of unity and purpose which is perhaps the most vital element in University life; secondly, the extension of the science laboratories and an increase in our present facilities for the teaching of science; and thirdly, the improvement and development of the University Library.' Gwyer went on to say that while the other and older universities of India were strongly rooted in their respective towns and provinces, 'Delhi University should not be afraid to draw its strength from a whole sub-continent. It should be a symbol of what India herself, above and beyond all her creeds or castes, can offer to the world.'

Gwyer also spoke of the importance of the university reducing its reliance on the public exchequer. He hoped that 'the time will come when to endow a chair of learning at Delhi University will seem to rich men a way, not less noble than others, of perpetuating their memory'. He ended his talk in words that rang true then, and ring truer now:

> I am speaking tonight more especially to the citizens of Delhi. Delhi University will always, I hope, be their University as well as a University for all India; and I look forward to the time when they will feel a great pride in its fortunes and in its work. I hope it will be a civic centre in the truest sense, and that those of its sons who are educated within its walls will learn there how to combine a love of their city with a love of their country, to look beyond the immediate conflicts of community and party to the greater unity which lies behind them, and to remember that of all the civic virtues for which a University should stand, a love of truth, a sense of proportion and a spirit of tolerance are not the least.

VI

Not very long ago, India had some fairly decent universities, but a very poor record in removing mass illiteracy. In the past two decades this situation has been reversed. There is a new energy abroad in the school sector, this driven in part by the state, in part by voluntary organizations, and most of all by parents. Once, many poor families chose to put their children to work rather than send them to school. Now, they wish to place them in a position from which they can, with luck and enterprise, exchange a life of menial labour for a job in the modern economy. As the educationist Vimala

Ramachandran pointed out in 2004, 'the demand side had never looked more promising. The overwhelming evidence emanating from studies done in the last 10 years clearly demonstrates that there is a tremendous demand for education—across the board and among all social groups. Wherever the government has ensured a well-functioning school within reach, enrolment has been high.'

Recent developments in primary education call for a cautious optimism. On the other hand, our best universities have steadily deteriorated in quality and capability. True, there remain a few well-functioning departments, some very fine scholars and many devoted teachers. Still, I think it is fair to say that in respect of the five criteria enumerated in this essay, the universities of Bombay, Calcutta and Madras probably functioned better in the 1930s and 40s than they do now. The halcyon period of Delhi University ran from the 1950s to the 1970s, that of the Jawaharlal Nehru University from the 1970s to the 1990s.

The deterioration that has set in, in these and other universities, has multiple causes. Among them are the varieties of parochialism and populism outlined above. These malign forces have been stoked by the political leadership. Ministers of education in the states work consistently to undermine the autonomy of their universities by interfering in appointments high and low. Ministers of education at the Centre have promoted personal favourites regardless of ability, and also used universities as tools of partisan politics.

In thinking of how best to renew our universities, we must, first of all, rethink our notions of size. Our big cities each have far too few universities for their own, and the public, good. The universities of Mumbai, Kolkata, Chennai, Delhi and Bangalore each have several hundred institutions affiliated to it, with a combined student population that runs into three lakhs and more. How can these institutions be effectively run, how can standards be maintained, by a single chain of authority headed by a solitary vice chancellor?

Second, within each university, big or small, all constituent units must not be treated alike. In particular, colleges and departments with a tradition of excellence in teaching and research should be accorded institutional autonomy, including the autonomy to raise their own funds. Each university must be encouraged to cultivate its own areas of distinction. Those words, 'distinction' and 'excellence', need to have their meanings restored. For, as we know only too well, in the realm of the academy, parochialism and populism work only to propel a race to the bottom. Why not instead work to ensure that some institutions of quality exist, and that those not yet there are encouraged to emulate them?

Third, to attract better teachers one needs more flexibility in recruitment policies. Now, most universities allow only full-time faculty, whose jobs are secure until superannuation, in exchange for which they must come to work every day and not take outside employment. However, a university in a city such as Mumbai or Kolkata can and must take advantage of the talent available in the public and corporate sector, in the media, and in voluntary organizations. If a scientist in an industrial laboratory, an editor in a newspaper, a senior lawyer in the high court, were all permitted to come one day a week to teach one course a year to young and keen students, there would, I think, be a profusion of volunteers. (A model here is the Social Communication and Media Department of Sophia College, Mumbai, which has made superb use of the multifarious talents of the working journalists of the city.) Likewise, with the increasing drift of the finest Indian scholars abroad, statutes and prejudices must be amended to allow some professors to teach for one term only, while spending the rest of the year where they like. The encouragement of adjunct and part-time faculty would, I think, greatly enrich the intellectual life of the university—and also help towards balancing its budget.

At the same time, with regard to full-time faculty our universities need to more seriously combat the pressures of parochialism. A policy of not appointing one's own graduates, at least at the lower levels, would aid a cross-fertilization of intellectual approaches and perspectives. A policy of setting apart a certain percentage of teaching jobs—say 30 per cent—for candidates from other states would make each university less parochial as well as more national.

By making one's teaching staff less parochial one can fashion a student body that is less parochial as well. One function that the best colleges and departments have historically served—and can be made to serve again—was to attract outstanding students from outside the state or region. In their pomp, the Delhi School of Economics, the Department of History at the JNU, the School of Fine Arts at M.S. University in Baroda, and the Department of Philosophy at the University of Puné, all had a catchment area that covered the entire country.

Which brings me, finally, to the question of funding. As of now, almost all universities in India are funded by the state and controlled by the state. In the long term, we need to have many more private universities, which might challenge the public universities to reform and redeem themselves. In the shorter term, colleges and universities in the state sector must more actively woo successful alumni and industrial houses for funds. The money, when and if it comes, can be tied to specific programmes and departments, but its ultimate use must be left to the discretion of the institution.

The ideals that I have outlined here are the product of an experience that is individual but I think not unrepresentative. My mind was quickened and shaped by the University of Delhi, which I was lucky to know and experience towards the end of its glorious period. But what I owe my *alma mater* is merely what other and greater Indians have owed their own universities. The national movement, and the building of a free and democratic India, were both nurtured and sustained by men and women whose minds were formed by the universities of India.

It is commonly argued that the impressive growth rates of recent years will be stalled by poor infrastructure: erratic power supply, potholed highways, inadequate public transport, and the like. My own view is that India's economic *and* social development depend as crucially on a renewal of its higher education system. What we Indians make of ourselves will depend, far more than we presently seem to realize, on what we make of our universities.

chapter twelve

IN NEHRU'S HOUSE: A
STORY OF SCHOLARSHIP
AND SYCOPHANCY

~

I

In the spring of 2005, I was in New Delhi for a meeting of the
Government of India's advisory board on culture, of which I was
then a member. Afterwards, the chair of the board—who was the
Union minister of culture, S. Jaipal Reddy—invited me into his
office. Mr Reddy had been reading a column I wrote for *The Hindu*
newspaper, and people he knew had praised the books I had
published. Would I, he asked, be interested in the directorship of
the Nehru Memorial Museum and Library (NMML)? I answered
that while I was flattered by his proposal, some of his colleagues in
government may not approve of his choice, since I was a critic of
the dynastic politics of the ruling Congress party. In any case, I added,
I would not be able to take the job, because I could not leave my wife
and children in Bangalore, and because I was a lousy administrator.

A few weeks later I wrote to the minister with a proposal of my
own. The NMML had been headless for about a year, its affairs
taken care of by a bureaucrat in the culture ministry. It certainly

needed a new, full-time director; however, I urged that the search be '*as transparent and open as possible*'. I recommended 'the following procedure for the selection of the Director of the NMML':

1. An Advisory Committee be constituted of eminent Indians of unquestioned ability and integrity. This Committee could consist of Professor André Béteille (representing the world of scholarship), Shri Gopalkrishna Gandhi (representing the world of public affairs), and Shri H.Y. Sharada Prasad (representing the world of letters). I doubt that you would find three other individuals so widely admired for their intellect and integrity. I should add that all three have a profound understanding of the principles that Jawaharlal Nehru stood for.

2. An advertisement calling for applications for the post of Director be placed in leading newspapers and journals. In particular, the advertisement should be inserted in the *Economic and Political Weekly*, India's leading journal of public affairs and social science research. Since the post is of the highest distinction, there should be no stipulation of minimum qualification (such as an MA in history); rather, all social scientists of quality, whether historians, political scientists, economists, or anthropologists, should be encouraged to apply.'

'The procedure I am recommending,' I continued, 'will ensure two things: first, it will allow and encourage qualified Indian scholars of all backgrounds (including those currently based abroad) to apply for this most prestigious post; second, it will lead to the best candidate being chosen, by a committee of the highest competence.'

When, a month later, I met the minister at the next meeting of the advisory board on culture, I asked why he had not replied to my letter. He said he had no answer to give, for (as he put it) 'sometimes one could not follow the highest academic standards'. I now asked whether he meant that since the NMML was named after Jawaharlal Nehru, and located in what was once his official home, it was Nehru's granddaughter-in-law and heir, Sonia Gandhi, who would decide who would be its next director, rather than a committee of scholars chosen by the ministry of culture, which funded the institution. I took Mr Reddy's silence to mean that my surmise was correct.

Not long after I met Mr Reddy, one of his Cabinet colleagues, K. Natwar Singh, took a senior journalist out to lunch. Mr Singh, then foreign minister, had, apparently, taken it upon himself to recommend a suitable new director for the NMML to Sonia Gandhi. He asked the journalist, whom he presumed to be more in touch with intellectuals than himself, for likely names. The journalist suggested mine. 'Ramachandra Guha has been critical of Indira Gandhi and the Emergency,' responded Natwar Singh; 'we can't have him.' His lunch companion then offered the name of the distinguished Kolkata historian and political theorist, Partha Chatterjee. 'I don't know Chatterjee's views on Indiraji, but he has been critical of Panditji [Jawaharlal Nehru],' said Mr Singh; 'so we can't have him either.'*

II

The Nehru Memorial Museum and Library is located in the grounds of Teen Murti House which, in colonial times, used to be the home of the commander-in-chief of the British Indian Army. It was the second grandest residence in New Delhi, smaller only than the viceroy's palace on Raisina Hill. When, in September 1946, Jawaharlal Nehru joined an interim government in the last year of colonial rule, he was assigned a decent-sized bungalow on York Road. After he became prime minister of India in August 1947, he stayed on in it. It was only in the middle of 1948 that he moved into Teen Murti House.

Cynics said at the time that Nehru had his eyes on the commander-in-chief's house all along, but so long as Mahatma Gandhi was alive he did not dare live in it. To be fair, Nehru's own needs were modest (if not quite as modest as the Mahatma's); he probably felt that his new home was better suited to the parties and official receptions that the prime minister of a large and sovereign nation would have to host. At any rate, when Nehru died, in May 1964,

*This story was told to me by the journalist, soon after his lunch with Mr Natwar Singh.

his daughter Indira Gandhi was determined that her father would be the first and last Indian occupant of Teen Murti House. Shortly after the mourning period was over, it was announced that Nehru's official residence would become a memorial to him. There was a precedent, of sorts—in the shape of a house half a mile to the east, which had once belonged to the millionaire Ghanshyamdas Birla. After Gandhi had been assassinated there in 1948, it became a museum to the memory of the Mahatma.

Fortunately, the man assigned to give shape to the Nehru memorial was the great Bombay jurist M.C. Chagla, who was then minister of education and culture in the Union Cabinet. Chagla thought that he had to do justice to Nehru the scholar and writer as well as statesman. So, Teen Murti House itself would become a museum; while in the spacious grounds a new archive and library would be established. Chagla and his advisers chose, as the first director of the Nehru Memorial Museum and Library, the historian and biographer B.R. Nanda. Nanda had been a senior official of the Indian Railway Service, who in his spare time had written first-rate biographies of Mahatma Gandhi and of Motilal and Jawaharlal Nehru. He knew how to manage men in an office; and he knew the value of primary source material.

On assuming charge, Nanda decided that the new museum and library would focus on the history of the Indian freedom movement. In the grand old home, Nehru's books and other artefacts would remain as they were, whereas in the rooms once devoted to state banquets a pictorial exhibition depicting the various stages of the independence struggle would be mounted. Meanwhile, a new building tucked away behind the mansion would house books, journals, magazines and private papers. Manuscripts and letters were sourced from families of nationalists all over India. The soldiers of freedom who were still alive—and there were then very many of them—were interviewed at length about their memories. Editors of journals and newspapers were encouraged to have their collections microfilmed; in exchange for their cooperation, they were given free copies of the microfilms for their use. Scholarly Indians with no heirs—or with heirs who disdained books—were asked to donate their collections. (Among the collections so acquired was that belonging to the Gandhi biographer, D.G. Tendulkar.)

By the time B.R. Nanda demitted office, in 1980, the library was well established. It was widely used by scholars living in Delhi, from other parts of India, and from across the world. Dozens of doctoral dissertations and books were being written on the basis of its collections. Nanda was succeeded as director by Ravinder Kumar, author of an important history of western India in the nineteenth century, and editor of a pioneering collection of essays on Gandhian protest. Kumar too knew the value of primary sources; moreover, he had interests beyond nationalist history, in such subjects as anthropology, social theory, cinema, art and literature. Nanda was a skilled and productive historian of the Indian freedom struggle; whereas Kumar was a genuine intellectual, whose scholarly concerns were unbounded by discipline or country.

Under Ravinder Kumar's direction, the scope of the NMML expanded in two important ways. First, the collections became more diversified—apart from politicians, the private papers of scientists, artists, social workers and performing artists were also acquired. This wider range of interests was also reflected in the journal and book collections. Second, a new Centre for Contemporary Studies was established, which gave three-year or five-year fellowships to historians and social scientists to write books on subjects of their choice. With thirty or so active scholars in residence, the NMML hummed with intellectual activity. A weekly seminar series was inaugurated, where the Fellows of the Centre for Contemporary Studies presented their research. Other speakers included university teachers in Delhi and beyond, and also visitors from abroad. Under the director's direction, the NMML became quite the liveliest place for scholarly work and debate in all of India.

In two respects, Ravinder Kumar stood out from the other Indian scholars of his generation. First, he was a genuine liberal, who encouraged quality work in all disciplines and from different points of the political spectrum. Second, he had a deep interest in the young. He chose the most promising scholars as his Fellows, and then encouraged them to host conferences on topics of their expertise.

The core strength of the NMML under Ravinder Kumar in the 1980s and 1990s was its intellectual diversity. This diversity was of five kinds: *disciplinary*, *ideological*, *methodological*, *geographical* and *generational*. Where B.R. Nanda and his team had focused on political history, now anthropologists, literary scholars and political theorists were as visible as historians, and social, cultural and environmental historians as likely to speak as students of the freedom movement. All varieties of intellectual and political opinion were represented. Liberals, Marxists, anti-Marxists and conservatives, all spoke. The only criteria were rigour and quality (and, especially, newness and originality of research). Presentations were based sometimes on archival research; at other times, on fieldwork or survey data. However, papers that were theoretical rather than empirical in nature were also welcome. Very many seminars were given by Indian scholars who came from outside Delhi, from Madras, Kolkata, and smaller towns. European, American and African scholars visiting India also spoke at the NMML. Those presenting papers ranged from young PhD students to emeritus professors in their seventies.

These multiple diversities were expressed in the regular Tuesday seminars, as well as in the thematic workshops held once every few months. The range of topics discussed was staggeringly wide. Social history, environmental history, labour history, gender studies, the history of art, educational reform, religious politics—on these and other subjects the most active debates in the Indian academy in the 1980s and 1990s were initiated or carried forward by the Nehru Memorial Museum and Library.

These seminars gave rise to papers and books of enduring quality. For instance, Aijaz Ahmad's widely discussed work on postcolonial literature, *In Theory*, and Sumit Sarkar's classic *Writing Social History* were both based on seminars first given at the NMML (and attended by a hundred or more eager if sometimes critical listeners).

Likewise, many other fine books and papers were produced as a consequence of this regular, diverse and rigorous seminar culture. A by-product under the NMML's own auspices were the couple of hundred Occasional Papers published by it, many of which later appeared in refereed journals in India and abroad. This production of books and essays was closely connected to the other major activities of the NMML—the augmentation of the manuscript collections, the conduct of new oral histories, the collection of new runs of old newspapers, and the publication of new series of historical documents.

B.R. Nanda and Ravinder Kumar came to the NMML in the right order. Nanda was a man of administrative detail who, with his civil service background, laid the systems in place. Kumar was a polymath and visionary, who through his range of interests and his own attractive personality took the work of the NMML beyond mere empirical accumulation into cutting-edge areas of scholarly research and argument. Both were helped by their staff, by the librarians, archivists, oral historians, and even clerks, security personnel and gardeners—all committed to their work and their institution. The NMML was also fortunate in having a series of excellent deputy directors—among them V.C. Joshi, D.N. Panigrahi and Haridev Sharma—who worked closely with the director in augmenting collections and guiding research. Their cumulative impact was colossal—one survey of published books found that as many as eight hundred had been based on the collections of the NMML.

III

I first entered the Nehru Memorial Museum and Library in the summer of 1982. I was just beginning research on my doctoral dissertation, which dealt in part with the social history of the princely state of Tehri Garhwal. In the files of the All India States Peoples Conference—one of several hundred separate collections housed at the NMML—I found fascinating material on peasant protests in Tehri Garhwal. In later years, the NMML proved crucial to the books and essays I was to write. My biography of Verrier Elwin drew in part on a collection of Elwin's papers that were housed at the NMML. My social history of cricket was based very largely on the fabulous newspaper archives maintained at the NMML, which included rare runs of Pakistani papers. My book *India after Gandhi* drew upon some forty collections of private papers at the NMML, as well as upon its microfilms of newspapers, its books and pamphlets, and its holdings of parliamentary proceedings.

By the time I met and wrote to the minister of culture, I had been working in the Nehru Memorial Museum and Library for more than two decades. I had known the place as a young student, as an experienced researcher, and, in between, as an employee. Between 1991 and 1994 I had been a Senior Fellow of the Centre for Contemporary Studies, when I had attended a series of stimulating seminars, argued with and learnt from my colleagues, and dipped into the archives in between. Among the thousands of beneficiaries of the selfless work of B.R. Nanda, Ravinder Kumar and their colleagues, I was but one individual, albeit, in my own eyes, a somewhat special one. In an intellectual and professional sense, no one owed more to the NMML than I. To be sure, there would be very many others who would insist that their debt was as great as mine—as great, perhaps, but certainly not greater.

Through the decades, as I had worked at the NMML, the staff had been knowledgeable, and unfailingly helpful. The surroundings were a delight; between spells consulting old files, one could walk around the grounds to see peacocks or hear the brainfever bird or simply admire the massive stone structure of the main building from the back or front lawn. True, the canteen served execrable tea and worse *samosas*, but here too, the conversation was never less than exhilarating.

Ravinder Kumar retired in 1997. The government in power, headed by the book-loving Prime Minister I.K. Gujral, appointed a committee to choose his successor. It came up with three names, of which at least two were credible: Mushirul Hasan, who like

B.R. Nanda, was a widely published empirical historian; and
Madhavan Palat, who like Ravinder Kumar, was a scholar of
cultured and cultivated tastes. Unfortunately, the government fell in
1998; and the regime that replaced it was headed by the insular and
parochial Bharatiya Janata Party. They rejected these two names—
Hasan's possibly because he was a Muslim, and Palat possibly
because he was, in a general sense, too broad-minded. They chose
instead the third name on the panel, which was of a bureaucrat
called O.P. Kejriwal who happened to have a PhD in history.

Kejriwal's tenure as director was colourless—he did not enhance
the NMML's reputation, but by respecting the autonomy and
capability of the staff, he did not damage it either. At the end of his
five-year term, a joint secretary in the ministry of culture assumed
temporary charge. By the time I wrote to Jaipal Reddy, Ravinder
Kumar had been gone for eight years. My (perhaps widely shared)
wish was that his legacy be renewed and even enhanced under a
new, and carefully chosen director. When Mr Reddy ducked the
challenge, I decided to approach the prime minister, Dr Manmohan
Singh, directly. This is the note I sent him:

Note for the Prime Minister on the choice of a Director for the Nehru
Memorial Museum and Library (NMML)

1. The NMML is the premier research centre for the humanities and
    historical research in the country. It has achieved its pre-eminence
    through the work of its first two Directors, B.R. Nanda and Ravinder
    Kumar, who cultivated an atmosphere of excellence and promoted
    scholarship of quality regardless of any prejudice in favour of or against
    any particular ideology.
2. The post of Director, NMML, has been vacant for some time now. It
    is imperative that this post is filled through an open, transparent process,
    with the Director chosen by a committee of acknowledged experts, and
    after candidates have been canvassed through advertisements in prestigious
    scholarly journals. As a member of the Advisory Board on Culture, and
    as a senior historian, the undersigned wrote to the Minister of Culture
    on the 11th of May urging such a process (letter enclosed). No reply was
    received to the letter.

3. It is believed that much lobbying is going on for the post of Director, NMML. This is worrying, given the predisposition of recent governments to fill such posts on grounds of patronage or ideology.

4. The heads of our scientific institutions are chosen by transparent considerations of merit and quality. The widely hailed appointment of Professor André Béteille as the Chairman of the Indian Council of Social Science Research gave rise to the expectation that the present government will uphold the same standards as regards the humanities and social sciences.

5. Were a careless choice be made as regards the NMML, it could have serious impact on the morale of the staff, and hence on the health of the institution itself. So many academic institutions in India have been undermined and even destroyed by patronage and politics. The NMML has thus far escaped this fate; it must be encouraged to escape it in the future as well.

Ramachandra Guha
Bangalore, 15th July 2005.

Once more, I received no reply. I heard from a friend in New Delhi that Dr Manmohan Singh had read the note, but that like Jaipal Reddy, he believed that this was Sonia Gandhi's turf, on which he would be wise not to transgress. Like Mr Reddy, he owed his own job to the chairperson of the United Progressive Alliance (and Congress party president). He was not willing to incur her displeasure by suggesting impersonal procedures for the selection of the new NMML director. From my (possibly naïve, certainly pig-headed) point of view, the NMML was a publicly funded institution that had to abide by professional norms. But in this regime the boundaries between party and government were fuzzy, and those between family and government fuzzy as well. Apparently, since the institution was named after Jawaharlal Nehru and based in a building where both Nehru and his daughter Indira Gandhi had lived, their heirs would have the final say.

IV

In August 2006, the Nehru Memorial Museum and Library finally got a new director. This was Professor Mridula Mukherjee of the

Jawaharlal Nehru University. She was chosen without an interview and not on the recommendation of a search committee. Rather, the selection had been made on the basis of the old Indian system of *sifarish*—that is to say, personal influence. Someone had suggested Professor Mukherjee's name to someone who knew someone who enjoyed the ear and the confidence of Sonia Gandhi.

Like some other scholars, I was disappointed by the manner in which the new director was chosen. Still, the deed was done; and the institution had to live on. Shortly after Professor Mukherjee took over, I wrote to her offering help in getting new collections of private papers for the library. I noted that since I did not teach in a university, the NMML meant more to me than any other Indian institution; and I would be delighted to do what I could to help it grow. There was no answer. A little later I wrote another letter to the director, this time with a fellow historian, Dilip Simeon. This urged that extended oral interviews be conducted of remarkable Indians now in their seventies and eighties. Among the names we mentioned were the social worker Ela Bhatt, the veteran worker for communal harmony Satyapal Dang, the environmentalist and founder of the Chipko movement Chandi Prasad Bhatt, the writer–activists U.R. Anantha Murthy and Mahasweta Devi, the security specialist K. Subrahmanyam, the Gandhian freedom fighter Narayan Desai, and the trade unionist Parvathi Krishnan. We volunteered to set up these interviews ourselves. There was no reply to this letter either. Letters offering support by other historians were likewise disregarded. The grandson of the great Tamil novelist A. Madhaviah wrote offering rare documents; he too received no reply. More shockingly, several letters sent by the Sabarmati Ashram suggesting the sharing of their respective collections went unanswered.

One can only speculate as to why these offers were scorned. What soon became apparent, however, was that Professor Mukherjee had her own agenda for the NMML. The family of which Sonia Gandhi was the most conspicuous and powerful legatee was to be made more visible in the programmes of the NMML. An exhibition was commissioned and mounted in the main foyer of the library. This was based on the letters exchanged between Indira Gandhi and Jawaharlal Nehru. For more than a year, every visitor to the library was greeted by the words and pictures of two former Congress prime ministers.

In the forty years of its history, the NMML had refused to identify itself with a particular party, still less a particular family. Its collections included the papers of the Hindu Mahasabha and the Communist Party as well as the All India Congress Committee. It had, under its own imprint, published the speeches and writings of Acharya Narendra Dev, who was a vocal critic of Nehru; and of Jayaprakash Narayan, who had been jailed by Indira Gandhi. The NMML was intended to be a serious centre of documentation and research, which paid attention to all political strands in modern India.

The Nehru–Indira exhibition was an artless attempt at ingratiation. Worse was to follow. The seminar room of the NMML was handed over to the Youth Congress, for meetings addressed by the family and party's presumptive heir, Rahul Gandhi. Meanwhile, the normal academic activities of the institution ground to a halt. There were no oral histories being conducted. In the past, the staff was sent on regular missions to different parts of India to seek out collections of private papers and old newspapers. The practice was disbanded; offers by individuals to donate important papers in their possession were ignored. The publication of books by Fellows and of series of historical documents also came to a standstill.

If some of the exhibitions and all of the Youth Congress meetings were intended to promote the family name, other efforts were aimed at protecting it from calumny and criticism. In May 2007 my book *India after Gandhi* was published. Among its sources were the private papers, housed at the NMML, of Subimal Dutt and Y.D. Gundevia, who had served in the foreign ministry under Nehru; and of Indira Gandhi's principal secretary, P.N. Haksar. These had proved crucial in reconstructing India's border disputes and wars with China and Pakistan. I had been the first to use these collections; but now, seeing my footnotes, other scholars wanted to consult them too. However, whereas I had free access, under the new director curbs were put in place, in case materials inimical to Nehru's or Indira's reputation were located in these papers. Every file relating to foreign affairs had now to be cleared by the director and by a senior official of the foreign ministry. This policy was probably illegal, for the donors of these collections of private papers had not imposed any such restrictions. 'Security reasons' were cited; but as the then serving foreign secretary (who was consulted by the NMML administration) told me, the director was being unnecessarily paranoid—at least 95 per cent of the files brought to his ministry for clearance, he said, had no bearing on national security at all.*

Meanwhile, the number of seminars organized by the NMML precipitously declined. Instead of one every week there was one every month (at best). The speakers were now mostly from Delhi. Likewise, the range of topics became much narrower, reflecting the new director's desire (as stated in a press interview) that her task was merely to promote the 'secular and scientific ideals of [Jawaharlal] Nehru'.

A further manifestation of the redirection of the institution was the decline of the library. The NMML was known for its excellent holdings of old and new books in history and the social sciences. It was the library of first or second recourse for thousands of students and scholars in Delhi, and the library of last recourse for students and scholars from other parts of India. The collections of old books had been steadily augmented by reaching out to families of deceased scholars. The purchase of new books was supervised by an acquisition committee composed of NMML Fellows from the various disciplines.

*At the time, I lodged a formal complaint against this policy of restricted access. In a letter dated 26th April 2008 to the chairman of the NMML's Executive Council, Dr Karan Singh, I wrote: 'My own self-interest might lie in curbs being placed on these materials on Kashmir, China, the Emergency, etc. For then I could aspire to *India after Gandhi* becoming the authoritative and uncontested version of these events. However, I was trained by Ravinder Kumar to welcome disagreement. I deplore the fact that the access granted to me under a previous dispensation is now being denied to other and often younger scholars. For I wish them to explore, more fully and more rigorously than I could, the riches of the NMML, even if in so doing they were to challenge or overthrow my own explanations and arguments.'

Shortly after the new director took over, the book acquisition committee was disbanded. The post of chief librarian, which had recently fallen vacant because of the incumbent's retirement, was left unfilled (and remained unfilled for the next five years). Opportunities to acquire collections were not taken; in a particularly sad, and shocking, instance, the NMML rebuffed the daughter of the literary journalist and bibliophile Sham Lal, when she offered to donate his collection for free. Meanwhile, with no one to lead or guide them, the library staff became apathetic and indolent. Books lay on tables for days, unshelved.

As compensation for the abandonment of scholarly work, the new administration of the NMML chose to start a Children's Centre. Groups of ten-year-olds were fed snacks and then taken through a library whose contents they must, given their age, have been completely confused by. This was done under the rubric of 'democratizing' access. The comment of a sceptical older scholar was that this was, at the very least, a safe and non-political alternative to critical intellectual activity; besides, it might make of these young Indians future Congress voters and family loyalists.

Perhaps because of the manner of her appointment, the new director was deeply insecure about her position. This was reflected in the somewhat obsessive urge to promote or protect the First Family of the Congress party. The director's insecurity was also manifest in the manner in which she bypassed the existing—and often very capable staff—by recruiting (often unqualified) consultants instead. These were very often from her own institution, the Jawaharlal Nehru University. The consultants were charged with such activities as putting up posters on trees around the campus (featuring the sayings of Jawaharlal Nehru and Indira Gandhi), and hosting lunches and teas for children. The staff, used to more substantive work such as the collection of manuscripts and the conducting of oral histories, were at first bemused. As the *tamasha* continued, however, their attitude went from resignation to cynicism.

In 2006 and 2007, I watched the institution deteriorate from very close quarters. I made at least half a dozen trips a year from

Bangalore to Delhi, each time spending a week or two working
through the priceless collections of the NMML. I saw the promotion
of the First Family come and grow; and the morale of a once-
devoted staff shrink and fade.

On one of these visits, I made a discovery that underlined the
staggering distance between the NMML as it once was and as it had
since become. In a back drawer of an upstairs hall, I found nine
microfilm reels containing records of the South African government
for the period 1893–1910. These had priceless information on the
life and labours of the Indian community in Transvaal and Natal, at
a time when Gandhi was working there. In a file of acquisitions
kept in the office, I was able to trace the process by which they
came to the NMML. The apartheid regime was in place then; and
no contact was possible between Indians and South Africa. However,
the visionary deputy director of the NMML, Haridev Sharma, had
located an American scholar who had trawled through the South
African archives. This man was prevailed upon to microfilm these
documents, and pass on a set to the NMML. For this, Dr Sharma
had to overcome not merely the diplomatic cold war between India
and South Africa, but the obdurate and unhelpful Indian bureaucracy
as well, out of whom he had somehow cajoled the necessary
permissions to compensate, in scarce foreign exchange, the American
scholar. That was the kind of work the NMML staff were once
motivated to perform. Now they were being instructed to distribute
barfis to schoolchildren and facilitate Youth Congress meetings.

V

In the summer of 2008, the deputy director of the Nehru Memorial
Museum and Library, Dr N. Balakrishnan, was abruptly divested of
his existing responsibilities. Like his predecessors, Dr Balakrishnan
had served as a crucial bridge between the director and the staff. He
was extremely knowledgeable and competent; and deeply committed
to the institution. One of his recent initiatives had been to rescue
a huge caché of Gandhi papers which were in the illegal control of

the family of the Mahatma's last secretary, Pyarelal. Under Dr Balakrishnan's supervision, these papers had been classified, sorted, preserved and indexed. This was the largest collection of Gandhi papers outside the Sabarmati Ashram; now, for the first time since Gandhi's death, officials of the NMML had made them accessible to scholars.

In the preface to his *War and Peace in Modern India*, the brilliant young historian Srinath Raghavan writes: 'In researching this book I have benefited from the expertise of archivists in fourteen institutions across four continents. But for their professionalism this book would never have got off the ground. It may seem invidious to single out an individual, but I am particularly grateful to Dr N. Balakrishnan, Deputy Director, Nehru Memorial Museum and Library.'

Why had this very capable archivist and administrator fallen foul of his boss? He had, it seems, expressed reservations about the Children's Centre, and the director's neglect of the staff in favour of outside consultants. Anyway, this humiliation of Dr Balakrishnan upset many users of the NMML, who could testify to his uprightness and competence. It seemed of a piece with the general decline of the NMML as a whole. A group of former Fellows now wrote to the chairman of NMML's executive council, Dr Karan Singh, expressing concern at the direction the institution was taking. Their note drew attention to the abandonment of the oral history programme, the lack of interest in acquiring manuscripts, the new-found political partisanship, and other signs of departure from the NMML's history and mandate. It concluded with these paragraphs:

A dynamic institution requires to keep abreast of change, whilst remaining true to its founding perspectives. This is especially true of the NMML, whose activities define it as a pro-active historical archive of modern India. We believe that six decades after Independence, the focus of this activity needs to go beyond the freedom struggle, important as it is. Oral testimonies of freedom fighters will soon become inaccessible. Meanwhile significant developments have taken place in the life of the Republic that require documentation and research. (The Centre for Contemporary Studies was established by Professor Ravinder Kumar to fulfil precisely this purpose.) These include social movements; new political alliances, civic activism; insurgencies; communal conflagrations; caste and class eruptions; changing gender relations; the media and communications explosion; the emergence of new business enterprises and new trends in education. The NMML should be active on these issues to retain its cutting edge.

If the NMML's governors consider our observations useful, they could establish an advisory committee of reputed academics charged with recommending institutional objectives. A strategic guideline of this kind might assist the NMML in making policy decisions and allocating resources. In any event, it will always require the care and retention of its existing instruments such as a fine library, ongoing oral history collections, an active manuscripts section, and a lively seminar for on-going work.

Our criticisms are not meant to detract from the valuable role the NMML plays in academic and intellectual life. There are many ways in which it continues to embody fine traditions and norms. All those who work there deserve credit for this. However, we are concerned about whether it is performing according to its past standards and pursuing its potential. The current practices may well lead the NMML into decline.

We have written this note in a responsible spirit and with respect. When a set of policies and decisions conflict with the core mission of an institution, it is time to think of a course correction. In our view an unfortunate administrative style and misguided decisions have been embarked upon that will corrode the NMML's strengths. Scholars, academics and citizens interested in the pursuit of knowledge have to try and rescue this internationally reputed institution. This is a task that we owe ourselves and future generations of researchers who have (and will) benefit from its fine services; it is also something we owe the great Indian intellectual and democrat after whom this institution was named and whom it was meant to honour.*

Dr Karan Singh was a former maharaja of Kashmir, who was now a senior Congress politician. The other members of his executive council included a journalist close to the Congress party, a newspaper proprietor close to the Congress party, and a bureaucrat close to the Congress party. None had any pretentions to scholarship, or any real

*The signatories to the note were Sumit Sarkar, Neera Chandhoke, Madhavan Palat, Mahesh Rangarajan, Prabhu Mohapatra, Ramachandra Guha and Dilip Simeon.

knowledge of the activities, past and present, of the NMML. All knew, however, that the present director of the NMML was the personal choice of the current president of the Congress party.

The letter by the former Fellows was met with a brief, non-committal answer. Dr Karan Singh was gracious enough to meet with some of its signatories. However, he showed little interest in what they had to say about the functioning of the NMML. The only concrete outcome of the meeting was a further humiliation of Dr Balakrishnan. Apparently, the director or the chairman of the executive council, or both, had come to the erroneous conclusion that the deputy director had instigated the note by the Fellows. So, in April 2009, Dr Balakrishnan was suspended from his post, and proceedings initiated aimed at his dismissal from service.

VI

The suspension of a central government officer is extremely rare in India. It occurs only when there is clear evidence of continuous and large-scale nepotism and corruption. This, however, was a vicious act of vengefulness; initiated by an insecure director, and carried out by a chairman whose attitude and actions betrayed the feudal background to which he owed allegiance. Dr Balakrishnan, from this perspective, was a rebellious and insubordinate serf, who had to be shown his place.

In May 2009, a month after Dr Balakrishnan was suspended, the Congress-led UPA won the General Elections. Manmohan Singh was sworn in for a second term as prime minister. This time, he chose to keep the culture portfolio for himself. This encouraged the group of scholars who wished to stem and if possible reverse the decline of the NMML; perhaps, as a scholar himself, the prime minister would see fit to support their efforts. The present director's term was to end in August; perhaps next time a capable successor could be chosen through an open and transparent process. The seven former Fellows who had originally written to Dr Karan Singh now solicited the support of other historians and social scientists who had worked in or been shaped by the NMML. The response was overwhelming. A letter to the prime minister/minister of culture was drafted and endorsed by fifty-seven scholars of distinction, young and old, living in India and abroad. The signatories included Rajmohan Gandhi, Veena Das, Sunil Khilnani, Tapati Guha Thakurta, Sanjay Subrahmanyam, Nayanjot Lahiri, Sumit Sarkar, Krishna Kumar, Partha Chatterjee, Sugata Bose, Srinath Raghavan, Joya Chatterji, Mushirul Hasan, Gyanendra Pandey, Nivedita Menon, Shahid Amin, A.R. Venkatachalapathy and Zoya Hasan. Never before had such a glittering array of (normally individualistic) scholars put their collective seal on a public activity. This was merely a reflection of what the NMML had once meant to the intellectual life of the nation. The operative paragraphs of their letter follow:

Sir, in your dual capacity as Prime Minister and Minister of Culture, we urge you to recognize that as the repository of our modern history the NMML is absolutely unique. The NMML contains within its walls the histories and memories of the very many remarkable people who made India a nation-state and who helped nurture it as a democracy. Some of these patriots are famous; others obscure. They came from all parts of the country and from a variety of social backgrounds. They owed allegiance to a wide variety of beliefs and ideologies. In giving all these trends a home, the NMML is a microcosm of India itself. In this sense the NMML is absolutely irreplaceable. If a private firm like Satyam collapses there are other private firms that shall take its place. If a once great college like Presidency in Kolkata or St. Stephen's in Delhi declines, other colleges will continue to provide quality education. If one political leader fails to honour his or her mandate, the voter or citizen can elect another in his or her stead.

But there is no possible substitute for the Nehru Memorial Museum and Library. Its decline is visible for all to see; its destruction will be a national calamity. We now ask you to immediately set in motion the steps necessary to save the NMML from becoming a failed institution. To revive the NMML, and to set in motion the process by which it can be restored to its former place of pre-eminence in the intellectual life of India, the Ministry needs to do the following things:

First, restore the morale of the dedicated and experienced staff by ending the tenure of all consultants, and by revoking the suspension of the Deputy Director;

Second, induct into the Executive Council (EC) three or more distinguished scholars. According to the bye-laws of the NMML, the EC must have an adequate representation from academics and scholars. However, at present the EC has only one scholar—this is Shri B.R. Nanda, whose advanced age (he is over ninety) and indifferent health has made it impossible for him to actively participate in the EC. The other members of the NMML EC are all from outside the academic community. Clearly, the absence of scholarly expertise in the body charged with supervision has contributed to the inability to stem the decline of the institution;

Third, once the present Director's term ends in August, her successor must be chosen through an open, transparent process. As with Directors of IIMs and IITs, the Director of the NMML should be chosen by a committee of acknowledged experts. This selection committee should consist of historians, sociologists or political scientists of national and international renown, and who are known to be utterly non-partisan. Applications for the post of Director, NMML, should be solicited through advertisements placed in leading academic journals in India and abroad. The selection committee can then short-list and interview candidates before choosing, through this rigorous process, the best person for the job;

Fourth, once a new Director takes office, he or she must be encouraged by the reconstituted EC to reach out once more to the scholarly community as a whole, thus to restore the NMML's non-partisan and plural character.*

The scholars who signed this letter sometimes expressed their sentiments in anguished personal communications to this writer. 'I know how important an institution the Nehru Memorial [Museum and] Library is,' wrote a senior art historian from Calcutta, 'and I'm distressed to hear of the kind of things happening there now. It is such a struggle to keep the life and dynamism of institutions going, especially as one generation of scholars and directors go away, and our generation must take over.' A sociologist and novelist based in Delhi, who is an exact contemporary of mine, and who had likewise been shaped and formed at every step by the institution, wrote that the

*The letter was published in its entirety in the *Economic and Political Weekly*, issue dated June 27–July 4, 2009.

Nehru Memorial Museum and Library has been a meeting ground for scholars for decades now. The Library was always the best kept, and the silence and the new books always meant that research was a priority for the staff, the fellows and the guests. The dichotomy between staff and fellows was always an artificial one, for the Director and the Deputy Director were meant to bridge this in their different ways. While Mridulaji is an old friend, I must admit that the polarity between staff and scholars (visiting the library or as fellows) is now very large. There is a great deal of discontentment since the staff is not given their due. The archives have been maintained for these many decades because of the commitment of the staff. The staff is the spine of the institution. They must be encouraged to speak their mind to the Board and to the Director, without fear of reprisal.

Dr Balakrishnan and his team have devoted their lives to the NMML. They had the total support of previous directors, and we as scholars from all over the country benefitted from that teamwork. Staff is permanent, directors rotate. The staff must feel that their work in keeping up the archives and library and resource materials of the NMML is acknowledged. The success of the institution, as museum, library and archives depends on the osmosis created between them. It is first of all a library and research archive, since the Museum houses these as a Trust to [Nehru's] contribution to the National Movement. Democracy rather than oligarchy must be its primary emphases.

Meanwhile, a very distinguished historian and founding member of Subaltern Studies said:

I feel really sad about the goings at NMML. I first began work there in 1972, when the library was in the old building, and seminars were held in a hall on the first floor. Dr Balakrishnan, and a clutch of senior lady administrators, librarians and manuscript handlers at the Teen Murti have all earned our respect. We must surely protest, and perhaps widen our intervention (at a later stage) by pointing out (as politely as possible) that the G[overnment O[f] I[ndia] has not thought fit to have a single practising scholar on the Board of Teen Murti.

And another remarked:

Dr Balakrishnan has been a huge support to scholars, particularly during the interregnum when the new Director had not been appointed for a considerable period. What is equally or perhaps more worrying is the way in which the current dispensation has operated there. This will, in the long run, leave precedents to be followed without any resistance for the worse kind of nepotism/oppression from the political class if not resisted at this juncture.

A British scholar wrote about how he

> vividly remember[ed] how awed I was by the NMML collections when I first visited there as a young scholar in the late 1980s and I owe a personal debt to Professor Ravinder Kumar (without whom I would never have been able to gain access to the MP State Archives in Bhopal, where I worked for a whole year in the early 90s). The NMML was always the best place to find the latest publications on the history, sociology or politics of any part of India. The collections were in fine condition and the NMML seminar programme used to be a lively centre for academic debate. Sadly, the NMML is now a poor reflection of this past excellence. The facilities for fellows are much deteriorated, the seminar programme is I understand entirely extinct, and it is a struggle to make use of the library's microfilm collection, with the limited and out of date equipment available and the weary and demoralized attitude of staff.

VII

The letter sent by the scholars to Dr Manmohan Singh was forwarded to the director of the NMML, who immediately—and naturally—canvassed her own supporters. These wrote in to the prime minister and the Congress president, saying that the criticisms of the institution's current functioning were personally and politically motivated. One letter accused the signatories to the memorandum of being 'self-professedly exclusivist and loyally wedded to the Euro-American pedagogic grid while remaining tactfully divorced from the Indian contexts upon which it feeds incessantly for the fame and glory it keeps garnering globally'. A second dismissed it as the handiwork of 'bureaucratic pin pricks and jealous people'. A third, written by a certain Arjun Dev, claimed that the memorandum sent by the fifty-seven scholars 'gives the impression that it was drafted to be addressed to the new government that the signatories thought would be formed in May under a new dispensation. That, unfortunately for them, did not happen. If it had, the Memorandum on this count at least would have won them great laurels and the new dispensation would have taken immediate steps to get rid of the malaise along with much else, if not the whole lot.'

The election of May 2009 had pitted the United Progressive Alliance, which was led by the Congress party, against the National Democratic Alliance, whose major constituent was the Bharatiya Janata Party. The incredible charge that the signatories to the letter to the prime minister—Rajmohan Gandhi, Sunil Khilnani, Nayanjot Lahiri, Partha Chatterjee, Neera Chandhoke, Sanjay Subrahmanyam, Nivedita Menon et al.—were closet or open supporters of the BJP was sought to be proven by a targeted reference to me personally. Thus Mr Dev wrote:

> The 'pluralism and ecumenism' of at least one of the signatories who appears to be the driving force, the representative of the 'representatives of the scholarly community', of the campaign against the NMML and its present Director perhaps needs some looking into. Shri Ramachandra Guha . . . [i]n his book, *India After Gandhi* [Picador, 2007] . . . deals with the killings of Sikhs in the aftermath of the assassination of Indira Gandhi. Following his version of 'pluralism and ecumenism' . . . he concludes that the mobs 'were led and directed by Congress politicians: metropolitan councilors, members of Parliament, even Union Ministers'. [P. 571] This is followed by a reference to the 'deeply insensitive' comment of Rajiv Gandhi. Later, he compares Rajiv Gandhi to Narendra Modi. He writes, 'In both cases the pogroms were made possible by the willed breakdown of the rule of law. The Prime Minister in Delhi in 1984, and the Chief Minister in Gujarat in 2002, issued graceless statements that in effect justified the killings.' [P. 657] In Shri Guha's view, Modi was guilty of issuing only 'graceless statements'; he was no more responsible for the Gujarat massacre than Rajiv Gandhi was for the killings in Delhi. Further, he writes, 'The final similarity is the most telling, as well as perhaps the most depressing. Both parties, and leaders, reaped electoral rewards from the violence they had legitimized and overseen'. [pp. 657–58] Rajiv Gandhi is thus accused of having not only legitimized the violence [by his graceless statement] but 'overseen' it, meaning 'supervising' it. Even the worst critics of Rajiv Gandhi have never made this accusation . . .

This letter was also copied to Sonia Gandhi. The parallels between the pogroms against the Sikhs in Delhi in 1984 and against Muslims in Gujarat in 2002 were marked—I would stand by every word I wrote on this subject in my book. But the twist, or spin, put by Mr Dev on my analysis was: 'This man is equating Rajiv Gandhi with Narendra Modi.' If there was one politician Sonia Gandhi detested, it was Mr Modi. As it happens, I don't particularly care for Mr Modi either, but this did not mean I would necessarily excuse or be an apologist for comparable crimes committed by other parties or politicians. In my book I had done what I thought was the historian's duty, but this had now come back to haunt, and possibly doom, the campaign to save the Nehru Memorial Museum and Library.*

In the end, Professor Mukherjee was granted an extension of two years. A senior official in the prime minister's office I spoke to said that the PM recognized the intellectual force of our argument—the mistake we had apparently made was to mention the portraits of the Congress prime ministers in the foyer and the fact that the NMML had been home to Youth Congress meetings. This permitted the director and her supporters to—*pace* Mr Dev—represent us as somehow being against the interests of the Congress party (and its

*The day after I wrote this paragraph, *The Hindu* published an article by Siddharth Varadarajan which compared the pogroms of 1984 and 2002 in the following words: 'The reality is that the Delhi and Gujarat massacres are part of the same excavated site, an integral part of the archaeology of the Indian state . . . In an act of conception which lasted four bloody days, something inhuman was spawned in the streets of Delhi in 1984; by 2002, it had fully matured. Paternity for the "riot system" belongs to both the Congress and the BJP, even if the sangh parivar managed to improve upon the technologies of mass violence. Both knew how to mobilise mobs. Both knew how to get the police to turn the other way. Both knew how to fix criminal cases. Both knew what language to speak, even if one set of leaders spoke of a "big tree falling" and the other paraphrased Newton. Both had the luxury of not being asked difficult questions by criminal investigators.' On the interrogation of the Gujarat Chief Minister Narendra Modi in March 2010, by a team appointed by the Supreme Court, Mr Varadarajan remarked that 'the reality is that the call for a leader to render account for mass crimes committed on his watch comes 18 years too late. Veteran journalist Tavleen Singh said recently that if Rajiv Gandhi had been interrogated in 1984 about what happened to the Sikhs [in 1984], Gujarat would not have happened [in 2002]. She is right.'

Fortunately, neither Tavleen Singh nor Siddharth Varadarajan were involved in seeking to rescue a public institution from the control of Rajiv Gandhi's heirs.

First Family). Members of Parliament who were office-bearers of the Youth Congress had also met the prime minister to press the director's case. Meanwhile, as with the controversial selection of Pratibha Patil as the President of India, criticisms of one of her appointees made Sonia Gandhi even more determined to protect her protégé. The Congress party, and its president especially, valued loyalty and length of service above all other virtues and characteristics. In India in general, and in this regime in particular, loyalty would take precedence over scholarship and institution-building, any time.

Soon after the director of the NMML had been granted a new term, the institution announced that it would hold a month-long celebration 'to commemorate the 120th birth anniversary of Jawaharlal Nehru'. A festival of films, inaugurated by the Congress chief minister of Delhi, purported to show how 'Bombay cinema took Nehru's vision of secularism to the masses and popularized it'. A seminar on Nehru's impact on Indian architecture was organized, where one speaker claimed that 'Jawaharlal Nehru wanted the buildings to reflect what he stood for . . . He was probably the last "ruler" in Delhi who has had a great impact on the architecture of his times and his city since Shahjahan.' Other seminars celebrated the 'Nehru Imprint' on music, drama, and education. Meanwhile, a children's fair was held to show young Indians how 'to make friends with Chacha Nehru in the twenty-first century'. The publicity material for this event noted that 'Pandit Jawaharlal Nehru was the first prime minister of India who had contributed much towards its freedom . . . [H]is love for children and emphasis on their education was outstanding.'*

Indians love anniversaries. Programmes marking the 50th, 60th, 75th, 100th, 125th or 150th anniversary of the birth or death of a famous writer, scientist or politician, or of the ending of a war, or

---

*The choice of examples was unfortunate. While Nehru made many contributions to national unity and democracy, architecture and the schooling of children were not among them. He disregarded building styles more adapted to Indian climates in favour of bloodless modernists like Corbusier. And he seriously neglected primary education. A more intelligent propagandist would have avoided these topics altogether.

the promulgation of a nation's independence, are ubiquitous. But this, surely, must be the first time a respectable scholarly institution, spent a whole month celebrating the 120th anniversary of anything. A brochure printed to record these events for posterity began with a selection of Nehru quotes, headlined, 'Nehruspeak'. Any echo of George Orwell's 'Newspeak' was wholly unintended.

VIII

In April 2010, just after I had finished writing the first draft of this essay, I received, in the post, a calendar printed by the Nehru Memorial Museum and Library, which like the 'Nehru Imprint' bulletin, was presumably proof of the tireless activities of the current administration. I was unimpressed, and wrote a letter to Suman Dubey, a close friend of Rajiv and Sonia Gandhi who had just been made a member of the NMML executive council. This is what I said:

Dear Suman,

I was recently sent a copy of the NMML calendar. I was disappointed by the production quality—as a bird lover, you must have noticed too that half the pictures were out of focus. But there is a larger question—should scarce public money be spent on this kind of product? It may be that a printing budget had to be spent—then why was this not spent on finally sending to the press the two volumes of the Rajagopalachari papers that for several years are awaiting printing, and for which very many scholars and ordinary readers are waiting? Or it may have come from a general budget, in which case we may ask, would not the money be better spent on books and journals for the library, or on a new microfilm reader?

You may also have noticed that the calendar starts in April, which means that hardly anyone is going to use it anyway.

With regards
Ram

I forwarded the letter to my friend Rukun Advani, who, within five minutes, had sent back this superbly satirical email:

Ram, hi,

I too got this wonderful NMML calendar. I don't know why you are so critical of it. I love it for its appropriateness. Surely even you can see that it is the only calendar in the world which starts with 1 April—such an auspicious day for the dispensation running the NMML. So heartwarmingly self-deprecating of them to alert us to the fact of All Fools. Such a nice thumbnosing of Oxford's All Souls. To think of printing a calendar which begins in the middle of the year is breathtakingly imaginative. Only an Indian babu of the highest pedigree could have thought of this. It can set a wonderful precedent for babudom generally and be sent off to all ministries as a reminder that the Christian era is passe. The BJP will love it. Others who have to learn to move with the times will learn that the year isn't a year unless it is seen as a financial year. Future editions of this work of brilliance can show Jan in red, Feb in orange, and March in green to remind babus they need to rush forward and spend their budget. I'm in a tizzy thinking of all the many possibilities opened up by this calendar. It is not a waste of money. Nehru would have loved it. He would have given one to Edwina, I'm sure. And Mridula Mukherjee can give it to all the little children who come to the NMML baal melas. Nehru loved children you see, and now his house is devoted to the cause of All Fools and children. A visionary new direction has been given to the institution. You are wrong to cavil.

Love
Rukun

Rukun Advani is a reclusive publisher who works out of the hill station of Ranikhet; although he publishes the works of India's best historians, he does not actually need the NMML himself. He could afford to be detached and sardonic. However, as someone who owed everything to the place, I continued to be despairing. Days after I received this priceless April–March calendar, the director of the NMML went on three months' leave. She appointed a recently recruited consultant to act as director in her place. The person in question had previously been an official of the India Tourism Development Corporation, in charge of duty-free shops at airports. Now, courtesy her contacts and her cronies, this person sat in the chair once occupied by B.R. Nanda and Ravinder Kumar.

And worse was to follow. In May 2010, I was sent a copy of an independent audit of the NMML, which had been recently submitted to the ministry of culture. The forty-three pages of this report were peppered with the words 'irregular' and 'profligate'. The audit report observed that since the new director took over in 2006, the NMML had recruited as many as sixty-four consultants, with several people being paid for the same job (while thirty-nine sanctioned staff posts remain unfilled). Meanwhile, there had 'been [an] abject failure on the part of the NMML so far as research work is concerned'. The financial implications of these irregular appointments were 'astronomical'; moreover, these favoured consultants often had 'no experience whatsoever'. As the audit report dryly observed, this 'shows the utter contempt with which NMML handles various economy instructions issued by the Ministry of Finance'. The report concluded that the 'NMML appears to be working with a mind set to provide benefit to individuals rather than to the Institution'.

IX

I suppose I should have been more realistic about, or more resigned to, the deterioration of the Nehru Memorial Museum and Library. I had myself written (in a book published in 1999) about how institutions in India worked well only for short periods of time. I had just been to the Christa Seva Sangh in Puné, a once-thriving centre of thought and action founded by the radical priest J.C. Winslow, which had sought to make Indian Christians more sensitive to the ideas and programme of Mahatma Gandhi. That was in the 1920s; however, I now wrote, 'to visit the Christa Seva Sangh is to be powerfully reminded of the iron law of Indian institutional decay. The average life of a reasonably well-functioning institution is twenty years; none, it seems, remains in good health after the death or disappearance of the founder. Gandhi's own ashrams, Sabarmati and Sevagram, still function in a desultory and decrepit way, but for all the influence they now command they might as well be dead. Why should Winslow's ashram be different? It requires an effort of the will to think of it as it once was, a centre of active and radical theological work, a bridge between the worlds of Anglican Christianity and an increasingly assertive Indian nationalism.'

Why did I think that the Nehru Memorial Museum and Library
would be exempt from this law? Personal engagement was certainly
one part of the answer. This institution had meant so much to me,
and to my generation of historians and social scientists. Why should
it not play the same emancipatory role for later generations of
scholars? Moreover, I continued to work there on a regular basis,
and felt the pain and anguish of the staff members who had once
devotedly served researchers but were now stifled by the atmosphere
of cronyism and nepotism that surrounded them.

But there were impersonal reasons why I thought, or hoped, that
the NMML could be revived. It had been lucky to have two good
directors in succession; with thirty years of solid foundational work,
perhaps it could survive a spell of lacklustre leadership—provided
the right successor was found. Then again, it was based in the
capital, and so exempt (in theory) from the pulls and pressures of
caste and regional considerations. This autonomy could—again in
theory—be guaranteed by the fact that a scholar, Dr Manmohan
Singh, was now prime minister and minister of culture. Nor were
funds a problem—the central government had always given it all it
wished for in this direction.

Finally, my hopes and desires for the NMML were also encouraged
by the fact that I knew a centre of scholarship which had been an
exception to the iron law of Indian institutional decay. This was the
Indian Institute of Science in Bangalore. I had worked there in
three separate stints (in 1984, 1987–88 and 2004), and done
extensive collaborative research with its professors. In 2009 the
institute celebrated a century of steady, consistent, high-quality
performance. Directors had come and gone. Some had been self-
effacing, others egocentric. All, however, had been efficient,
non-partisan, and committed to serious research and teaching.

Why could the NMML not be a humanities version of the Indian
Institute of Science? In some other culture and country this might
have indeed been possible. But not in the India of the twenty-first
century. Here, directors of IITs and science institutes would be
chosen by their peers. But the direction of the softer disciplines

operated at the whims and fancies of the political class. Sycophancy, not scholarship; connections, not credibility, would largely determine who would be chosen to head centres of social science and historical research.

Things were once otherwise, in Jawaharlal Nehru's time, when (for example) V.K.R.V. Rao built the Delhi School of Economics into a world-class centre of scholarship. Nehru had an indifferent second-class degree in science from Cambridge; however, this was compensated for by his respect for the autonomy of intellectuals and intellectual practice. Our present prime minister, on the other hand, has a first-class degree from the same university, where he was awarded the prestigious Adam Smith Prize to boot. And he went on to take a PhD in economics at Oxford. This scholar–politician knew of the importance of the Nehru Memorial Museum and Library. Several fine scholars whom he respected had independently drawn his attention to the institution's decline. His could have been the critical, redemptive intervention—but it would not come.

A cautiously hopeful postscript: This essay was drafted and completed in the summer of 2010. In December of that year, the Indian National Congress celebrated its 125th anniversary. At a function attended by the prime minister and the party president, an official history of the Congress was released. The finance minister, Pranab Mukherjee, was identified as the 'chief editor' of the book; but the main work had been done by five academic advisors. These included Mridula Mukherjee, her husband Aditya Mukherjee and her sister Sucheta Mahajan.

Fortunately for these historians' reputations, this book is not easily available at bookstores. I was, however, able to obtain a copy from the party's office, and was struck by how slight (in both senses of the word) the volume was. Five historians with PhDs had collectively produced a book that, in size and substance, was substantially inferior to the official history of the Congress published in 1935 by the medical doctor, Pattabhi Sitaramayya.

Still, *Congress and the Making of the Indian Nation* was not written without a motive, or perhaps several. One was to rescue Indira

78   PATRIOTS AND PARTISANS

Gandhi, the revered mother-in-law of the Congress president, from
the charge of being authoritarian. The excesses of the Emergency of
1975–77 were therefore attributed exclusively to Sanjay Gandhi. A
second motive was to cast the current Congress president in the
halo of sainthood. Of her decision not to become prime minister in
2004, it was said that 'not since the days of the freedom struggle was
such a complete separation of the objective of personal power and
the objective of achieving social ideals seen. People looked upon
Sonia Gandhi's renunciation of power as reminiscent of the Mahatma.'

For the NMML director to help write the official Congress
history was in clear violation of conduct rules, which explicitly
prohibit 'any government official from being a member of, or be
otherwise associated with, any political party or any organization
which takes part in politics; nor shall he [or she] take part in,
subscribe in aid of, or assist in any other manner, any political
movement or activity.' In the light of what had passed in the past
five years, it may not be too cynical to read the NMML director's
participation as a gesture of thanks to her political patrons, as well
as a coded application for a further extension.

As it happened, the application (if it indeed was one) was not
heard—or heeded. In the first week of February 2011, it was
announced that the executive council of the Nehru Memorial
Museum and Library had appointed a search committee to choose
a new director. Scholars of distinction were asked to recommend
candidates, a selection of whom were then interviewed by the
search committee. The committee's choice finally fell on Professor
Mahesh Rangarajan of Delhi University.

Mahesh Rangarajan had made major contributions to environmental
history and to the analysis of Indian elections. He was young,
energetic, and non-partisan. Moreover, he had been a Fellow at the
NMML during Ravinder Kumar's tenure; as a regular user of the
library since, he knew what the institution was like at its best, and
at its worst. Chosen fairly, and with a credible reputation based on
serious scholarly work, the new director could command the
support and goodwill of other serious scholars, and, perhaps more
crucially, of a still capable and qualified staff.

In September 2011, shortly before departing for a year overseas, I visited my favourite library-cum-archive in the world. Professor Rangarajan had been in office barely a month, yet change was in the air, and humming on the ground. The consultants were being disposed of, one by one. The oral history programme was being revived; the quest for manuscript collections being resumed. The staff were more energized than they had been in years, their enthusiasm renewed by, among other things, the belated revocation of the suspension of the much-admired deputy director, Dr N. Balakrishnan.

Professor Rangarajan and Dr Balakrishnan had reactivated the weekly seminar series; the day I was there, a historian of science from Bangalore was presenting a paper to an audience of historians, sociologists, physicists and economists from all the major universities in Delhi. The discussion was intense, even electric; it carried on afterwards in the corridor and the café, with new arguments being made and new friendships being forged.

The buzz was in part a tribute to the dynamism of the NMML's new director; in greater part, a tribute to the heroic hard work of the NMML's first two directors. The foundations they had laid were so solid that the NMML seemed set to defy the iron law of Indian institutional decay. Those who knew not or cared not for these visionaries could disturb and shake these foundations, but not destroy them altogether. After five years of despair, I left Delhi that September day in a mood of cautious optimism. Now, with luck, persistence, and the absence of partisan political interference, perhaps the Nehru Memorial Museum and Library might yet be restored to *something* like its former glory.

chapter thirteen

LIFE WITH A DUCHESS: A PERSONAL HISTORY OF THE OXFORD UNIVERSITY PRESS

~

I

In the 1990s, I spent many weeks in what must, or at any rate should be, every Indian's favourite city—Bombay, a city whose depth of history and richly lived (and intensely felt) cosmopolitanism is in such stark contrast to the even-tempered blandness of the town where I live, Bangalore. I would go there twice a year, in February and November, and book myself into a room in the Cricket Club of India. Every morning, I would walk across the oval, dodging joggers and the odd flying cricket ball, and then skirt round the high court to the side entrance to Elphinstone College where, after climbing a staircase stinking with piss, I would arrive at the reading room of the Maharashtra State Archives. Three or four hours of work on the files was a reward in itself, though I often gave myself the further bonus of a Rajasthani *thali* at Chetna restaurant, before returning for some more digging.

In those days the Maharashtra State Archives were moderately well run (I remember in particular an experienced hand named Lad), and their collections were very rich indeed. Still, my warmest memories of research in Bombay are linked to a private archive that lay down the road, in Apollo Bunder off Colaba Causeway. This was housed in the third (and top) floor of a sturdy stone building owned by the Indian branch of the Oxford University Press, the world's oldest (and greatest) publisher.

A British historian once said that being published by the Oxford University Press was like being married to a duchess—the honour was greater than the pleasure. My experience was otherwise. Not long before I began working in their archives, the OUP had published my first book. As scholarly books go, it was a work of art. It was set, using hot-metal type, in an elegant Baskerville by the legendary P.K. Ghosh of Eastend Printers, Calcutta. The cover was arresting—a photograph by Sanjeev Saith of a Himalayan oak forest cut up by the designer to represent the 'unquiet woods' that the book documented. The prose inside, jargon-ridden and solemnly sociological in its original incarnation, had been rendered moderately serviceable by the intense (and inspired) labours of the book's editor, a young scholar with a PhD in English literature from the University of Cambridge.

To enter the Bombay office of the OUP in 1993 and 1994 was, for me, like entering an ancient club of which I was a privileged new member. The honour was manifest, but so also the pleasure. In the foyer were displayed the works of the best Indian sociologists and historians—André Béteille's *The Idea of Natural Inequality*, Ranajit Guha's *Elementary Aspects of Peasant Insurgency*, Ashis Nandy's *The Intimate Enemy*, Irfan Habib's *An Atlas of the Mughal Empire*. Also on display were the works of OUP authors who were not Indian, among them such colossally influential scholars as Isaiah Berlin, Ronald Dworkin and H.L.A. Hart. The gentry and literati of Bombay came to this showroom, and I spent some time there myself. But my main work lay upstairs where, in a locked cupboard, lay the correspondence between a writer whose life I was writing about and a publisher who had once dominated the building where I now sat.

This writer and his publisher were both Englishmen who had gone native. They were expatriates of standing, who knew, or knew

of, the most powerful Indians of the day. Their own relationship
was personal as well as professional. They were (as in those days
writer and publisher sometimes could be) really close friends. In their
correspondence they discussed books, but also food, music, politics,
and occasionally, sex. Their letters were sometimes businesslike, at
other times warm and gossip-laden. Reading them, fifty or sixty
years after they were written, was an exhilarating experience.

Occasionally, hearing me chuckle or gasp, the occupant of the
next cabin would come to have a look. Named Rivka Israel, she
was a senior editor at the OUP, and the person who was in charge
of—and lovingly tended—the archive. (She came from a family of
Bombay Jews who made their living as craftsmen of learning—her
father, Samuel Israel, had been an admired editor himself.) Rivka,
in turn, would sometimes call in the branch manager, a cheerful
Gujarati named Ramesh Patel, and have me read out once more
that passage about, for example, life with Gandhi's 'sexless and
joyless entourage'.

A historian's happiest days are always in the archives. In the case
of this now somewhat elderly historian, the days have accumulated
into years. Yet of all these days and years, the weeks in the OUP
archive in Bombay may have given me the most joy. The letters I
found there were, for my purposes, infinitely rewarding; but the real
pleasure (and honour) lay elsewhere, in seeing (and sensing) oneself
as being part of a great, continuous scholarly tradition; a freshly-
minted OUP author entering a building stocking the works of the
greatest OUP authors to work on the letters of a long-dead OUP
author—all for a book that would one day be published by the
OUP itself.

II

The year 2012 marked the centenary of OUP in India. In the
history of the Press, two men stand out: one white, the other
brown. In 1930 an Oxford graduate named R.E. Hawkins came
to teach in a school in Delhi. The school closed down during the

non-cooperation movement, so Hawkins found a job with the OUP in Bombay instead. In 1937 he was appointed general manager. By now he wore *khadi*, though this may have been a mark of gratitude rather than an affirmation of political solidarity—by closing down that school in Delhi, the Gandhians had given him a new life.

When Hawkins became general manager, the Indian branch of the Oxford University Press had been in existence for a quarter of a century. In its first year, 1912, it published the first book of a then obscure academic—S. Radhakrishnan's *Essentials of Psychology*. However—as described by Rimi Chatterjee in *Empires of the Mind*, her history of OUP India's early years—the branch was viewed by Oxford as more vendor than publisher. It was set up chiefly to sell textbooks written by Englishmen in England, and prescribed by the Raj for schools and colleges in the subcontinent. Sensing the mood, Radhakrishnan himself soon moved to another publisher, Allen and Unwin.

Under Hawkins, the OUP continued to make its money selling textbooks. However, this Englishman recognized that some Indians were now producing serious works of scholarship. He published a few such—A. Appadorai's *The Substance of Politics*, A.A.A. Fyzee's *Outlines of Muhammadan Law*, and, most notably, K.A. Nilakanta Sastri's *A History of South India*, which, seventy years later, is still in print and still indispensable.

While not antipathetic to intellectuals, Hawkins's real interests lay elsewhere, in nature and natural history. The three authors he most enjoyed publishing were the ornithologist Salim Ali, the anthropologist Verrier Elwin, and the hunter-turned-conservationist Jim Corbett. Their writings gave him much pleasure, and their books made the OUP a good deal of money. (None more so than the books by Corbett—*Man-Eaters of Kumaon* was bought by the American Book of the Month Club, whose first print run of 250,000 sold out in weeks. This book, commissioned by Hawkins, was translated into twenty-seven languages, and was even made into a Hollywood film, of which Corbett commented that 'the best actor was the tiger'.)

In the 1940s and 1950s, Bombay was the intellectual capital of India. It had the country's best social scientists, and its only decent English-language poets and writers. In this literary culture, an Englishman known affectionately as the 'Hawk' set new standards of editing and publishing. The writer Laeeq Futehally, working at that time with the magazine *Quest*, remembers that when they had to choose a printer they settled on the Inland Press, 'for it was also patronised by the Oxford University Press, whose General Manager, R.E. Hawkins—in spite of having only one functioning eye—was known to be the best editor and proof-reader in South East (sic) Asia'.

The books published by Hawkins were carefully edited, rigorously proofread, and often beautifully produced. In the works of his favourite authors, words and pictures were exquisitely matched. No books produced in India before or since, equal in this respect, such gems as Verrier Elwin's *The Tribal Art of Middle India* and Salim Ali's *Indian Hill Birds*.

Hawkins retired from the OUP in 1970. Five years later, he was present when the tenth and final volume of the *Handbook of Indian Birds* was released in the presence of the prime minister. Asked to speak, the Hawk read out the following verse:

> *William Shakespeare's a master of words*
> *And a tusker a leader of herds*
> *But wherever you fare*
> *Over land, sea or air*
> *Salim Ali's the raja of birds*

In his last years as general manager, Hawkins was assisted by two gifted young Indians. Girish Karnad was a mathematician by training and a playwright by temperament. Ravi Dayal was a history scholar who had read widely in the social sciences. After seven years in the press, Karnad left to make a career in films. Dayal stayed on, and in 1971, moved to Delhi to start a branch of the OUP there. The city was coming to replace Bombay as the intellectual capital of India. An air of self-confidence was abroad. Scholars in Delhi University and the Jawaharlal Nehru University thought they were among the best in the world. Some certainly were—such as the sociologists M.N. Srinivas and André Béteille, the historians Sarvepalli Gopal and Romila Thapar, the economist Sukhamoy Chakravarty, and the unclassifiable social scientist and social critic Ashis Nandy.

Meanwhile, Hawkins was succeeded as general manager of the OUP by Charles Lewis, a gentle, understated Englishman with an effervescent and politically active Indian wife. Lewis took the sensible decision to move the firm's headquarters from Bombay to New Delhi, from where it could focus on the scholarly list. In 1975, the Emergency was promulgated, and Mrs Lewis was put in jail by Indira Gandhi's police. The OUP thought it best now to move Lewis back to Oxford. Ravi Dayal was appointed general manager in his place.

The early works of the best Indian historians and social scientists had often been published overseas—by Cambridge, Chicago, Blackwell and other presses. Ravi Dayal persuaded them to offer their next books to the OUP, so that they would be edited and printed in the country where the scholars lived and about which they wrote. Most agreed, because they recognized that there were now more Indian than foreign readers of their books, and because it was impossible to refuse Ravi Dayal.

A small, dapper man dressed (by choice) in *churidar-kurta*, Ravi Dayal had a great (if subtly subdued) intelligence, and a greater (and visibly manifest) charm. He was a Kayasth, from a community that produced north India's best scholars and scribes, but also its finest cooks. The Kayasths were also keen patrons of Hindustani classical music. Dayal himself could talk food like an Indian and talk Dickens like an Englishman. He was both vernacular and cosmopolitan, a mixture that characterized the scholars whose books he was seeking. For, men such as André Béteille and Irfan Habib were likewise *desi* and *videsi* in equal measure. They were naturally drawn to a publisher who bridged their worlds.

By the end of the 1970s, Ravi Dayal and the OUP had shifted the locus of scholarly publishing on South Asia out of the West. This was the stamp that scholars working on the subcontinent most craved. Historians and social scientists, whether living in India or overseas, of whatever nationality or ideological affiliation, were, so to say, lining up outside the OUP's offices in New Delhi. Their manuscripts were subject to rigorous vetting—scrutiny by the editor concerned, and by at least two external referees, in a process that saw perhaps four out of five proposals turned away to other, lesser, publishers.

In the summer of 1979, Dayal, now the most respected publisher in India, received a proposal from a middle-aged, middle-ranking Bengali academic based in England. His name was Ranajit Guha. At that stage Guha had published one rather obscure book, and that too twenty years previously. This was a very specialized study of a single aspect of agrarian policy in eighteenth-century Bengal. As a student in Calcutta, Ranajit Guha had been a fiery orator, and as an academic, he continued to work for the most part in the oral tradition. So, although he had himself published little, he had gathered around him a group of bright young devotees who promised to publish a great deal.

Ranajit Guha's proposal to Ravi Dayal was that he and his acolytes would publish a series of collected essays under the running title 'Subaltern Studies'. Where other editors might have been deterred by Guha's lack of distinction, and turned off by the confusing (not to say bizarre) series title, Dayal saw here an exciting move away from the elite-centred narratives of Indian historiography. For, Guha and his disciples were genuine interdisciplinarians— historians who reached out to anthropology and political theory to make meaningful sense of the past. They had also moved beyond the colonial archive to seriously explore sources such as vernacular tracts and oral testimonies.

A first volume of *Subaltern Studies* was commissioned, and duly appeared in 1982. Three more volumes appeared in quick succession. Although some librarians persisted in placing them in the military section, the first four volumes of *Subaltern Studies* were to radically alter our understanding of Indian history. For the first time, the voices of peasants, tribals, workers—those hitherto excluded from the standard narratives—were brought to centre stage.

The OUP had also begun publishing the works of creative writers. Girish Karnad persuaded Vijay Tendulkar and Badal Sircar to pass on the English translations of their plays to the OUP. An even greater coup was the rendition in English by A.K. Ramanujan of U.R. Anantha Murthy's Kannada novel, *Samskara*, which may by now have sold more copies than any other Indian work in translation, the writings of Tagore and Gandhi only excepted.

To the scholars he wooed, Dayal was a publisher who understood scholarship. To his staff, he was a boss with no sense of hierarchy. One who worked with him wrote that Dayal 'refused an airconditioner in his room because it would have made the organization inegalitarian in a way he considered unacceptable. This was the sort of Gandhian trait that earned him huge respect, and which made his organization congenial and unhierarchical. It created a sort of "Dayal Bagh" in which everyone grumbled about low salaries but where everyone stuck it out because the bidi-smoking boss at least looked like he was in the same boat as the bidi-smoking chaprasis. No one cultivated unglamorous socialist fellow feeling with as much perverseness as Dayal. Most people who worked with him secretly hoped he would one day see the light of capitalist hedonism. But he never did.'

It was not, of course, merely a matter of personality. The subordinates respected Dayal because he knew every side of the business—finance, marketing, sales, etc.—and cultivated an atmosphere of professional pride all around. The scholars trusted Ravi Dayal because he was a superbly skilled editor. After he retired from the OUP and set up his own list, he published the early novels of Amitav Ghosh, who says that Ravi Dayal was the best editor he has worked with.

Ravi Dayal may have left the OUP in part because the prose of academics requires far more work than the prose of novelists. He had stayed long enough in any case, so long that (as one protégé claimed) Dayal 'coauthored and ghost-wrote and may well have rewritten more books and authors than any editor in the history of Indian publishing'.

There is a story that nicely illustrates Ravi Dayal's integrity as well as his achievement. Sometime in the 1990s, a young journalist went to interview the man who had been India's most respected academic publisher and was now India's finest publisher of literary fiction. She found him walking in the small—fifty feet by hundred feet—park that lay outside his apartment. Since the capacious (and glorious) Lodi Gardens lay just down the road, the journalist asked Dayal why he didn't take his exercise there instead. 'Too many rejected manuscripts,' was the answer.

Shortly after this I went to meet Ravi Dayal myself. I had come to ask for a favour—that he recommend me for membership of the India International Centre. The IIC needed 'full' not 'associate' members to provide recommendations, and I knew only two such grandees, an old family friend and Ravi Dayal. He suggested I find another signatory. 'I would be happy to recommend you,' he said, 'but I fear it won't help your case, since I have offended all the trustees of the IIC.' I took this to mean that he had turned down their various, and variously mediocre, book proposals. But I didn't know any other full member, so asked him to sign on the form any way.

My application was approved, whereupon a friend commented that the IIC trustees perhaps hoped that they could now make fresh approaches to Ravi Dayal with me as their messenger.

III

In 1989, two years after Ravi Dayal had moved on to start his own firm, my first book was published by the OUP. It was commissioned by Rukun Advani, an introverted scholar from Lucknow who was recruited by Dayal immediately on completing a Cambridge PhD on the non-fiction writings of E.M. Forster. Advani lacked—and still lacks—Dayal's charm, but in my view he was, and is, an even better editor of historians and sociologists. Like Dayal, Advani is deeply attentive to language. Unlike his mentor, he has a scholarly background. To write and defend a PhD thesis, and convert it into a book, means that one can conceive of a large, complex project, break it up into discrete parts, do a great deal of original research, and then write it up as a coherent and connected narrative.

It took a Ravi Dayal to see the potential of *Subaltern Studies*; and it needed a Rukun Advani to edit the volumes and see them through the press. As a well-trained scholar, Advani knew what made a book (or essay) credible, original, readable, and saleable. It was fortunate for the OUP, and for the world at large, that he was the main editor for the Subaltern Studies series, and that he edited, too, the individual monographs that the Subalternists published under their own names, among them such influential works such as David Hardiman's *The Coming of the Devi* and Shahid Amin's *Event, Metaphor, Memory*.

To be sure, Advani published some superb studies by non-Subalternists, too. These included Harjot Oberoi's dazzlingly original *The Construction of Religious Boundaries*; Chetan Singh's *Region and State*, which radically altered our understanding of the later Mughal Empire; Vasudha Dalmia's important work of literary history, *The Nationalization of Hindu Traditions*; and Mahesh Rangarajan's fine environmental study, *Fencing the Forest*.

Speak to any or all of these writers, and they will tell you that they were profoundly fortunate to have had an editor like Rukun Advani; that, in fact, he rewrote their books as effectively and elegantly as his mentor rewrote the books of an older generation of scholars.

Speaking for myself, when I wrote a first draft of my biography of Verrier Elwin—the writer whose correspondence with the 'Hawk' lay in the building in Apollo Bunder—Advani told me to tear it up and start afresh, since a biography had to be approached differently from the sociological treatises I was accustomed to writing. As advised, I went back to my notes, and wrote them up chronologically, rather than by theme. This draft came back marked up everywhere in red ink, with a final comment: 'This is fine as a study of Elwin the scholar and public intellectual, but where is Elwin the man?'

I now read, more closely than before, my subject's correspondence with his mother, sister and friends, writing this all into the next draft. Advani had, as before, very many stylistic suggestions, ending with the remark that 'this is fine as a book about Elwin the son, brother, friend and husband, but where is Elwin the writer and polemicist?'

I went back to my desk and rewrote the damn thing again. Advani approved, on the whole, of this version, but before it went to press he inserted some references to (among others) Eliot and Handel, references that enriched the narrative while giving the impression that the historian who was its author was a connoisseur of modernist poetry and classical music.

What I owed to Rukun Advani, other OUP writers owed, more or less, to their editors. Ashis Nandy speaks with much affection of Salima Tyabji, the lady who edited his manuscripts. And my late friend, the combative Bangalore critic T.G. Vaidyanathan, became an OUP author only because his editor, Anita Roy, had great skill and even greater patience.

In 1988, the year after Ravi Dayal left, his successor as general manager, Santosh Mukherjee, was persuaded by Rukun Advani to launch the 'Oxford India Paperbacks'—the attractive republication in soft cover of the less recondite of their scholarly books. Advani also conceived a 'Themes in Indian History' series, under which appeared collections of pioneering papers, edited by an acknowledged expert in the field. These books also appeared in paperback, thus continuing the work of the 'Hawk' and Dayal in bringing the fruits of Indian scholarship to a wide audience of scholars, students and thinking citizens.

I have spoken so far of the editors, but the production and marketing staff of the OUP also had a proper respect for the books they printed, bound, displayed and sold. Whether working in editing or printing or sales or finance, the staff had a noticeable sense of belonging. As publishing houses go, this was a very high quality operation. It was also an organization at peace with itself, its sense of cheer radiating the OUP's branches around the country—in

Mission Row in Calcutta, on Mount Road in Madras, in Koramangala in Bangalore, in Daryaganj in Delhi, and, not least, in Apollo Bunder in Bombay, all places which this Indian who read and wrote books in English once regarded almost as an extension of his own home.

IV

In 2011, the Indian branch of the Oxford University Press entered its hundredth year. Plans for an extended celebration were afoot: new releases of classic works by OUP authors in India, seminars and conferences, a great big bash at the World Book Fair in New Delhi in February 2012, to be attended by the Delegates of the Press, men of distinction in British intellectual life.

As it turned out, in the middle of its anniversary year, OUP India had what may, in retrospect, be viewed as the worst episode in its history. In November 2011, the University of Delhi withdrew an essay by the poet, folklorist, translator and theorist A.K. Ramanujan from the BA History syllabus. The essay explored the many renditions of the Ramayana in India, an exercise in scholarship (and ecumenism) that offended right-wing dogmatists seeking to impose a single, authorized, invariant text on the public.

The decision sparked outrage, for Ramanujan was a truly great scholar, whose work has had a profound, enduring influence on Indian and global scholarship. That his essay was being suppressed due to pressure from Hindutva extremists was particularly ironic— for his majestic translations of medieval Hindu poetry had done much to make the world aware of the beauty and depth of our mystical traditions.

The essay had originally appeared in a volume edited by Paula Richman called *Many Ramayanas*, and then in Ramanujan's *Collected Essays*. Both books were published by the OUP. However, they had been allowed to go out of print after a petition filed in a court in the small Punjab town of Dera Bassi claimed that Ramanujan's essay offended religious sensibilities. In withdrawing the books, OUP assured the litigant that it 'very much regret[ted]' publishing the essay, apologized for causing him 'distress and concern', and assured him that the books containing the essay would be withdrawn.

As it happens, the vice chancellor of Delhi University had justified his decision to drop Ramanujan's essay on the grounds that since the books containing it were no longer being sold, teachers and students would not be able to access it. When these facts were made public, a series of critical articles appeared in the press. A petition urging the OUP to bring the essay back into circulation was endorsed by more than five hundred scholars, many of them very distinguished indeed.

The anguish over the OUP's betrayal of Ramanujan was in part because of the Press's reputation; in part because of Ramanujan's own distinction; and in part because it followed on other such examples of the betrayal of scholars and scholarship. In recent years, the OUP has withdrawn books on the law, on medieval history, and on Indian nationalism under pressure from fanatics and from the state.

Admittedly, Indian courts are ever willing to entertain frivolous or tendentious petitions, and fighting them can be costly in terms of time and money. On the other hand, the OUP has on occasion been willing to engage in a battle in court. While it lately acquiesced in the suppression of A.K. Ramanujan's work, it recruited some of the country's most expensive lawyers to fight a tax case on its behalf in the 1990s.

When the first series of articles on the Ramanujan controversy was published, the OUP dismissed it as the work of malicious or motivated individuals. Fresh articles appeared, highlighting previous instances of the suppression of books by the OUP in India. Then came the cross-continental signature campaign. In personal meetings with the company's CEOs in Oxford and New Delhi, OUP authors expressed their anger and dismay. Eventually, the publishing house agreed to reprint A.K. Ramanujan's *Collected Essays* as well as Paula Richman's *Many Ramayanas*.

The original disavowal of Ramanujan in court forces us to ask whether there is anyone working in the OUP today who has read his books and essays. Anecdotal evidence suggests that the focus on scholars and scholarship, so evident in Ravi Dayal's day, is not any more a conspicuous hallmark of the OUP's functioning. I was myself alerted to this some years ago, when a book of mine appeared for the first time in paperback. Sent an advance copy, I found that excerpts from the reviews of the hardback had been inserted after the prelim pages; in fact, in between the prologue and the first chapter. The editor to whose attention I brought this lapse had a hard time comprehending what I was complaining about. Other OUP authors have their own stories, of works of scholarship published without an index, with pages transposed, and the like.

About a year ago, I asked the OUP for access to the files in their archives dealing with the abridged edition of Mohandas K. Gandhi's *My Experiments with Truth*, which they had published in the 1930s. I knew from other references that there were many letters to R.E. Hawkins from Gandhi's secretary Mahadev Desai, perhaps some from the Mahatma himself. The letters could not be located— worse, I was told that the archive, sections of which I had consulted in Apollo Bunder, no longer existed. It had been a casualty of the OUP's decision to sell the property in south Bombay and move their office to the suburbs. The acts were of a piece—the abandonment of that wonderful old building and of all that it contained and represented.

chapter fourteen

TURNING CRIMSON AT PREMIER'S

~

I

It was a fellow writer, Achal Prabhala, who called to tell me that Premier Bookshop was closing down. 'Mr Shanbhag seems quite determined,' said Achal: 'The landlord is giving trouble again. He has to undergo an eye operation himself. And his daughter is keen that he come visit her in Australia. The nice thing is that he seems very calm about it.'

I claim a long connection with Mr T.S. Shanbhag and Premier Bookshop, but Achal's connection was deeper. Since he is some fifteen years younger, he had known them all his life. (I was already a teenager by the time I made my first acquaintance with bookseller and bookshop.) Like me and countless other residents of Bangalore, he had come to regard them as indispensable and immovable. When, after many years overseas, Achal had moved back to his home town, it was in the knowledge that Mr Shanbhag and Premier's would take care of at least one part, perhaps the most critical part, of his life. To see the shop close and the owner retire was for him as unanticipated, and as hard to bear, as the death of a revered family elder.

One of the attractions of Premier's was its closeness to the café known as Parade's to the old Bangalorean, but as 'Koshy's' to the new immigrant. Premier's and Parade's were a cricket pitch's distance away from one another. In between lay Variety News, where one could buy magazines in all the languages of the Eighth Schedule (and then some). The usual drill was to start at the bookshop, proceed to the newsagent, and end in the café, where one placed the material newly acquired on a chair, before ordering a coffee and perhaps a vegetable patty to go with it. (The routine used to be more elaborate—and more fulfilling—in the days when the floor above Parade's was occupied by the British Library.)

I first began to patronize Premier's in the 1970s, at a time when, unbeknownst to me, the lady who is now my wife began to patronize it as well. My first clear memory of the bookshop is of a day in January 1980 when my wife—then my girlfriend—took me there to buy a parting gift. I was off to begin a PhD in Calcutta, and she was due to rejoin her design school in Ahmedabad. At my request she bought me a copy of Isaiah Berlin's biography of Karl Marx. Somewhere before or after buying the book she gave me a gentle peck on the cheek. By the standards of Bangalore today that gesture was timid. However, by the social norms then prevailing, it was outrageously provocative. Unfortunately, she was caught in the act by the bookshop's owner, who turned a deep shade of red in consequence.

I was back in Premier's on my first holiday from graduate school. It took longer for my girlfriend to return, not because her love of books was any less, but because it took her a while to overcome the embarrassment of that perceived transgression. So, we usually went there separately. In any case we had—and have—different tastes, she reading literary fiction and a little poetry, me going in for history and the harder—or more boring—stuff. Fortunately, Premier's had plenty to suit us both. In time, our children began going there as well, to develop as keen a sense of ownership as we had.

II

Among Premier's lesser attractions was that the shop gave decent discounts—10 per cent to the first-time visitor, 15 to the regular, and a hefty 20 per cent to the true old-timer. Among its greater charms was the charm of the owner himself. T.S. Shanbhag had learnt his trade from his uncle, the legendary Mr T.N. Shanbhag of Strand Book Stall, Bombay. Our Shanbhag first set up shop in Bangalore in 1970, opposite the Technological Museum on Kasturba Gandhi Road. A year later he moved to the ground floor of a building on Church Street, in the very heart of the city.

T.S. Shanbhag is of medium height, with a round face. He is clean shaven and does not wear spectacles. For as long as I have known him, he has not had a hair on his head. He is a reticent man, who says just enough to let you understand that he knows a great deal. He has a sly wit, infrequently expressed verbally, but doubtless always at work in words thought if unspoken. As it is, so long as he ran the shop most of what he said was about books, usually to alert you to a new arrival that his experience suggested might be of special interest.

Also among Premier's attractions were the wild eccentricities of its layout. The shop extended over a single room, this twenty-five feet long and fifteen feet wide. In the centre was a mountain of books, seven or eight layers deep, these representing the sediment of knowledge discarded or scorned by Bangaloreans down the years. The last layer of the mound—the only one that was visible—showcased modern classics: Graham Greene, Gabriel Garcia Marquez, P.G. Wodehouse, and the like. One had to walk around the hill to view the other books on display, set in piles against the walls of the shop. As one entered one saw, first of all, the new hardbacks, these carefully chosen: not books on cheese and chicken soup but, rather, works of history and biography that Mr Shanbhag felt would attract the more elevated among his readers.

Then one began a ritual circumambulation of the mountain. The wall to the left featured, as one went along, first, fiction; then

sociology and political science; then history and economics and
ecology. Now it was time to walk around the mound, to consult,
on the other wall, first, children's books; then books on nature; then
works of spirituality, and resting appropriately next to them, of science;
and last of all, paperbacks on current affairs and military history.

There was a method to this mayhem, but one needed years of
experience to know it. Still, even if one were to find a book on
one's own, without Mr Shanbhag one could not easily take it off
the shelf; else, dozens of other books would come tumbling down
with it. There were frequent traffic jams as one went around the
hump in the middle. This happened when visitors ignored the
shop's unspoken rule, which was that walks of discovery be
undertaken clockwise only.

The crowd of customers and the cramped quarters were, however,
redeemed by the character of the man in charge. Once, I went to
buy some books for a friend in America who wanted to acquaint
himself, long distance, with modern India. I ordered Sunil Khilnani's
The Idea of India and a volume of *Subaltern Studies*. Assessing the
train of my thought, Mr Shanbhag then pulled out a breezy book
on India by a not unknown Indian. 'Not that,' I said, 'I am looking
for serious stuff.' 'Wait a minute,' said Mr Shanbhag, 'we don't
want any more fights in *The Hindu*.' Titters of laughter broke out
from the men and women in the shop who had caught the put-
down, which referred to a bloody polemic which I had then just
started in the pages of that newspaper. Now, it was *my* turn to turn
crimson at Premier's.

III

In January 2001, my wife and I threw a party to celebrate thirty
years in the life of Bangalore's best-loved bookshop (and bookseller).
She had printed a card with a photo of the shop's inner circle,
looking even madder than we had imagined it. Those who were
invited all intimated that they would attend, but I was very nervous
that the chief guest would not show up. The party was scheduled

for a Sunday, on which day Mr Shanbhag usually kept his shop open in the mornings. I was there at 9.30, chewing my nails until he arrived. He came at 10, and for the next two hours I hovered around him. At noon he gave in, closed his shop, and drove his car behind mine to our home.

The scientist C.V. Raman liked to say that his greatest discovery was the weather in Bangalore. Fortunately, the day of our Premier party was in keeping with this—a cloudless sky, a gentle breeze blowing, and the Green Barbet calling in the middle distance. After the *bisi bélé* had been consumed, it was time for the speeches.

The first tribute was offered by Chiranjeev Singh, a Kannada scholar of Sikh extraction, and one of the state's outstanding civil servants. Chiranjeev recalled how he and his senior in the service, Christopher Lynn, built the secretariat library more or less from the selection at Premier's. Then he added: 'There is one thing that I want to tell you about Mr Shanbhag, which speaks to the kind of man, or businessman, that he is. He has never entered a government office.'

Following Chiranjeev was Tara Chandavarkar, for long one half of the city's most reputed architectural firm, for long also a great patron of music, and servant of the suffering and the elderly. 'Those of you present here,' began Mrs Chandavarkar, 'know of Premier's as a bookshop. But I have also known it as a crèche run for charity.' Apparently, she would leave her grandchildren in Shanbhag's shop while she herself went off for a meeting with a client.

Other speakers that day included Narendra Pani and Janaki Nair, who remembered how, when they were impecunious students, Mr Shanbhag would allow them to take away books and pay when they could. (Years later, they became established authors, and Premier's proudly displayed, and sold, their books.)

In the end, though, it was the sly old man who had the last word. As the party dispersed he commanded us to wait, disappeared into his car, and returned with a gift for each of us, this, of course, a book.

At the risk of sounding snobbish, I should say that Premier's had the most cultivated tastes of all the bookshops in India. It is only here that works of literature and history outnumbered (and outsold) books designed to augment your bank balance or cure your soul. When it came to fiction, Shanbhag stocked not merely the latest Booker winner but the backlist of the author (if he or she had one). When J.M. Coetzee won that prize, even the pavement seller was selling *Disgrace*, but only in Premier's would one find *The Master of St. Petersburg* as well. Shanbhag kept more, and better, hardback history than any other Indian shop I know; more, and better, literary fiction; and more, and better, translations.

The quality of his stock was, as I have said, enhanced by the quality of the man himself. One winter I was in and out of Bangalore, one week in town, the next week out of it. Taking a plane back home, I suddenly remembered that I owed Mr Shanbhag 500 rupees. The next morning I went into the shop to pay it back. Mr Shanbhag denied that I was in the red; to the contrary, he said it was he who owed me the money. In his version he did not have the change for a larger note, which I had said I would collect the next time. I was certain that the debt ran the other way. We argued back and forth, till ultimately I gave in. I still think I owed him the money. However, my guilt at having done so was substantially exceeded by the guilt felt by Mr Shanbhag at the mere possibility that it was he who was the debtor. The entire conversation was conducted to the growing bemusement of the customers present. Which other shopkeeper would refuse an offer of money owed, and claim that it was he who had to settle accounts instead?

Sadly, the Bangalore that T.S. Shanbhag represented appears to be dying. Some years ago, a journalist rang to ask me to recommend a book that all Bangaloreans should read, 'You know, like all people from Los Angeles must read *The Wrath of Grapes*.' I told her that the novel was actually called *The Grapes of Wrath*, and that it was set in rural California, not LA. She persisted: 'But Mahesh Dattani says when a group of Bangaloreans meet they should read Maya Jayapal's *Bangalore: Portrait of a City*. Next I will ask Anita Nair. *Please* give me your choice.'

We seem to live in an age where more books are sold, but less books read, than ever before. Books are bought to gift as presents and adorn drawing room tables, but not, it seems, to read or discuss. To be fair, the journalist's question seemed to display an almost guilty awareness of this. It might even have been the product of a desire to uplift and educate, to promote the idea that Bangaloreans should not merely drink alcohol or write computer software, but also improve their minds. Perhaps she thought: let me get a group of writers to each recommend one book that 'every Bangalorean *must* read'—and read collectively, around a table stacked with beer cans. In time they might even come to read books alone, in their rooms.

However, that the question was asked at all shows a depressing lack of familiarity with the most civilized pocket of what was once a very civilized city. So long as T.S. Shanbhag was around, and selling books, residents of Bangalore, whether journalists or otherwise, had no reason not to know of the works of John Steinbeck, and of other great writers past—such as Ivan Turgenev and Evelyn Waugh— or present—such as Milan Kundera and Ian McEwan—or home-grown—such as R.K. Narayan and Shivaram Karanth.

There was only one bookshop anywhere in India that matched Premier's: that run by Ram Advani in the Hazratganj locality of Lucknow. That place too was adjacent to a library run by the British Council and down the road from a famous coffee house. The owner was a refugee from Sindh with a keen interest in golf and western classical music. He started his shop in the Lucknow of the 1940s, a very different place from the Lucknow of today. The city's university was then first class; with superb sociologists, historians, literary scholars, and musicians. Sensing the city's decline, the British Council closed down its library. The Hazratganj coffee house fell victim to a strike and a lockout. But Ram Advani is still there, pushing ninety, still attending to books and book buyers, the strains of Mozart in the background.

IV

After Achal Prabhala called with the news that Shanbhag was shutting shop, I went to Premier's the next day, to find the owner

almost as stoic as I had been told he would be. He rehearsed his
reasons for retirement, but when I found a book to buy (Simon
Winchester's essay collection, *Outposts*), he said, with some emotion:
'I will *not* let you pay for this.' When he insisted, I asked only that
he inscribe the book for me.

When I went back the following day, Mr Shanbhag had regained
his composure. I bought some books and paid for them, and he
made me sign some copies of a book I had written. He had, he said,
a week more to run, before he put down his shutters and put
himself in the hands of the eye surgeon. By now, word of his
closure had spread. Every day the number of visitors grew. The
great mound in the middle of the shop became shorter and slimmer.
The top layers on the side shelves were peeled off by paying
customers, to reveal books published in the 1980s and before, that
had lain buried, unseen and unsold.

On the first Sunday after Mr Shanbhag had made his decision
known, a city magazine organized a photo shoot. Several writers
were called to feature in the frame, among them the distinguished
Kannada novelist U.R. Anantha Murthy. As he sat himself down
among us, Anantha Murthy asked, 'Why is Girish [Karnad] not
here?' I knew the answer: that great patron of Premier's could not
come because his daughter was getting married the next week. I said
that Girish's wife sometimes told him, when he came home with
the day's loot, that their house had begun to resemble Shanbhag's
shop, with books on the steps, books on the window sill, books on
the kitchen counter, books everywhere including on one's head. I
added that my wife sometimes told me the same thing. There were
laughs all around, the loudest from Mr Shanbhag.

I went back several times the next week. Once I took my
daughter along, so that she could buy her own last books from
Premier's, and also take some photographs of the shop and its
owner. It did not look at all like a store that was soon to go out
of business. Customers bumped into one another on the narrow
walkways. Some faces were known to me—I had seen them, and
they, me, in the same place for the last twenty years, and more. But

there were strangers too, as well as surprises. A lady peeked in and asked Mr Shanbhag whether he bought old computer books. He quietly answered that he did not.

In those last days and weeks at Premier's, the friends and patrons of the shop suppressed their own feelings. For them, as for Achal Prabhala, Girish Karnad, my daughter and myself, the passing of the shop meant a void in their lives. Mr T.S. Shanbhag was not merely the most knowledgeable bookseller in Bangalore, but also the most likeable. But, taking our cue from the man, we would not display our emotions. We would see things as he, silently and by example, encouraged us to see them. A bookseller had carried out his calling with pride and integrity for four decades. Had he not earned himself a dignified retirement?

Mr Shanbhag's dealings with publishers, retailers, customers and strangers were always exemplary. Still, nothing became the man so much as the manner of his leaving. The last stages of the careers of our politicians, cricketers and film stars tend to be embarrassingly extended. Contrasting Mr Shanbhag's behaviour with theirs, we were inspired to subsume our private sorrow in a public celebration for a career conducted with honesty and dignity, and always on its own terms.

chapter fifteen

THE GENTLE COLOSSUS: KRISHNA RAJ AND THE *EPW*

~

A magazine is a despotism or it is nothing. One man and one man alone must be responsible for all its essential contents.

—H.L. Mencken

I

The British historian E.P. Thompson once remarked that 'India is not an important country, but perhaps the most important country for the future of the world. Here is a country that merits no one's condescension. All the convergent influences of the world run through this society: Hindu, Moslem, Christian, secular; Stalinist, liberal, Maoist, democratic socialist, Gandhian. There is not a thought that is being thought in the West or East which is not active in some Indian mind.'

Thompson must have been reading the *Economic and Political Weekly* (*EPW*), the Bombay journal where these thoughts and influences converge and meet. Rich in information and glowing with polemic, its pages are an index to the life of India. On subjects as varied (and important) as the economy, caste politics, religious violence, and human rights, the *EPW* has consistently provided the most authoritative, insightful, and widely cited reports and analyses. Among the journal's contributors are scholars and journalists, but also activists and civil servants—and even some politicians.

Like other such journals around the world, the *EPW* commands an influence far out of proportion to its circulation. It has shaped intellectual discussion in India, and has had a profound impact on policy debates. Can one see it then as an Indian version of the esteemed New York weekly, the *Nation*? There are some telling similarities. For one, both are appallingly bad looking. The well-loved columnist Calvin Trillin said of the *Nation* that it was 'probably the only magazine in the country if you make a Xerox of it, the Xerox looks a lot better than the original'. More substantively, they have a similar philosophy or credo, this, in the words of the former *Nation* editor Victor Navasky, being 'to question the conventional wisdom, to be suspicious of all orthodoxies, to provide a home for dissent and dissenters, and to be corny about it, to hold forth a vision of a better world'.

Newsmagazines are mostly written by a staff of experienced and full-time reporters. On the other hand, opinion journals draw much more on freelance contributors and university scholars. As the historian Christopher Lasch pointed out, with the onset of television and the dumbing down of the mass media, these journals had become 'the only surviving media in which scholars can talk to each other. They give the intellectual community what little unity and coherence it retains.' That is true of the *Nation*; and even more so, one thinks, of the *EPW*.

There is another way in which the profitable glossy is to be distinguished from the poorly circulated journal of opinion. In the words of the critic Dwight Macdonald, 'a "little magazine" is often more intensively read (and circulated) than the big commercial magazines, being a more individual expression and so appealing with a special force to individuals of like minds'. These journals are to be judged not by the bottom line, but by their (often considerable) impact on shaping public policy and public debate and, beyond that even, by the love and loyalty of their readers.

The *EPW* may be superficially compared to the *Nation* of New York or to the *New Statesman* of London. Think deeper, and the comparison is all to the *EPW*'s favour. For one thing, it has never allied itself (however loosely) to a political party. (The *Nation* is for Americans who vote Democrat; the *New Statesman* for Britons who vote Labour.) For another, it does not have a sugar daddy. Run on less than a shoestring budget, it has been chiefly sustained by the goodwill of its subscribers. But perhaps the most vital difference lies in its intellectual weightiness. Here were, and are, published the first and sometimes the finest essays of India's most eminent intellectuals: of Jagdish Bhagwati, Krishna Bharadwaj, André Béteille, Amartya Sen, M.N. Srinivas and the like. Moreover, the quality (and influence) has been sustained now for more than half a century.

The *EPW* is a unique three-fold mix of political prejudice, dispassionate reportage, and solid scholarly analysis. The weekly begins with a few pages of unsigned commentary, arch reflections on the events of the past few days. The second part of the journal is taken up with signed reports from around the country. Here we find the 'news behind the news', so to say, stories of conflict between landlords and labourers in Bihar or of ethnic and secessionist movements in North-East India. These reports are generally longer than what a newspaper would allow, and (but not for that reason alone) also more informative. The journal's back pages are filled each week with book reviews and two or three academic papers, soberly presented and massively footnoted.

The *EPW* represents an emphatic triumph of content over form. For, no journal I know is more depressing to look at. The cover has black type upon a white background, with a red band on the top left-hand corner representing a pathetic attempt at colour. The text inside is printed in nine-point size, with sixty lines to the page—these made less readable still by being set in columns. A recent 'redesign' has left the *EPW* looking much the same as before. The type remains small, the paper is still faded, the covers still wearyingly similar, but the articles as astonishingly diverse and unpredictable as ever.

II

The *EPW* began life in 1949 as the *Economic Weekly*. Its founder was Sachin Chaudhuri, a Bengali grandee from a talented family. One brother was a successful film-maker; another, a celebrated sculptor. Sachin himself was by turns a nationalist volunteer, an ascetic in the Himalaya, a PhD student in economics, and a market researcher. He was even, for a time, general manager of the pioneering film company, Bombay Talkies.

This experience came in handy when Chaudhuri decided to start his journal. His timing was exquisite, for India had just become independent. The *Economic Weekly* quickly emerged as the focal point of intellectual arguments about the shape of the new nation. As befitting the times, much of the debate was about economic planning and development. But from the beginning the journal was about more than the dismal science. Thus in its first few years, it ran a series of essays (later collected in a book) demonstrating the continuing influence of caste on political life in India.

In August 1966, the journal changed its name to the *Economic and Political Weekly*. By the end of the year, Chaudhuri was dead. He was succeeded by the economist R.K. Hazari, but within a couple of years, Hazari left for the Reserve Bank of India. The job was now handed over to one of the assistant editors, Krishna Raj. A Malayali from Ottapalam in Kerala, schooled at the Delhi School of Economics, he had worked with Chaudhuri since 1960. His tenure as editor was even longer than the founder's, extending from 1969 until his death in 2004.

I was first properly introduced to the *EPW* by my friend Bernard D'Mello. I had seen the journal as a student in Delhi University, but never opened it. In 1980, however, I joined the Indian Institute of Management (IIM), Calcutta, for a doctorate in Sociology. The same year Bernard joined the IIM. for a doctorate in Economics. But for some years past he had been an attentive reader of the *EPW*. His copy of the weekly, like so many others, was recycled. It was first read by Bernard's father in Bombay, then passed on to him and, in turn, to me.

When I went home to Dehradun for the summer, I missed the *EPW* terribly. After some days of searching I found a newsagent who stocked it. He was sited deep in Paltan Bazaar, a dense and particularly unattractive part of town, and at the other end from where I lived. To get there I had to walk a mile and a half in the sun, wait for a bus, sit twenty minutes in it when it did come, get off at the terminus and then trudge into the middle of the bazaar. Not that I minded. For, I was just discovering ideas, and discovering India. And where else would I find the most richly contentious ideas about India? On the way to Paltan Bazaar, I was driven by the anticipation of acquiring the new copy of the *EPW*, and on the way back by the enchantment of reading it.

When I returned to the IIM after the holidays, I took out my own subscription. Now there were times when Bernard borrowed my copy. For, his own copy, diverted via his father in Bombay, arrived three or four days after mine, and often there was an essay or polemic of particular interest to him. At any rate, for both of us the *EPW* was the item in the post we most looked forward to. This was an experience that we had in common with a majority of the journal's subscribers.

Some two years after I joined the IIM, I was walking down the corridor, when I passed the office of Nirmal Chandra, a professor of economics known for his command of several European languages (Russian among them) and of the complete oeuvre of Lenin. His door was open, and he was sitting reading a book, a half-burnt cigarette in his left hand. He happened to look up as I passed and, to my surprise, called me in. (At that stage we had not exchanged more than half a dozen words.) As I entered his room, Professor Chandra searched for a piece of paper on his table, and handed it over, saying: 'Here, this must be for you.' I took it and walked out. The paper was coloured pale green; on closer inspection, it turned out to be an inland letter. The typed contents ran roughly as follows:

Dear Nirmal,

Jim Boyce was in the office recently, and told me of his meeting with a young scholar doing research on the history of forestry in India. They were working on adjoining desks in the National Library. Jim has forgotten his name, but thinks that he might be a student at your Institute. Can you locate him and see if he has something suitable for the *EPW*?

Many thanks, and with regards,
Krishna Raj

After reading the letter, I walked back into Professor Chandra's office. 'Sir, what do I do about this?' I inquired nervously. 'Write back to him yourself, and tell him about your work,' was the answer. I did as instructed, and received in reply a green letter, which said that the editor of the *EPW* was coming to Calcutta next month, and would be happy to meet me.

My first meeting with Krishna Raj took place in an unlikely location—the Great Eastern Hotel. (He was staying there as a guest of the West Bengal government, who were hosting the seminar he had come to attend.) What struck me most forcibly was his reserve. His manner, his tone, his speech, all denoted a man of the utmost shyness. Was this the same person who wrote those sharp and pungent editorials, the same person who ran a journal known for the abrasive directness of so many of its articles?

These first impressions were to persist, even when I later met Krishna Raj in his own office in Bombay. Here the austerity of the surroundings matched the asceticism of his own personality. Here he spoke somewhat more. But he still spoke softly. So softly, indeed, that one began sometimes to wonder: did he ever lose his temper at his wife, his children or his staff?

The answers, most likely, were No, No and No. But the gentleness could be misleading. It was manifestly true, so far as his personal manner went. But it did not preclude decisiveness in his professional duties. To run a journal of this significance, of this diversity in contributors and contributions, and to do so week after week, required an authority, and authoritativeness, of a very special kind.

The green inland letters that, for many years, were Krishna Raj's chosen mode of correspondence had printed on it the journal's

address: Hitkari House, 284 Frere Road, Bombay 400038. In time
the street, city and pin code all changed: to Shahid Bhagatsingh
Marg, Mumbai, and 400001 respectively. Inside, the editor stayed
the same. Visiting him in his office was a kind of secular pilgrimage.
Hitkari House lay between Victoria Terminus (VT) and the head
office of the Reserve Bank of India: in a part of Bombay dense with
memory and history, and, above all, humanity. VT and the RBI
were joined by a street chock-a-block with shops, the road overrun
with cars and cycles and pedestrians.

It was with some relief that one turned away from the street into
the building that housed the journal. An unlit lift took one up to
the sixth floor. It opened out into the *EPW* office; this a mass of
cubicles linked by a narrow passage. Right at the end lay the cubicle
of the editor. It was like any other: six feet by four feet, with a
single small desk and two or three chairs. There was, of course, no
question of air conditioning; the only luxury was a window which
on a good day allowed in the elements of a breeze.

The austerity went beyond mere appearances. For, Krishna Raj
insisted that his own salary must not be more than five times that
of the lowest-paid employee. In 2002, after thirty years in the job,
the editor was paid Rs 12,000 a month. In that year the trustees of
the journal doubled his salary, to match that of a university
professor's. It was still shockingly inadequate, when one considers
the importance of the work, or the fact that he put in at least twice
as many hours as did the most hard-working academic in India.

Like most of his other writers, I knew Krishna Raj best through
correspondence. As a subscriber, it was exciting enough to get the
copy of the journal each week; as a contributor, it was even more
thrilling to find one of those green inlands from the editor in the
mail box. Unusually for a man of his generation, Krishna Raj took
quickly and expertly to electronic communication. This was probably
a relief to his foreign writers; but I speak for most of the desi ones
when I say I missed those inland letters, distinctively coloured and
still more distinctively worded. For, his signed correspondence, like
his unsigned editorials, displayed a masterly economy of expression,

one altogether rare among Indians who write in that still foreign tongue, English.

In the two decades that I knew Krishna Raj we must have met on perhaps eight or nine occasions. The first time, as I have recalled, was in Calcutta; the last time, in Bangalore a few months before he died (he was in the city to visit his daughter, who lived there). All other times we met in Bombay, in his office. The editor was an oval-faced, handsome, white-haired man, with inquiring eyes peering out from behind his spectacles. On his desk there was a pile of papers two or three feet high: submissions to be considered or rejected. On a shelf was a row of books, one or two of which would be offered to the visitor for review.

On my last visit, as on my first, I could not get over the sense of wonder as I entered the lift at Hitkari House. Who would have ever thought, when I used to go to Paltan Bazaar to get my cherished copy of the *EPW*, that I would one day go into the journal's office, there to parley on more or less equal terms with the journal's editor?

As I grew older, the *EPW* gave me a promotion I esteemed highly. From 'contributor' I now became 'contributor and talent spotter'. Much as I was once introduced to the journal via the economists James K. (Jim) Boyce and Nirmal Chandra, it now became my duty to pass on names of bright young things to the *EPW*. There were many others who were similarly elevated in the course of their own careers, and doubtless they were all as tickled as I was. But this device of Krishna Raj's was no mere flattery; it was very good business. Indeed, this is precisely how he maintained the quality of the *EPW* over the long run. For, one of his very special gifts (which he shared with his mentor, Sachin Chaudhuri) was the ability to bring to the journal the best of the emerging talent in the social sciences.

I have called Krishna Raj a 'gentle colossus'. The appellation is, I think, apposite in itself. But I also consciously evoke here the title of a book on Jawaharlal Nehru by the Communist Hiren Mukherjee. Mukherjee disagreed, sometimes profoundly, with Nehru's politics. But he saluted the man's personal decency and integrity, and the fundamental role he played in nurturing the democratic traditions of independent India. Likewise, among the friends of the *EPW*, I was not alone in being at times exasperated with the journal's obsession with intra-Marxist debate. Yet we all admired the editor for his charm and gentleness of manner and, more so, for producing, in such inhospitable circumstances, a journal that has almost single-handedly sustained an intellectual culture in India.

Between them, Sachin Chaudhuri and Krishna Raj helped construct a community of the thinking Indian. It was through their weekly that one kept in touch with the work of one's friends, as well as one's enemies. It was lucky, if no accident, that the editors of this remarkable journal came from Bengal and Kerala respectively. For, these are, in an intellectual sense, the most vigorously active states in India—and also the most disputatious. In both states, the Communists have enjoyed long spells in government, placed there by the ballot box. They have been bitterly opposed by the extreme left, by those who think that the road to revolution lies through armed struggle. And they have been opposed from the other side, too, by liberals and conservatives dismayed by the attacks by Communists (of all kinds) on liberty, property, and tradition. The polemical nature of these debates in Kerala and West Bengal has spilled over into the rest of the country. A prime vehicle for this spread has been the *EPW*. Had its editors been from other parts of India, perhaps the journal would have been more genteel, but scarcely more readable.

When the *Economic Weekly* began, India was ruled by Jawaharlal Nehru, a man who was socialist in his economic beliefs but liberal in his political outlook. Most times, his commitment to the procedures of democracy outweighed his commitment to the ideals of socialism. This was not to the liking of the younger Indian intellectuals. The *EW* inevitably became the vehicle for their views. If industry was still under monopoly control, they argued, or if the progress of land reforms was slow, it was owing to the class character of Nehru's Congress party, a party dominated by rich peasants and funded by the bourgeoisie.

As I have said, the journal has never been allied to a single party. But its orientation has always been politically charged. Under Sachin Chaudhuri's editorship, the contributors divided themselves almost equally into two camps: the liberals and the leftists. Chaudhuri's own credo may be summed up as: 'We Admire Nehru, But Do Not Necessarily Follow Him.' Revealing here is an editorial he wrote in August 1966, in the inaugural issue of what was now the *Economic and Political Weekly*. Nehru was dead, but his aura lingered on. 'Many underdeveloped countries in the post-War period,' said Chaudhuri, 'have had a brief spell of elation or whatever we may call it, induced by the charisma of a leader and a concatenation of circumstances but how many have maintained their pace, and how many fallen by the way? Circumstances may throw up such leaders but it is thinking men and women who aspire and do not acquiesce who alone can mould a people into a nation and keep them going.'

Within a few years Nehru's liberalism had been seriously challenged by, as it happens, his own daughter. As prime minister of India, Indira Gandhi crushed dissent within and outside her own party, expanded the role of the state in the economy, and promoted partisanship in judges and civil servants. These developments culminated in the notorious Emergency of 1975–77.

Among Mrs Gandhi's critics were old-fashioned liberal democrats and right-wing Hindu conservatives. Under Krishna Raj, the *EPW* threw in its lot with a third class of dissenters: the Marxists. The editor himself was deeply impressed by the idealism of the young Naxalites, who, inspired by China, were challenging the parliamentary orientation of the established Communist parties. Among the gains of the journal's leftward turn were the detailed reports on human rights excesses by the state. Among the losses was the excessive space devoted to doctrinal dispute: to exegeses of what Marx or Lenin or Mao really said or meant.

When I first came to read it, in the early 1980s, the *EPW* gave space equally to the Old and New Lefts. Soon it was profiling the work of the Newer Left, as contained in the environmental and feminist movements. All this put off some previously loyal supporters.

In 1991, the historian Dharma Kumar, who had been a friend of Sachin Chaudhuri, called for an end to Marxist hegemony and a return to the old catholicism. Her letter, printed in the *EPW*, brought forth a host of angry responses. Particularly noteworthy was a letter signed by about two dozen western academics, the product of some frenetic trans-Atlantic phone calls, which suggested that Professor Kumar's protest was part of the larger IMF–World Bank conspiracy to destabilize India. But there were also some letters of support. These asked the Indian Left to take heed of the winds of liberalism then blowing through eastern Europe.

As ever, the *EPW* was happy to give over its letters and discussion pages to inter-academic abuse. The debate continued for months, but its ultimate effect was salutary. For, Krishna Raj realized that it was not just Russia that had changed. So had China, and India. The twentieth century had demonstrated that, compared to the state, the market was a more efficient agent of economic change. Liberal economists once more began to find their voice in the *EPW*. At the same time, the journal also reached out to younger historians and sociologists, who unlike their teachers were unburdened by party dogma. But the *EPW* was careful not to go to the other extreme. Advocates of globalization had their say, but so too did its critics.

The *EPW* remains a broad church of intellectual opinion in India. The contributors to its pages range from free-market liberals on one side to Naxalite sympathizers on the other. However, there is one kind of perspective that the journal has consistently excluded: that of religious extremism. In this sense it is not wholly representative of the political spectrum, since in contemporary India, Hindutva forces exercise much influence. But then, religious radicals are not especially keen to have their say in the *EPW* either. In this they are much like their counterparts elsewhere. (The *Nation* will not commission an essay by Rush Limbaugh, but then Rick Santorum doesn't want to write for the *Nation* either.) In any case, in spreading their word, Hindu chauvinists would much rather use the medium of oral gossip and innuendo than a journal printed in the language of the élite, English.

After Krishna Raj died, the trustees appointed as his replacement the economist Rammanohar Reddy. The son of a Socialist who had been jailed during the Emergency, Reddy had studied in Chennai, Kolkata and Thiruvananthapuram. Under his stewardship, the *EPW* has maintained its standards and its catholicism. The new editor has introduced some important innovations, two of which honour his predecessors. One is a column that excerpts an article or editorial from the archives of the *Economic Weekly*; the second, a paragraph that appears every week under the masthead and reads: 'Ever since the first issue in 1966, *EPW* has been India's premier journal for comment on current affairs and research in the social sciences. It succeeded *Economic Weekly* (1949–1965) which was launched and shepherded by SACHIN CHAUDHURI, who was also the founder–editor of *EPW*. As editor for thirty-five years (1969–2004), KRISHNA RAJ gave *EPW* the reputation it now enjoys.'

To me, Krishna Raj was both friend and mentor; but in the two decades (and more) of our association, there were two extended periods when we were not in communication. For, in 1991, and again in 1999, I fought with the journal on matters which I thought were of high principle but others would think were of mere ideology. Much later, Krishna Raj was kind enough to write to me that 'the fights, as you called them, were very good for the *EPW*'. But it is noteworthy that each time it was I who sued for peace. The *EPW* could do without me; I could not do without the *EPW*.

SOURCES

~

The original provocation for, and/or publication of, each of the various essays in *Patriots and Partisans* is listed below:

'Redeeming the Republic' is based on two essays commissioned by *Outlook* magazine, the first published as an *Outlook* Nano booklet in 2008, the second published as the cover story in the magazine's Republic Day issue of 2011.

'A Short History of Congress Chamchagiri' is a greatly expanded version of an essay first published (under a different title) in *Seminar*.

'Hindutva Hate Mail' was specially written for this book.

'The Past and Future of the Indian Left' was originally published (under a different title) in *Caravan*.

'The Professor and the Protester' draws in part on columns previously published in the *Telegraph*, here expanded (and rid of topical references) to form an integrated essay.

'Gandhi's Faith and Ours' is a revised version of an essay written as the introduction to the Indian edition of J.T.F. Jordens's *Gandhi's Religion: A Home-Spun Shawl* (New Delhi: Oxford University Press, 2012).

'Verdicts on Nehru: The Rise and Fall of a Reputation' is a revised and expanded version of the V.K.R.V. Rao Lecture, delivered at the Institute of Social and Economic Change, Bangalore, in

May 2005. Shorter versions of the present text were published in *Prospect* and in the *Economic and Political Weekly*.

'An Asian Clash of Civilizations? The Sino-Indian Conflict Revisited' is based on the Ingalls Lecture, delivered at the Harvard-Yenching Institute, in March 2011. It was later published in full in the *Economic and Political Weekly* and, in abbreviated form, in the *National Interest*.

'The Beauty of Compromise' is based on the inaugural Himal Lecture, delivered at the India International Centre, New Delhi, in December 2007. A shorter version was published in *Himal Southasia*.

'The Rise and Fall of the Bilingual Intellectual' was delivered as a lecture at the India International Centre, New Delhi, on 15th May 2009, to mark the birth centenary of the librarian B.S. Kesavan. It was later published in the *Economic and Political Weekly*, where it attracted several printed responses, the main points of which have been incorporated in the present version.

'Pluralism in the Indian University' is based on the inaugural address to the symposium on 'The Quest for Excellence: Great Universities and their Cities, Mumbai, Kolkata, Chennai', organized by the Department of History, Mumbai University, in January 2007. An earlier version was published in the *Economic and Political Weekly*.

'In Nehru's House: A Story of Scholarship and Sycophancy' was specially written for this book.

'Life with a Duchess: A Personal History of the Oxford University Press' was published (under a different title) in *Caravan*.

'Turning Crimson in Premier's' is a lightly revised version of an essay first published in Aditi De, editor, *Multiple City: Writings on Bangalore* (New Delhi: Penguin India, 2008).

'The Gentle Colossus: Krishna Raj and the *EPW*' is a substantially expanded version of a tribute to Krishna Raj first published in *Himal Southasia*.

ACKNOWLEDGEMENTS

~

I would like to thank, for variously provoking, commissioning, facilitating, or commenting on the essays that make up *Patriots and Partisans*, the following individuals: Aditya Bhattacharjea, Swapan Chakravorty, Gill Coleridge, Aditi De, Sudhanva Deshpande, Kanak Mani Dixit, Mariam Dossal, Gopalkrishna Gandhi, the late Anjan Ghosh, David Goodhart, Keshava Guha, David Hardiman, Diya Kar Hazra, Peter Heehs, Cara Jones, Vinod K. Jose, Mukul Kesavan, Sunil Khilnani, Nayanjot Lahiri, Charles Lewis, Vinayak Lohani, Shajahan Madampat, Swapan Majumdar, Sharan Mamidipudi, J. Martinez-Alier, Vinod Mehta, Shiv Shankar Menon, Rudrangshu Mukherjee, Anil Nauriya, Mohandas Pai, Jonathan Parry, Elizabeth Perry, Anjali Puri, Srinath Raghavan, Alok Rai, Niranjan Rajadyaksha, V. Ramani, Mahesh Rangarajan, S.L. Rao, Rammanohar Reddy, Justine Rosenthal, Chiki Sarkar, Jonathan Shainin, Shanuj V.C., Geetanjali Shree, Dilip Simeon, Malvika Singh, K. Sivaramakrishnan, Rupert Snell, Sugata Srinivasaraju, Nandini Sundar and Akhila Yechury. A special word of thanks is due to Nandini Mehta (of Penguin India) and Rukun Advani (of Ranikhet), for their patience in listening to long harangues on the phone, and for reading (and most valuably commenting on) multiple drafts of more or less all the essays in this book.

INDEX

~